A DEATH RETOLD IN TRUTH AND RUMOUR

Kenya, Britain and the Julie Ward Murder

The series is now open to submissions from the disciplines related to literature, cultural history, cultural studies, music and the arts.

African Articulations showcases cutting-edge research into Africa's cultural texts and practices, broadly understood to include written and oral literatures, visual arts, music, and public discourse and media of all kinds. Building on the idea of 'articulation' as a series of cultural connections, as a clearly voiced argument and as a dynamic social encounter, the series features monographs that open up innovative perspectives on the richness of African locations and networks. Refusing to concentrate solely on the internationally visible above the supposedly ephemeral local cultural spaces and networks, African Articulations provides indispensable resources for students and teachers of contemporary culture.

Please contact the series editors with an outline, or download the proposal form www.jamescurrey.com. Only send a full manuscript if requested to do so.

Stephanie Newell, Professor of English, Yale University stephanie.newell@yale.edu
Ranka Primorac, Lecturer in English, University of Southampton r.primorac@soton.ac.uk

Previously published

Achebe & Friends at Umuahia: The Making of a Literary Elite, Terri Ochiagha, 2015

A DEATH RETOLD IN TRUTH AND RUMOUR

Kenya, Britain and the Julie Ward Murder

Grace A. Musila

JC JAMES CURREY

James Currey
is an imprint of
Boydell & Brewer Ltd
PO Box 9, Woodbridge
Suffolk IP12 3DF (GB)
www.jamescurrey.com
and of
Boydell & Brewer Inc.
668 Mt Hope Avenue
Rochester, NY 14620-2731 (US)
www.boydellandbrewer.com

British Library Cataloguing in Publication Data
A catalogue record for this book is available on request from the British Library

ISBN 978-1-84701-127-5 (James Currey cloth)

The publisher has no responsibility for the continued existence or accuracy of
URLs for external or third-party internet websites referred to in this book, and
does not guarantee that any content on such websites is, or will remain, accurate
or appropriate

This publication is printed on acid-free paper

For

Henry Oketch, E. Munyasya, J. Midenga, Joyce and Alfred Nyairo,
James Ogude, Bhekizizwe Peterson – *teachers, mentors, friends*

Gladys Chematya E. Kipsongok – *my fiercest fan and toughest critic*

James Chebaibai Kipsongok – *who prays for me, 'irregardless'*

Elijah Musila Murundu – *mentor, inspiration, best friend*

May I remember to pass it on

Contents

Julie Ward, taken 3 June 1988 in *Station de Capture d'Epulu* (now Epulu Conservation and Research Center), in Zaire (now the Democratic Republic of the Congo). Copyright and reproduced by kind permission of Alastair John Spurr.

Julie Ward Case Timeline 1988–2012

1960	20 April	Julie Ward's date of birth.
		Education.
1980–88	January	Working for Rowland Phototypesetting Ltd.
1988	7 February	Leaves home in Suffolk on a seven-month overland trip to/in Africa.
	27 June	Arrives in Nairobi.
	2 September	Drives from Nairobi to Maasai Mara Game reserve with Dr Glen Burns (planned to return 4 September)
	3 September	Game drive. Jeep breaks down near Mara Serena Lodge; seems to need new fuel pump.
	4 September	Glen Burns flies to Nairobi, with faulty pump.
	5 September	New fuel pump flown to Mara from Nairobi.
	6 September	Jeep fixed. Drives to Sand River Camp in Mara to collect tents left there.
	2.30 p.m.	Last seen by Constable Gerald Karori.
	6–10 September	Whereabouts unknown.
	10 September	Reported missing.
	12 September	John Ward arrives in Nairobi to search for his daughter.
	13 September	John Ward arranges search in the Mara, with volunteers.
	10.30 a.m.	Jeep found stuck in a gully in the Mara.
	4.00 p.m.	Partly burnt remains found at Oseropia: jawbone (split in two), left leg, lock of hair. Skull found about a month later.

	15 September	Kenyan police pathologist Dr Shaker autopsy concludes Julie Ward was murdered. Police insists she committed suicide or was attacked by wild animals. Suggestion that she was struck by lightning was seemingly supported by British Foreign Office & MI6.
	22 September	Chief Government Pathologist Dr Jason Kaviti alters Dr Shaker's post-mortem report.
	13 October	John Ward seeks second opinion from UK Pathologist Dr Roger Thorpe and Prof. Austin Gresham. Both arrive at same verdict as Dr Shaker, i.e. murder.
1989	6 April	Kenyan investigating police officer Supt Wanjau Muchiri reports that according to his investigations, Julie Ward committed suicide.
1989	9 August – 27 October	Inquest into Julie Ward death in Nairobi courts under Magistrate Joseph Mango.
	27 October	Magistrate Mango concludes Julie Ward was murdered.
1990	February	Scotland Yard detectives go to Kenya to investigate. Recommend trial of two suspects.
1992	January–June	Game wardens Peter Kipeen and Jonah Magiroi tried for the murder, and both acquitted.
	April	Valentine Uhuru Kodipo, an alleged renegade from secret militia, in government employ, submits detailed statement of his activities to Forum for the Restoration of Democracy opposition party. Testifies at the Kiliku Parliamentary Commission of Inquiry into the 1992 'ethnic clashes'. Claims to have witnessed Julie Ward's murder by high-placed politicians in Moi government. Offered UN asylum in Denmark.
1995	24 September	Kodipo offers detailed eye-witness account of Julie Ward's murder to the UK *Daily Mail*.

1996	2 March	Kenya Attorney General Amos Wako orders new inquiry into Julie Ward's murder.
1998	July – **1999** September	Chief Game Warden Simon ole Makallah charged, tried and acquitted.
2004	2 March	Inquest into Julie Ward's death in Suffolk UK resumes. Investigates the conduct of the Scotland Yard detectives and the Foreign Office.
	April	British SIS agent testifies at inquest; admits covert involvement in the case.
2005	4 February	New task force by new National Rainbow Coalition Government to investigate Julie Ward's murder
2009	April – **2011**, 4 November	New Scotland Yard team visits Kenya for new investigations into Julie Ward's murder. Additional evidence and DNA technology renew hopes of new findings.
2012	3 March	John Ward publishes report in *Nairobi Law Monthly* claiming *Mr B.* killed his daughter.
	8 March	*Mr B.*'s lawyers publish denial of claims in a response published in *The Nairobi Star*.

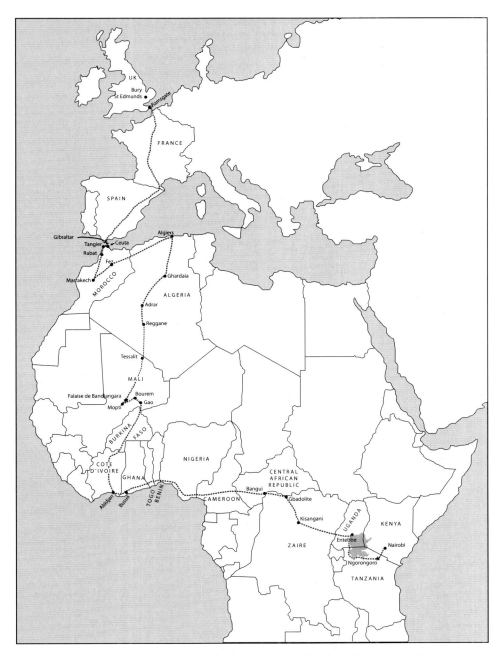

Map 1 Retracing of the route taken by Julie Ward and the Hobo Trans-Africa group of travellers to Nairobi (Kate Kirkwood)

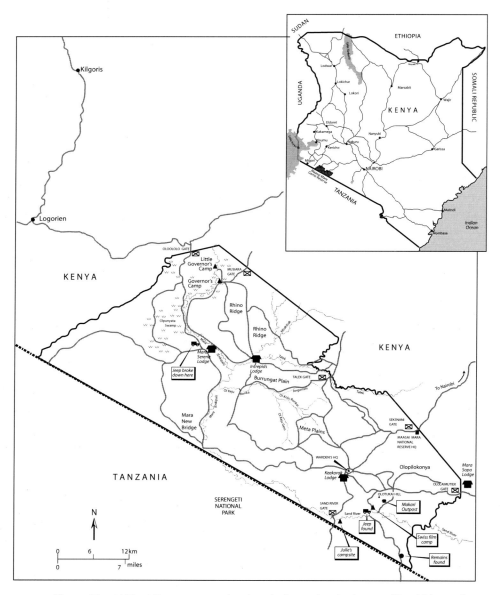

Map 2 Maasai Mara Game reserve, showing the key points in the case (Kate Kirkwood)

Acknowledgements

While working on this book over the years, I have been blessed beyond the most optimistic promise of my name. Every step of this book's journey, from a half-thought thought to its current shape has been a constant reiteration of God's grace. I am grateful to Him for this and for much else.

This book's childhood was nurtured by financial and intellectual resources from Wits University through the African Literature Department. I am grateful to my teachers, Professors James Ogude, Bhekizizwe Peterson, Isabel Hofmeyr and Dan Ojwang for many years of mentorship, inspiration and commitment to ideas. A special 'thank you' to Professors Ogude and Peterson for allowing me to impose on your time, and for regularly asking about the book, with an unwavering conviction that I was up to the task. I must confess that many times, it was the version of me reflected in your eyes that gave me the strength to take that next step ... and the next one. If I can be half as inspiring a teacher to my students as you two are to me, I will be most grateful to the ancestors.

I am also grateful to my previous teachers who have known and supported my work and thought for decades: Profs Tom M. Mboya, Tirop Simatei, Joyce Nyairo, Christopher Joseph Odhiambo, Basil Okong'o, Busolo Wegesa and Peter Amuka, all of Moi University. Thank you for the solid foundation.

My colleagues in the English Department at Stellenbosch University have been such a wonderful source of support, both directly and indirectly. I am grateful to Jeanne Ellis, Annie Gagiano, Tina Steiner, Louise Green, Megan Jones and Tilla Slabbert for regularly asking about the book. Thanks too to Nwabisa Bangeni, Lynda Spencer and Hale Tsehlana for etcSA/Breakfast for Coloured Girls Only; Dirk Klopper, Shaun Viljoen and Sally-Ann Murray for gentle leadership, faith and fostering an affirming research culture in the English Department at Stellenbosch University; Colette Knoetze for countless interventions; and Carol Christians for her calming presence, irreverent laughter and assurance that things will always work out eventually. Carol, thank you for your strength, wisdom and sheer delight in life. Travel well, my friend. Travel well.

In its later life, this book has benefited from countless opportunities for thinking space, writing, feedback and collegial discussion in different places, thanks to a number of institutions and people. I am particularly grateful to the African Humanities Programme, particularly Andrezj Tymoski, Eszter

Csicsai and Barbara van der Merwe; to the Institute of International Advanced Studies at the University of Ghana, Legon, particularly, Professor Irene Odotei, Ebi Kanga Landry, Sabina Akwei Yeboah, Edward Nanbigne, George Opiata and Victor Yankah of the University of Cape Coast; the Cadbury Fellowship at the University of Birmingham, particularly Karin Barber, David Kerr, Rotimi Fassan and Adebayo Mosobolaje; the Institute for African Studies at University of Georgia, with special thanks to Akinloye Ojo and Karim Traore; and the National Research Foundation in South Africa.

I am grateful to my friends Mutuma Ruteere and Jacob Aketch for many hours spent discussing my work and sharing insights over a beer in Nairobi. Special thanks too, Mutuma, for generously sharing your contacts and tips on archival research in Nairobi. My acquired brothers Godfrey Chesang, Collins Miruka, Litheko Modisane, Khwezi Gule, Chris Ouma, Anthony Ambala, Grace Lubaale, and Lawrence Ngoveni walked with me for much of this journey, always knowing just what amount of reassurance, rebuke, laughter or prayer was necessary at which stretch of the road. My acquired sisters Dina Ligaga, Flo Sipalla, Sharlene Khan, Pumla Dineo Gqola, Silindiwe Sibanda, Carli Coetzee, Naomi Barasa and Wakasa Barasa: I give thanks every day, for you.

Stephanie Newell, Ranka Primorac and Lynn Taylor: I could not have asked for a better team to work with on this project. Thank you for your generosity, patience and integrity at every step of this project, and for lending me your energy and faith in this book on the many occasions I ran short of both. My sincere gratitude too, to Nicholas Jewitt, who edited the manuscript with such an eye for detail, and a fine ear for what I was trying to say. I also owe a huge debt of thanks to Alastair Spurr, who kindly shared his photographs of Julie Ward and allowed me to use one of them in this book, and to Kate Kirkwood for the wonderful maps reproduced in the book.

This book would not exist without the combined generosity in time, cash, ideas, friendship and faith, of James Chebaibai Kipsongok, Mary Chebet Kipsongok, Gladys C.E. Kipsongok, Eveline Kipsongok, Susan Kipsongok, Hannah Chepkemboi, Lucy Chepkemboi, Chelagat Kipsongok, Cherop Kipsongok, Chebichi Kipsongok, Betty Chemutai, Risper Kariuki, John Midenga, Mrs Munyasya, Joyce Nyairo, Alfred Nyairo, Pravin Bowry, Ambreena Manji, John Harrington, Jackie Sipalla, Godwin Siundu, Tom Odhiambo, George Ogola, Nicholas Boro, K.K. Kabui, Judith Chepkemboi Songo and Samuel Okola: each of you is an embodiment of undeserved kindness. Judith, how I looked forward to showing you this book. I hope you like it. Travel well, my sister and friend. Travel well.

This would have been a much poorer book without the thoughtful feedback and suggestions by the two anonymous peer reviewers who read an earlier version, and several other anonymous peer reviewers of sections of the earlier work that appeared in journal articles. Sections of Chapter 3 appeared in 2008 in *The Journal of Commonwealth Literature* 43 (1) as 'Between the Wildebeest, Noble Savages and Moi's Kenya: Deceit and Cultural Illiteracies in the Search for Julie Ward's Killer(s)'. Parts of Chapter 4 were published in 2008 in the *Journal of Postcolonial Writing* 44 (1) under the title 'Remapping Urban Modernities: Julie Ward's Death and the Kenyan Grapevine'. A version of Chapter 3 appeared in 2008 in the *Journal of Eastern African Studies* 2 (3) under the title 'Inscribing Memories on Dead Bodies: Sex, Gender, and State Power in the Julie Ward Case'. Sections of Chapter 6 appeared in 2012 in *Rethinking Eastern African Literary and Intellectual Landscapes* under the same title. Parts of chapter 7 were published in 2012 in *Kunapipi* 34 (1) under the title 'Submerged Fault Lines: Interests and Complicities in the Julie Ward Case'. I am grateful to the editors and reviewers of these publications.

On 17 September 1988, the *Daily Nation* featured a short article titled 'British tourist eaten by beasts'. The Kenyan newspaper quoted Kenyan police as saying they did not know how the woman had died or which animals had eaten her, but that lions, hyenas, cheetahs and leopards were among the animals in the Maasai Mara Game Reserve where the remains had been found five days earlier. The woman in question was Julie Ann Ward, a 28-year-old British tourist. She had been reported missing on 6 September, before her remains were found on 13 September. This book is about Julie Ward's death.

I did not set out to write about Julie Ward. My journey to the story of her life and brutal death was far less deliberate. In fact, Julie Ward found me. Initially, I wanted to write about rumours of political and politicized assassinations in Kenya. Growing up in Kenya, rumours about politicians' misadventures and high-profile court cases rubbed shoulders with tales of Abunuwasi's[1] escapades in our story-telling worlds. Some of these tales found their way into what T. Michael Mboya terms 'soundtracks of our youth'.[2] So, while the state broadcaster Kenya Broadcasting Corporation religiously flooded the airwaves with 'patriotic' songs in praise of the then ruling party, Kenya African National Union (KANU), and the Daniel Toroitich arap Moi presidency, the rumour networks collaborated with rugby fans and students, to produce cover versions of such songs. In place of patriotic songs like '*Kenya Nchi, yangu / Kenya Nchi yangu na ninaipenda!*'[3] we sang '*Kenya Nchi, yangu / Kenya Nchi, yangu na 'toto Jonathan!*'[4] We never realized it at the time, but on hindsight, these songs were accurate commentaries on the political elite's sense of its ownership of the country: Kenya belonged to the political elite and those in their networks, as a culture of personal rule and patronage took root, first in the Jomo Kenyatta regime of 1963–1978 immediately after flag independence, then in the Moi regime of 1978–2002, later to be perfected by the Mwai Kibaki regime of 2002–2012 and then the current Uhuru Kenyatta regime that took over in 2012. This prompted Kenyan rumour mills to update the terminology for this plutocracy by coining new terminology:

---

[1] Abunuwasi is a popular figure in Swahili folklore, largely drawn from *Arabian Nights*.
[2] T. Michael Mboya, personal communication.
[3] 'Kenya is my country / Kenya is my country and I love it!'
[4] 'Kenya is my country / Kenya is my country, mine and my son Jonathan's!' – President Moi's son.

wananchi (ordinary citizens) and *wenyenchi* (owners of the country). But back then, the social truths of these soundtracks of our youth were hardly legible to us. We were more interested in their witty humour as they indexed the Kenyan grapevine's perspectives. [5] This is where my interest in rumours began.

Years later, as I began to explore the subject of the rumours of political and politicized assassinations in Kenya, it became clear to me that, while the more-prominent Kenyan politicians and outspoken clerics who had died under suspicious circumstances had received significant attention, Julie Ward remained an ephemeral figure in the grapevine, appearing and disappearing in an unpredictable pattern; when she did appear, she seemed to be a 'placeholder' for other concerns. In a sense then, Julie Ward's story found me. I, on the other hand, have not quite found her. I have had glimpses of her life's journeys, her joys, her pleasures, her pain and her death from the extensive range of media reports, court transcripts, true crime books and rumours about her. Yet, even after several years of thinking about these multiple portraits of her life and death, she remains both familiar and mysterious to me. In recognition of this familiar-stranger position, my book is anchored in the same incompleteness that marks Julie Ward's life and death. Like the circumstances surrounding her brutal death, Julie Ward remains elusive. I embrace her elusiveness.

Julie Ann Ward was a 28-year old British tourist and wildlife photographer who visited Kenya's Maasai Mara Game Reserve in September 1988, to watch and photograph the annual wildebeest migration from Tanzania's Serengeti National Park into the Maasai Mara. On 6 September 1988, she was reported missing. Six days later, her partly burnt remains were found in the game reserve. Kenya-based Egyptian Police Pathologist Dr Adel Shaker performed the first autopsy on the remains. In his report, Dr Shaker noted that the remains had been severed with a sharp object, after which attempts were made to burn them (Ward 1991: 121). Subsequently, the then Chief Government Pathologist Dr Jason Kaviti purportedly altered Dr Shaker's autopsy report.[6] Dr Kaviti would later insist that the alterations were made in consultation with Dr Shaker, and that they jointly instructed the typist to make these alterations (Kaviti n.d.). Dr Kaviti's alterations appeared to validate the Kenyan police's official position that Julie Ward had been attacked and killed by wild animals, and/or struck by lightning. It was subsequently to emerge that the lightning theory was first put forward by a British Intelligence agent based in Nairobi. (I explore this in greater detail later in the book.) With the manner of death thus contested, an inquest was held between 9 August and 27 October 1989 in Kenya, presided over by Chief Magistrate Joseph Mango. The inquest revealed that Julie Ward

---

[5] I use 'grapevine' in this study in reference to the local rumour(-mongering) networks.
[6] The autopsy report, showing the alterations, is reproduced in John Ward's *The Animals are Innocent: The Search for Julie's Killers*: 121.

had been murdered by persons unknown. A second inquest in April 2004 in Ipswich, Suffolk, UK echoed this finding. This revelation in 1989 was followed by a protracted search for her murderers, by Kenyan police and British investigators from Scotland Yard. In 1992, two Maasai Mara game wardens John Tajeu Magiroi and Peter Metui Kipeen stood trial for the murder. The two were acquitted by Judge Abdullah Fidahussein on 29 June 1992. After a second round of investigations and extensive media coverage of an alleged eye witness's claims, a third suspect – Chief Game Warden at the Mara Reserve, Simon Basha ole Makallah was charged with the murder in 1999. Makallah was acquitted by Judge Daniel Aganyanya on 17 September 1999.[7] At the time of writing this book, Julie Ward's killers, if living, are still at large, and the investigation continues.

Julie Ward's death is the subject of three true crime books by her father and two journalists: John Ward's *The Animals are Innocent: The Search for Julie's Killers* (1991), American Michael Hiltzik's *A Death in Kenya: The Murder of Julie Ward* (1991) and British Jeremy Gavron's *Darkness in Eden: The Murder of Julie Ward* (1991). At the time, Hiltzik was the *Los Angeles Times* Bureau chief in Kenya while Gavron wrote for the *Economist* and *Daily Telegraph*. In Kenya, the death captured the local imagination, resulting in various rumours, speculation and gossip regarding the possible culprits and the reasons behind her murder. The case also attracted significant media coverage in both local and international print media. Apart from these sets of texts, a 1989 feature film *Ivory Hunters*, and a 2001 novel, *The Constant Gardener* – both set in Kenya – show striking resemblances to some versions of speculations about the circumstances surrounding Julie Ward's death. Indeed, the narratives in both texts closely approximate certain aspects of the Julie Ward case, in ways that prompt a close reading of these fictional texts alongside the other texts on the case.

This book is about versions of truths and their attendant fictions in the Julie Ward case. I am interested in locating the place and meanings of Julie Ward's murder in Kenyan public memory, with a view to tracing the significance of her murder and responses to it on one hand, and on the other, the echoes and resonances that her murder sets off across Kenyan history, both with hindsight and subsequently. Using the three true crime books, print media reports, court judgements, *Ivory Hunters*, *The Constant Gardener* and the various rumours and speculations retrieved from print media in Kenya and Britain, I examine the discourses these narratives inscribe onto Julie Ward's life and death, and what

---

[7] In a recent memoir titled *The Judicial Purge 2003 that Never Was* (2014) the now-retired judge sharply rebukes the Kenyan judiciary as having been steeped in deep corruption. He claims to have been frequently offered bribes both in cash and kind (which he declined) to influence his judgements, including an alleged attempt by a lawyer retained by John Ward, on a trip to London during the Makallah investigations: 'whether it was with John Ward's knowledge or not, I cannot tell. The lawyer said I'd get free accommodation and meals for seven days in one of Ward's hotels.'

these reveal about cultural productions of truth and knowledge. In effect, both the *readings of* and *inscriptions on* Julie Ward's life and death become important windows into British and Kenyan imaginaries on a wide range of issues. I read the various textual sources both along and against the grain, occasionally adopting what Rita Felski terms 'the hermeneutics of suspicion' (2011: 574), in reference to 'the technique of reading texts against the grain and between the lines, of cataloguing their omissions and laying bare their contradictions, of rubbing in what they fail to know and cannot represent' (ibid.). While her interest is in interrogating what can be termed the tyranny of context in certain strands of literary critical practice which subscribe to 'the clarifying power of historical context' (ibid.), I opt to use her against the grain of her concerns, as I am interested in mapping the constellations of ideas that emerge when we read Julie Ward's life and death in different permutations of the various texts about her, both along and against the grain of their stated logics and intentions.

The book attempts to answer questions such as: what were the ideas sparked by Julie Ward's death? What was it about this particular death that made it a favoured arena for expressing these concerns? How were these ideas woven into a seemingly straight-forward case of the brutal murder of a tourist? Broadly speaking, I am interested in three key concerns. First, how narrative works as a critical intervention in understanding social reality, by not only mediating reality, but also attempting to influence its meanings and interpretations. Second, and related, I am interested in the ways in which the Julie Ward case and the layered discourses it inspired offer a critique of rationality, the unity of the subject and its related logocentrism as key tenets of a colonial modernity that continues to mediate metropolitan readings of postcolonial Africa. Third, I am interested in revisiting the seeming tensions between the particularity of local epistemes and their interactions with so-called universal discourses. This book reads the Julie Ward case as illustrating how narrative works as a cognitive device which sometimes excavates repressed knowledges in an unexpected enactment of the return of the repressed. I argue that underpinning Julie Ward's presence as a tourist in Kenya, her murder in Maasai Mara, the failure of modern state institutions (science and the law) to get to the bottom of the case, and her father John Ward's relationship with Kenyan and British state institutions, lay various co-ordinates of colonial modernity mapped in a troubled relationship with Africa. As such, I suggest that a riskier, more adventurous, reading of the ostensible tensions between local particularities and conventional 'universal' epistemes can offer important insights into contemporary interactions between Africa and the rest of the world, and the attendant knots of collaboration, contestation and complicities in these interactions across different vectors of interests and agencies.

It is important to underline two issues regarding the various texts analysed in this text, and especially the rumours: this is not a work of investigative journalism. First, I do not seek to determine who murdered Julie Ward. Second, rumours can be untrue, or contain a grain of truth, or the whole truth waiting to burst out. In this book, I examine an intertextual process, by looking at how rumours relate to the evidence available in published books and newspaper articles on the murder.

Given our interest in the workings of narrative as a medium for understanding historical reality and influencing its meanings and interpretations, an important concern for this book becomes the fictive/*fictive*[8] processes that were enacted in the various narratives, and the ways in which narrative mediated Kenyan and British attempts to make sense of the murder. To this end, Hayden White's (1987: 1) observation that 'narrative might well be considered a solution to a problem of general human concern, namely … the problem of fashioning human experience into a form assimilable to structures of meaning that are generally human', succinctly frames this book's interest in the deployment of narrative as a tool for mediating truth(s) and knowledge(s) in understanding Julie Ward's murder. On this basis, the book reads narrative as an intervention on historical reality which must not be read in terms of how faithfully it represents a given historical reality but rather, what knowledges, truths and insights it yields into these realities. In effect, the book is not so much interested in the actual circumstances surrounding Julie Ward's death, but in the representations of the death in a range of narratives which straddle the overlap between literature and history. Although the relationship between literature and history has always been fraught with contested claims to legitimacy regarding the use of the past and the kinds of truths contained in the respective disciplines,[9] one important point of consensus is the role of narration in rendering past events and experiences legible and accessible in the present. Hayden White (1987) terms this 'emplotment', in reference to the arrangement of raw, otherwise meaningless, information into meaning-making units. Stuart Hall too underlines the centrality of narrative in all forms of communication as a vehicle of transmitting and making meaning out of reality. In his view, a 'raw historical event' cannot be transmitted in that form; it must 'become a story before it can become a communicative event', a process he terms 'encoding' (2002: 302). For both Hall and White, narration is a search for and expression of meanings and truths. This process of encoding a raw historical fact into a 'communicative text' – a narrative – is not a technical one. It involves the mediation of historical reality, a process informed by the ideological perspectives and interests of the 'narrators'. The idea of emplotment of historical reality into narrative provides

---

[8] The terms 'fictive' and 'fiction' are used both in the literary sense of fiction as narration, and in the pejorative sense of fabrication. Where the former applies, regular font is used, while I use italics to denote the pejorative sense of the two terms.

[9] See for instance White (1987) and Bennett (1990).

an important conceptual handle for decoding the various narratives' discursive imprints, which tinted their rendering of the death of Julie Ward in Kenya.

In essence then, this book explores the meaning-making processes in Kenya and Britain that went into the interpretations of Julie Ward's death, processes that I see as simultaneously decoding the death and encoding new narratives around it, as the various narrators filtered through the available information to craft their own meanings and preferred truths on the matter. For Hall, this is also the process by which texts 'contract relations with the universe of ideologies in a culture [and] domains of social life, the segmentations of culture, power and ideology are made to signify' (2002: 306).

In the Julie Ward case, various fictive/*fictive* interpretative processes were implicated in plotting the available facts into coherent and meaningful structures which would bear particular truths, witnessing to the legitimacy of specific positions on the murder. Cutting across the various interpretations of the case was a concern with logical cohesion and motive. The various narratives were carefully plotted around a particular logic supported by credible cause-effect patterns on the one hand, and accompanying motive(s) behind possible actions taken on the other. Evidence, then, became the unifying factor between the two elements that would lend further legitimacy to versions of truths in a case where, with the paucity of information, all narratives dabbled in significant degrees of speculation. The various narratives underline shifting terrains of power relations and interests, which often overlapped, contradicted each other and sometimes created new gaps in the case, allowing rich glimpses into processes of negotiating knowledge production and the accompanying de/legitimization of truth(s) in contemporary Kenya.

Notably, the available narratives of Julie Ward's death reveal a sharp dichotomy between the genres Anglo-American narratives adopted, contrasted with the Kenyan narratives. While the available Kenyan narratives on the Ward case take the form of media reports, court transcripts and rumours, the Anglo-American narratives further included true crime books, and one novel, all authored by white male writers. Equally notably, as I discuss later, these books – by Ward, Gavron, Hiltzik and le Carré – all deliberately locate themselves in a distinctly white library of narratives about Africa, with regular intertextual nods to celebrated expatriate writers, colonial explorers and colonial icons such as Mungo Park, Karen Blixen and Lord Delamare.

White writing on Kenya has received a fair amount of scholarly attention.[10] Much of this scholarship examines key figures in settler writing on Kenya, with Karen Blixen, Robert Ruark, Elspeth Huxley and Beryl Markham enjoying almost all the attention to the exclusion of contemporary white writing

---

[10] See for instance Duder (1991); Maughan-Brown (1985); Lewis (2003); Whitlock (2000); Horton (1995).

on Kenya, much of which offers interesting engagements with contemporary Kenya – albeit often from the same vantage points that marked this earlier writing.[11] The representational trends underlined by Ngugi wa Thiong'o's (1993) reading of Karen Blixen's *Out of Africa* remain prevalent in much white writing on Kenya, which has historically deployed certain templates of the colonial gaze; the current texts on Julie Ward's death are no exception. Yet much of the scholarship on white writing on Kenya is largely 'separatist' in impulse. With the possible exception of David Maughan-Brown's seminal *Land, Freedom and Fiction: History and Ideology in Kenya* (1985), most of this scholarship examines white writing in isolation from black Kenyan writing. In this book, I explore the productive potential of setting these bodies of work in conversation with each other by reading British and Kenyan narratives on the Ward case alongside each other. Although little has been done in terms of exchanges and conversations between white/settler texts on Kenya and local textualities, one fascinating aspect of the narratives on Julie Ward's death is the manner in which these narratives point towards the blurring of such polarities. The narratives studied here further gesture towards the ways in which unbending investment in patronizing ways of reading Africa and Africans sometimes works against Anglo-American interests. It is against this background that I see Julie Ward's death as an important case which convened an interesting zone of negotiation of social truths and meanings between Anglo-American and Kenyan imaginaries, inspiring narrative interventions from both the British and the local populace. This approach is consistent with Michel Foucault's views on the ways in which discourses function:

> Discourses are not once and for all subservient to power or raised up against it, any more than silences are. We must make allowance for the complex and unstable process whereby discourse can be both an instrument and an effect of power, but also a hindrance, a stumbling-block, a point of resistance and a starting point for an opposing strategy. Discourse transmits and produces power; it reinforces it, but also undermines and exposes it, renders it fragile and makes it possible to thwart it [Foucault 1979: 100–101].

In the course of speculating on the circumstances surrounding Julie Ward's death, the narratives on the case comment on race relations in postcolonial Africa, wildlife tourism and conservation in Africa, perceptions on female sexuality,

---

[11] Examples of such writing include peace corps romance such as Terri Richards' *Mission of Desire* (2012); Robin Jones Gunn's *Finally and Forever* (2012) and Heather Clarke's *Chai Tea Sunday* (2012); thrillers such as Alex Berenson's *The Night Ranger* (2013) and memoirs of hostage encounters in the region such as Jessica Buchanan, Erik Landemalm and Anthony Flacco's *Impossible Odds: The Kidnapping of Jessica Buchanan and her Dramatic Rescue by SEAL Team Six* (2013) and Judith Tebutt and Richard Kelly's *A Long Walk Home: One Woman's Story of Kidnap, Hostage, Loss and Survival* (2013).

the workings of state power and modern state institutions in Africa and Britain, and transnational capital as a mediating factor in relationships between empire and former colonies – among other issues. In the process, the narratives also engage with a number of assumptions on these questions, which are variously challenged, modified, discarded or reinforced. Against this backdrop, I read the narratives on the Julie Ward death as an insightful example of the processes and practices of knowledge production and contestation in contemporary Kenya.

There is no such thing as a good death. This truism notwithstanding, Julie Ward's was a particularly terrible death. While the autopsy reports were unable to determine exactly how she died, the manner in which her body was disposed of – dismembered and burnt in the wild savannah using a flammable liquid, possibly petrol – graphically suggests an excruciating death. Further, there was a six-day gap between the day she was last seen alive (6 September 1989) and the time of her death as determined by Dr Shaker's autopsy (12 September 1989). To date, her whereabouts and experiences during these six days remain unknown. But if the manner of disposal of her body is anything to go by, the possibility of unimaginable horrors looms large.

What worsens the brutality of Julie Ward's murder is not only that, three decades later, her murderers and their motive remain unknown, but also her family's determined attempts to find answers have been consistently scuppered by both Kenyan and British institutions, often with great insensitivity to the family's grief. John Ward's *The Animals are Innocent* describes one such instance at Serena Hotel, Nairobi, which took place approximately a month after some of her burnt remains were found in the game reserve:

> There was a knock on my room door. Two men stood in the corridor. I recognised one of them as a plain-clothes policeman who often went around with [the Kenyan Detective assigned to the case] Wanjau.
>
> 'Good evening, sir. I have been instructed to bring you this.'
>
> He held out an envelope. Opening it I saw it was the death certificate I had re-quested from [Kenyan Commissioner of Police, Phillip] Kilonzo.
>
> 'This is for you, too', he continued, handing me a plastic shopping bag.
>
> 'What's in there?' I asked, taking the bag from him.
>
> 'It's your daughter's skull', he replied without expression.
>
> And I hadn't even had time to take a deep breath.
>
> I called John Lee [mortician] who couldn't believe what I had in my room, but he hurried over from his home and took the plastic shopping bag to his mortuary, with my instructions to send the contents to Prof. Gresham [UK-based pathologist] with all speed [Ward 1991: 176].

While the policemen may have intended no harm, this incident is deeply trou-bling. There is something bizarrely chilling about a parent unexpectedly receiv-ing his daughter's decapitated skull in a plastic bag, in a hotel room, at night. A month earlier, Ward had had a similar encounter, at the worst possible moment in the case when, searching for a daughter he believed to be alive, but stranded somewhere in the game reserve, the search party found his daughter's burnt remains. At the time, still trying to process what the 'foul sweet smell of burnt flesh' and the 'jaw-bone in two halves' meant, in the company of Mara employees and Kenyan policemen, he reports how these men walked off, and started their cars, assuming he would leave his daughter's remains there in the bush. Ward had to improvise a bag out of a helicopter seat-cover, then use his hands to collect the ashes and pieces of burnt bone, along with his daughter's jaw-bone and leg; before one of the policemen, Insp. George Odhiambo of the Mara Bridge Police Post decided he would take charge of the remains (Ward 1991: 83–4).

From these two incidents, the emotionally loaded nature of this case hardly needs explaining. For the Ward family, the desire for closure remains, both in terms of finding answers on how she died, and getting justice. John Ward's anger is palpable when he remarks, 'she must have died in a lot of pain and I feel it was completely unacceptable to do that to her and get away with it. I will feel a certain contentment if I get a murder verdict, but there is no sense of pleasure in finding out who murdered my daughter. It has been grisly, unpleasant and nasty work.'[12] Elsewhere, in his account of his investigations into his daughter's death, *The Animals are Innocent: The Search for Julie's Killers*, John Ward writes of the constant battle to retain objective distance from the personal tragedy, to restrain his emotional response, in the pursuit of truth and justice, even as he tells of the anguish that has rocked his family and its struggle to deal with the tragedy: 'You don't really have any option. You say to yourself, no matter what it is going to take, these people are not going to get away with it. But in the end you are one individual against a state and it is not easy.'[13] For anyone who has followed the case closely, John Ward's resolute commitment to the search for truth and justice in his daughter's death is spell-binding. In addition to countless trips to Kenya, he has travelled to Spain, Canada, Sweden and Australia in search for answers, and written many letters to people across the world, searching for clues to his daughter's last hours. It is hardly an overstatement to say he is one individual against a state – in fact, two states – which systematically marshalled several institutions and powerful figures towards frustrating his family's quest for answers.

Julie Ward's mother, Jan Ward tells of a similar struggle to accept her daughter's cruel death. In her preface to *Julie Ward: Gentle Nature* (1998), a coffee-table collection of Julie Ward's letters to her family with her wildlife photographs, published in her memory, Jan Ward writes:

[12] Quoted in Helen Carter 'I will feel a certain contentment if I get a murder verdict' *The Guardian*, 22 July 1998: 12.
[13] Ibid.

Ten years on, the sadness of her loss remains but the agonising pain has faded. I can remember so many happy times and funny moments, and enjoy talking about her with those who knew and care about her … I don't think there will ever be an end because there is always an empty space. I think in the early days the feeling is overwhelming. You have got to know why and how and who and where. And you think when you know all that, you will understand and accept it. But I will never in a million years understand how anybody could kill Julie. You do feel that somehow when you know everything you will be able to accept it but it's not true. It's just a stepping stone along the way [1998: n.p.].

These sentiments on the personal anguish of the Ward family underline the difficulty of an emotionally-laden project such as the current one. While the focus of this book is on the range of discourses that gained expression either through her death or were inscribed on Julie Ward's life and death, we cannot overlook the tragedy, its horror and the anger, frustration and desperation that continue to haunt the Ward family. Nick Buckley captures these sentiments in his introductory remarks to *Julie Ward: Gentle Nature:*

Nothing brings the continuing reality of their loss home more to the Wards, who have two grown-up sons, than basic questionnaires, censuses, or bank forms that call for the simplest details about where you live, and how many dependants you have. Jan said: 'I remember once I had to fill in this form for a dog club. Are you married? Where do you live? How many children have you got? And I put down three automatically because I have three children, and I thought 'that's not right'. And I crossed it out and put two. And I thought, 'how can I deny Julie?' So I crossed out two and put three again. They must have thought I was mad. But it's silly things like that that catch you out' [ibid. n.p.].

It is hard to overemphasize the terrible horror and brutality of Julie Ward's death. I would like to argue that the various individuals discussed in this book – including those who may have actively blocked the Ward family's quest for the truth – at some level grasped and empathized with the human tragedy that was Julie Ward's death. John Ward reports several such encounters with some of the key players in the case who would, years later, admit to lying to him. One such example is Supt Muchiri Wanjau, the first Kenyan police officer charged with investigating the case immediately after the remains were found in the Mara Game Reserve. On 6 April 1989, Supt Wanjau reportedly lodged a formal report to the effect that, according to his investigations, Julie Ward had committed suicide. Ward reports that twenty years later, in March 2009, Wanjau sought a meeting with him during one of Ward's investigative visits to Nairobi. At the meeting, an ailing Wanjau explained in detail the pressure he was under from powerful figures in the Kenyan police and the Criminal Investigations Department to ensure that his investigations pointed away from foul play and murder. Wanjau's complicity in the cover-up of this brutal murder would seem to sit uneasily with the subsequent voluntary acknowledgement of deceit in ways that provide yet another glimpse of the interface between the misuse of state power and the everyday fortunes of ordinary civil servants and, ultimately, the gaps between the grapevine truths and science and the law, which were to prove decisive in the case. Such a gap is underlined by John Ward's titling of his cover story in the March 2012 issue of the *Nairobi Law Monthly*: 'Mr B. Killed Julie'.[14] This widely read article offered a detailed discussion of the Julie Ward case and explicitly painted a picture of *Mr B.* as the much-rumoured 'big man' behind the murder. But it never translated to a legal charge against the well-known, prominent and politically powerful *Mr B.*, beyond a short response from him, published in the local papers, firmly denying all accusations of involvement in the murder (Koross 2012). These gaps between different bodies of knowledge and truths are a core concern of this book.

While the academic nature of this book necessitates an emotional distance that is hopefully reflected in the discussion, this should by no means be read as disregard for the magnitude of the tragedy, nor an attempt to reduce Julie Ward's life and death to its 'afterlives' as merely a textualized subject.[15] On the contrary, the human tragedy at the centre of this discussion was often intellectually and emotionally paralysing, and the pursuit of balance between the intellectual project of the book and the human tragedy at its core was a constant struggle. One anecdotal moment in this book's writing process underscored for me the complex challenge of writing it.

In 2012, while attending the African Studies Association of the United Kingdom (ASAUK) conference at Leeds University, I presented a paper on a project I was working on at the time – the work and thought of Kenyan writer, Parselelo Kantai. I was part of a panel convened by Stephanie Newell and Onookome Okome on popular arts in Africa. At tea break, I got a chance to chat with Stephanie. We had been in touch by email, but this was the first time we were meeting. I knew her in relation to her work, which was mainly on West Africa, so, I had never associated her with East Africa or Kenya. As we chatted, she asked me what else I was busy with apart from the paper on Parselelo Kantai's work, and I told her I was working on a book project about a British tourist murdered in Kenya in 1988. She stared at me silently, but this was a look I was used to. Not many non-Kenyans were familiar with the case. So, I started explaining: 'her name was Julie Ward. She was in the news regularly, in UK, as her father

---

[14] While Ward gives this person's real name in the magazine article, which remains in public circulation, I opt to anonymize him as *Mr B.* because these accusations have not been proven in a court of law. This is not so much to privilege legal truths over other truths, which the book takes seriously, but rather, in acknowledgement of the seriousness of Ward's allegations, which I discuss in detail later in the book.

[15] I gratefully borrow the term 'afterlives' from one of my anonymous peer reviewers.

sought to get to the bottom of her death. Have you ever heard of her?' After another moment's silence, she said, 'I knew her. I was on that trip to Africa.' It was my turn to be stunned. Over the years, I had 'lived' with Julie Ward, traced her movements, her thoughts, other people's thoughts about her. But having elected not to interview her family or anyone else involved in the case – as I was interested in the textual interpretations on the case – I had never met anyone who had known her alive. So, for me, there was something astonishing about meeting someone who not only knew Julie Ward, but had been on the same fateful road trip from the UK, across the continent to Kenya. Someone who could remember her voice, her laughter, where she sat on the truck that took her to Kenya, what clothes she wore. This encounter was shocking, intriguing and difficult for me.

My consistent hope over the years of working on this book has been that it is not only a defensible intellectual project, but that it reflects a fair engagement with not only the human tragedy of Julie Ward's brutal murder, but also the layers of prejudice, betrayal and disregard for human life that undermined the pursuit of justice for the Ward family and the many families of those who were murdered both before and after Julie Ward in Kenya, as I discuss in the next chapter.

Who was Julie Ward?

The one enduring question in all the narratives on Julie Ward studied here is who she was. This question arises in relation to who she *really* was, as part of attempts to understand the logics behind her death, but at the same time, to the more obvious aspects of her identity – a young, white, British woman – became important concerns that activated different constellations of thought in various sections of Kenyan and British imaginaries.

From the three books on the case, court transcripts and the letters written by Julie Ward to her family on her trip to Africa and published in the coffee-table book, *Julie Ward: Gentle Nature*, a certain portrait of her journey to Kenya, her death and the subsequent search for her killers emerges. In keeping with the incompleteness of her story, sections of this portrait are clear and uncontested, while others remain subject to speculation and multiple truths.

Julie Ward was the first-born in a family of three children. At the time of her death, her father, John Ward, was a successful businessman in the hotel industry and owned a chain of hotels in the United Kingdom. Ward's economic standing was to be an important saving grace in the search for truth and justice following his daughter's death, as, faced with reluctant Kenyan and British state institutions, he had to not only finance investigations, right from the moment his daughter disappeared, but also spend a lot of time personally carrying out and/or overseeing investigations. As at July 1998, John Ward had reportedly spent GBP 500,000 investigating the case.[16] Indeed, it is the family's persistence for justice, and their investment of huge amounts of time, money and effort, that gave the case the public profile it came to acquire in Kenya and Britain.

Julie Ward was born on 20 April 1960. In his introductory remarks to *Julie Ward: Gentle Nature* (1998), Nick Buckley describes her mother, Jan Ward, as a 'devoted animal lover' (n.p.) who nurtured a similar interest in animals in her daughter. The two shared a strong love of animals and wildlife which later shaped the younger woman's interest in wildlife photography. At the time of her death, Julie Ward had been working as a personal assistant to Ian Rowland, the owner of Rowland Phototypesetting Ltd, for close to nine years, since leaving school. In 1988, she decided to take a year off and travel to Kenya, on an overland trip organized by Hobo Trans-Africa Expeditions, which was based in Halesworth, England. She had been to Kenya on shorter trips on two previous occasions: in 1986, she flew to Nairobi, then had a two-week camping trip in various game parks, organized by Guerba Expeditions. The second trip lasted two months, during the Christmas holidays of 1987, again through Guerba Expeditions. On this third trip, she opted for an overland trip across the continent, with Hobo Trans-Africa Expeditions. On 7 February 1988, the truckload of twenty-six travellers from all over Britain left for Africa. The group drove to Spain, then crossing the Mediterranean, passed through Morocco, Algeria, Mali, Burkina Faso, Ivory Coast, Ghana, Togo, Benin, Nigeria, Cameroon, Central African Republic, Zaire, Uganda and Tanzania, finally ending the trip in Nairobi on 27 June 1988. From Nairobi, the travellers dispersed, with most electing to briefly explore Kenya before taking their flights home. Julie Ward was one of these.

In Nairobi, the driver of the Hobo truck, Dave Tree – whom Julie appears to have dated during the overland trip to Kenya[17] – introduced her to Paul and Natasha Weld Dixon, whose home stood on close to fifty acres of land in the suburb of Lang'ata, Nairobi. The Weld Dixons, who often rented out their grounds as a campsite for travellers, became fond of Julie Ward, who shared their love for dogs. She camped on their grounds for much of July 1988, and later rented a cottage from their neighbour, a pilot named Doug Morey in August. She also bought a second-hand brownish Suzuki jeep, for getting around in Nairobi. During this visit, she met two Australian friends she had made on a previous trip, Beth Symonds and Murali Varatharagan. The two introduced her to another Australian, Glen Burns, a biologist, and together, the four young people planned to drive to Maasai Mara Game Reserve, south of Nairobi to watch the

---

[16] Quoted in Helen Carter 'I will feel a certain contentment if I get a murder verdict', *The Guardian*, 22 July 1998: 12.

[17] In his judgement on The State vs John Tajeu Magiroi and Peter Metui Kipeen, Judge Fidahussein Abdullah writes 'Dave Tree, it would seem, was boyfriend of Julie' (1992: 4).

annual wildebeest migration from neighbouring Tanzania's Serengeti National Park into the Mara. At the last minute Beth and Murali changed their plans but Julie Ward and Glen Burns decided to take the trip nonetheless.

On Friday 2 September 1988, the two drove to Maasai Mara in her second-hand Suzuki jeep. Ward and Burns set up camp at the Sand River Camp Ground. The two drove across the park on Saturday 3 September 1988, but the jeep broke down near the Mara Serena Lodge. A tour-truck, driven by a man they came to know as Stephen Watson, towed them to Serena Lodge. As they had left their tents at the other end of the park, Watson lent them a spare tent which Ward and Burns shared. The two had planned to return to Nairobi on Sunday 4 September 1988, but the broken jeep could not be immediately fixed, as a mechanic advised that the problem was with the fuel pump, which had to be replaced. Glen Burns was forced to fly back to Nairobi because he had to attend a conference at the Nairobi Museum, leaving Julie Ward behind. He took the faulty fuel pump with him and promised to liaise with Paul Weld Dixon in securing a new one. Weld Dixon bought a new fuel pump and sent it down to Maasai Mara on one of the charter flights on Monday 5 September 1988, but it arrived too late in the day for Julie Ward to get the car fixed and take the drive back to Nairobi, so she elected to spend the night at Serena Lodge. That afternoon, she met Stephen Watson again at the Lodge and they spent the afternoon together. Ward invited Watson to share her room at Serena Lodge and they made love to each other. The following day, Tuesday 6 September 1988, the jeep would still not start despite the new fuel pump. The mechanic realized that the problem was a loose wire connected to the starter, which he immediately fixed. Meantime, Watson, a tour leader, had to take a group of tourists to Lake Naivasha. Watson and Ward had agreed that she would join him at Lake Naivasha on her way back to Nairobi, once her jeep was fixed. At about midday, Julie Ward left Serena Lodge for Sand River Camp Ground to collect the two tents she and Glen Burns had left there three days earlier.

From this point, Julie Ward's whereabouts and movements are shrouded in controversy. According to the clerk at the Maasai Mara's Sand River Gate, David Nchoko, she arrived at the campsite a few minutes past 2 p.m. and dismantled the two tents. She then paid for the three extra nights during which the tents had stood on the camp, before driving off towards Keekorok Lodge on her way to Nairobi, at about 2.30 p.m. Gerald Karori, a police constable attached to the Mara made similar claims, adding that he had helped her dismantle her tents before she drove off towards Keekorok Lodge. The two, who appear to have been the last people to see her alive, insisted that she drove off alone. In the subsequent investigations, the question of whether she left Keekorok Lodge alone was an important and largely unconfirmed issue. In 2004, an unnamed witness claimed that he saw her drive off with an armed man in military fatigues on the day she was last seen, Tuesday 6 September 1988 (Nation Reporter 2004: 3).

Back in Nairobi, the Weld Dixons knew their guest had booked a return flight to England for Saturday 10 September. They had arranged to have her over for dinner on Friday 9 September and planned to drop her off at the airport to catch her flight home the next morning. When there was no sign of her on Tuesday 6 and Wednesday 7 the elderly couple became anxious and started to phone hospitals and police stations along the Nairobi-Mara road asking about her, fearing that she had been involved in a road accident. On Saturday 10 September, John Ward happened to call the Weld Dixons to find out what his daughter's plans were, as she was expected home sometime the next day, Sunday 11 September 1988. This was when he learnt that she was missing. Ward took a flight to Kenya arriving on Monday 12 September. By then, his daughter had been missing for six days. Once in Kenya, he organized a search party in Maasai Mara, with the help of the Weld Dixons and other friends his daughter had made in Nairobi, and several Mara game wardens and policemen. On Tuesday 13 September mid-morning, Ward's jeep was found abandoned in a gully at a stream known as Makindu, in the Mara. A few hours later, her remains were found in a remote area of the reserve known as Oseropia by the Chief Game Warden, Simon ole Makallah. The circumstance under which Makallah was able to find the remains is one of the contentious matters in the case. Reports indicate that Makallah joined the search party soon after the jeep had been found; and drove from the scene of the jeep to the scene of the remains. Once there, he sent a radio message to Ward and the rest of the search party about his discovery. During his murder trial, Makallah insisted that they went in that direction after driving in a random manner around the abandoned jeep, hoping to find the lost tourist; and when they spotted vultures rising from the ground and flying off, they decided to go investigate what had drawn the vultures, before making their horrifying discovery. For John Ward though, subsequent tests of how long it takes to drive from the jeep to the scene of the remains suggest that Makallah drove there directly from the jeep. This, to him, suggested someone who knew in which direction to drive, and not a random search. According to Ward then, Makallah knew the location of the remains, long before they were discovered. It remains unclear how Julie Ward's jeep got to be stuck in the gully, in the middle of the game reserve, far from visible road tracks – though there were several attempts by witnesses in court to claim there was a clear track.

This is the widely accepted version of Julie Ward's life and the events of her last months. However, her identity was a subject of much speculation in the Kenyan grapevines. In some of these speculations, there is the conviction that she was not the tourist she appeared to be, but rather, she was a British intelligence agent, who was in possession of sensitive intelligence on the activities of Kenyan political elites in the Maasai Mara (I explore this angle in greater detail later). Interestingly, while John Ward and the Scotland Yard detectives dismissed these rumours as baseless, John Ward was later to learn of the possible complicity of the British Secret Intelligence Service in covering up the truth behind his daughter's death, as I also discuss later.

Beyond these speculations about a double identity, who was Julie Ward, and how did her identities influence the framing of her death? Julie Ward was a young white British woman, and a tourist in Kenya. These identities placed her presence in Kenya in a grid marked by multiple intersections between race, gender, nationality, sex and Africa. In her death, these intersections were activated by both Kenyan and British imaginaries, each of which read the case from specific perspectives, firmly dependent on their respective popular archives. Thus, as we see in Chapter 3 of this book, the idea of a young white woman murdered and burnt up in the wild savannah in Africa mobilized discourses of the black peril in British imaginaries, despite the absence of evidence pointing to rape by black men. On the other hand, this same combination – young white woman murdered in Kenya – coupled with government attempts to frame the murder as a natural death, activated ideas of a British spy who posed the risk of exposure to a criminal political elite. In essence, Julie Ward's identities – obvious as they were – remained decisive in determining the kinds of ideas and interpretations her death would attract in the various social imaginaries as revealed in this book.

Exchanges in Contact Zones: Modernity and Africa

Julie Ward's death in Kenya scaled a range of topographies, both physical and discursive, all of which had an important bearing, not only on the unfolding quest for truth and justice by her family, but also on the kinds of ideas, anxieties, desires and prejudices that came to be articulated through the case. Against this background, Mary Louise Pratt's concept of 'contact zones' provides a useful starting point in framing this discussion.

Pratt defines contact zones as 'social spaces where disparate cultures meet, clash, and grapple with each other, often in highly asymmetrical relations of domination and subordination' (1992: 4). While Pratt uses the concept in relation to transculturalism, the notion of sites of contact marked by both difference and unequal power relations is equally applicable to the Julie Ward case. Her presence in Kenya, her death and the ensuing quest for truth and justice convened multiple zones of contact: between tourist and host; Kenya and Britain; the Ward family and Kenyan state institutions; official and unofficial terrains. Discursively, each of these intersections came laden with ideas, values, cultures and assumptions that 'met, clashed and grappled' with each other. The shapes of interactions and the ideas mobilized at these points of contact that form the interest of this book.

In view of our reading of the Julie Ward case as convening a site of negotiation of meaning between Kenyan and British imaginaries, Pratt's (1992: 6) description of the contact zone as 'the space in which peoples geographically and historically separated come into contact with each other and establish ongoing relations, usually involving conditions of coercion, radical inequality and intractable conflict' to a large degree describes the sets of interactions that unfolded in the various sites of contact in the Ward case. In a powerful resonance with Pratt's work, our case was marked by coercion and conflict coupled with deceit and collusion, which Pratt associates with power imbalances in contact zones.

In its exploration of these contact zones created by the Ward case, this book is further framed by a concern with the logics and assumptions of modernity about Africa. To this end, Simon Gikandi's (2000a: 23) reminder that 'we cannot take full stock of the problematic of modernity in Africa, clearly one of the most complex subjects of our time, without identifying the sensitive points of the encounter between the hegemonic culture of the West – moving relentlessly towards what Max Weber would later call the rationalization of the world – and African subjects trying to re-orientate their cultures in the new order of things' is instructive. In a subsequent essay titled 'Reason, Modernity and the African Crisis', Gikandi revisits this question, noting:

> In spite of our comfortable assumption that such distinctions as traditional and modern society, modern and postmodern polis, colonial and postcolonial cultures, do not tell us anything more than the self-reflexive desire by the West to master its others in order to understand itself, *the problem of modernity and the opposition it generates remains the most powerful explanatory mode in which the politics of culture in Africa can be apprehended* [2002: 141; emphasis added].

Gikandi's arguments here are particularly relevant to this book's discussions. Indeed, at the core of the Julie Ward case lay an overriding privileging of science and reason, explicitly associated with Britain and British institutions, which were seen to be a failed project in Kenya, as the typical postcolonial African state. In the same vein, Gikandi might as well be referring to the Julie Ward case when he writes about the need to reflect on 'the black subject's precarious position inside and outside modernity' (2002: 136), as a similar ambivalent positioning of Kenyans emerges in the Ward case. Equally noteworthy here is the duplicity and complicity of both Kenyan and British subjects in the Ward case, challenging binary logics about modernity and Africa in important ways.

In *African Modernities: Entangled Meanings in Current Debates* (2002), Deutsch et al. evoke Jurgen Habermas' (1981) phrase 'the unfinished business' with reference to Africa's relationship with modernity. This relationship has sparked much debate, around issues such as assumptions about Europe as the womb of originary modernity, the value-laden tensions between modernity and tradition, Africa's alleged position outside history – and therefore modernity, and African 'cannibalization' of modernity among other issues.[18] Elsewhere, Gikandi insists that 'while we live in a world defined by cultural and economic flows across formally entrenched national boundaries, the world continued to be divided in stark terms between its 'developed' and 'underdeveloped' sectors. It is precisely because of the starkness of this division that globalization seems to be perpetually caught between two competing narratives, one of celebration, the other of crisis' (Gikandi 2001: 628–9).

Existing literature on modernity in Africa emphasizes what Elísio Macamo describes as Africans' resistance to and selective appropriation of modernity (2005a: 3). In recent decades, a body of literature on hybridity has emerged, which celebrates the creative ways in which Africans have domesticated modernity and 'developed their own culturally embedded definitions of what they consider to be modern' (Deutsch et al. 2002: 3). Despite this literature celebrating African inventiveness, there still exists an enduring master narrative of modernity which clings to an unyielding Africa–Europe binary. In this binary, Africans are scripted playing catch-up to a normative European modernity, while African realities continue to be read through distinctly Eurocentric epistemological lenses, and invariably found wanting. Francis Nyamnjoh captures this state of affairs, in his observation that 'most accounts of African experiences have been a look from above, with the consequence being the devaluation or outright rejection of a lot of social experiences valued by African people (2001: 363). Valentine Mudimbe prefigures these sentiments when he notes that

> even in the most explicitly 'Afrocentric' descriptions, models of analysis explicitly or implicitly refer to categories and conceptual systems which rely on a Western epistemological order … as if African traditional systems of thought are unthinkable and cannot be made explicit within the framework of their own rationality [Mudimbe 1985: 150].

To be sure, this trend is neither unique to Africa nor entirely limited to the academy or even exclusively sustained by European prejudice. Dipesh Chakrabarty's work on India for instance, reveals that 'Indian history, even in the most dedicated socialist or nationalist hands, remains a mimicry of a certain "modern" subject of "European" history and is bound to represent a sad figure of lack and failure. The transition-narrative [of conversion from "medieval" period to "modernity"] will always remain "grievously incomplete"' (2010: 65). The interactions between Kenyans and the British in the Julie Ward case eloquently bear witness to this scenario. As our discussions here reveal, the quest for truth and justice in the Ward case was framed by assumptions about British institutions and their ostensibly normative scientific knowledge, rationality, legal apparatuses and morality, to which Kenya was assumed to be transparent. This epistemological

---

[18] See for instance Larrain (1994); Comaroff and Comaroff (1993); Appadurai (1996).

posture failed to heed Hebe Vessuri's caution that 'it is necessary to go beyond conventional claims to the universality of scientific knowledge and introduce into analyses the dimensions of power and domination. Throughout history, science has fashioned a very powerful narrative that has been instrumental in delegitimizing other descriptions of the world, while consolidating its own position as the preeminent form of knowledge' (Sörlin and Vessuri 2007: 157). This privileging of British epistemologies resulted in an epistemological disarticulation which became a stumbling block to the search for truth and justice.

The privileging of science and modern law in a polarized framing of Kenya and Britain recurs over and over in the Ward case, in ways that gesture at British imperial assumptions about Africa broadly, and Kenya in particular. But how do we explain the resurgence of colonial archives in the British imaginaries on the Julie Ward case? And how do we understand the failure of the modern state institutions, science and law – both Kenyan and British – to get to the bottom of the Julie Ward case? One way of understanding this is by re-examining the foundational tenets of modernity and their configurations in the various contact zones that were convened by the Julie Ward case. Of particular interest here are the workings and underlying assumptions of the key co-ordinates of modernity, including rationality/reason, the unity of the subject and its implicit logocentricism.

If we take Elísio Macamo's contention that colonialism was the historical form through which modernity became a real social project in Africa (2005: 8), then we begin to see the ways in which what Abdul JanMohammed (1983) has termed 'Manichean structures' lay at the core of the enlightenment project and, by extension, colonial modernity. The one figure that lucidly captures this is the 'noble savage' who scales the contours between what Hayden White describes as 'civilisation and wildness' and the associated couplet of 'humanity and animality' (1978: 151).

In the British imaginaries, as revealed by the narratives on the Julie Ward case, these tropes of wildness, 'noble savages', humanity and animality form recurrent motifs in the construction of the Maasai and Maasai Mara as the 'noble savages' and the Edenic wilderness respectively, which provide a perfect escape to nature from the over-modernized Europe. In his discussion of what he terms the picturesque in South African landscape, J.M. Coetzee defines the wilderness as a world over which 'the first act of culture, Adam's naming, has not been performed [yet] a place of safe retreat into contemplation and purification … a place as yet incorrupt in a fallen world' (1988: 49). This is the kind of Edenic rhetoric around which Maasai Mara Game Reserve is framed. On the other extreme are the callous 'savages', the (black) killers, who are seen to have lost their humanity and degenerated to an inhuman status, largely owing to a failed encounter with modernity and modern state institutions. A similarly troubled relationship with modernity emerges in the passion for wildlife conservation and protection of wildlife against African violence, which is an important co-ordinate in the construction of postcolonial whiteness in Kenya as seen in Chapter 6. Underpinning this investment in wildlife conservation is cynical disillusionment with the project of modernity in Africa; indeed, a discourse of disengagement from African humanity whose ostensible violence and compromised state institutions seem to underscore the failure of the 'civilizing' mission. This disengagement is coupled with a compensatory recourse to protecting wildlife from African violence.

At the same time, from our discussion, the interactions in the various contact zones confirm Macamo's (2005a: 8) processes of selective appropriation and rejection of modernity. In fact, the Ward case is instructive on the ways black subjects negotiate the core paradox of colonial modernity which seems to have transposed itself into the current wave of globalization: that it 'dislocated the African subject by propagating its tenets as a universal model, while at the same time denying Africans, on political and social grounds, the possibility of its realization' (Gikandi, cited in Deutsch et al. 2002: 13). For Gikandi, to understand the collapse of modern state institutions in postcolonial Africa, it is important to revisit the question of modernity. He writes:

> In order to think about the African present as a conceptual problem, we have to reflect on the origins and status of many of the theoretical problems inherited from modernity and its rationality; but because the African has historically been located inside and outside the normativity of the modern ... a reflection on African debates on rationality and what it means to be modern implies a rigorous questioning of the privileged position of modern reason [Gikandi 2002: 142].

The rumours circulated in Kenya on the Julie Ward case would seem to take up Gikandi's challenge, by offering a critique of the workings of Western rationality, science and modern state institutions in Africa, institutions which, as both Frantz Fanon (1967) and Mahmood Mamdani (1996) have argued, were never adequately reformed to serve the needs of post-independence societies. For Dipesh Chakrabarty, writing in the case of India, this is in part because both Indian nationalist elites and the British imperialists saw India through the lens of 'transition from a "medieval" period to "modernity" [but] within this narrative [of transition] shared between imperialist and nationalist imaginations, the "Indian" was always a figure of lack' (2010: 57). A similar sensibility would appear to have informed Kenyan nationalist elites' thought in the 1960s, a sensibility captured in the popular motto of fighting poverty, illness and ignorance. The rumours on the Ward case move beyond notions of the failure of modernity in Africa, by critiquing the paradoxes that lay at the core of colonial modernity, and which continue to be reproduced in postcolonial Africa. Indeed, one of the main insights from the case is the kind of trajectories that result from the paradox Gikandi (2001), Macamo (2005a) and Mamdani (1996) have all identified, in the exclusion of the African from modernity, while simultaneously being politically forced into its institutional apparatuses. For Gikandi, 'the irony about the culture of modernity … is that, even in the era of colonialism and enslavement, it sought to promote a universal narrative of freedom and rights, even as it recklessly promoted ideologies of difference' (2000a: 24). His sentiments here echo Jean-Paul Sartre's earlier paraphrase of Fanon's searing critique of French colonialism in his preface to *The Wretched of the Earth*: 'you are making us into monstrosities; your humanism claims we are at one with the rest of humanity but your racist methods set us apart' (Fanon 1967: 8). Nowhere is this more eloquently articulated than in the positioning of the Maasai at the intersection between wildlife tourism, state power and a predominantly white tourist clientele, in the Julie Ward case.

A second, equally fascinating insight is presented when considering the ways in which the Ward case debunks the myth of the unity of the subject, illustrating how capital often forges unlikely partnerships, which undermine the notion of a shared moral superiority and commitment to truth, justice and human rights, as exemplified by the seeming complicity of the British High Commission in Nairobi, the Foreign Office and British Intelligence in foiling John Ward's attempt to find the truth behind his daughter's death. These dimensions recall Ann Stoler's work on the competing political and economic agendas that marked European colonial communities, contrary to popular assumptions about a homogeneous colonial authority with common interests (Stoler 2010: 178). Indeed, Gerald Loughran writes, there was palpable animosity between the settlers and the administrative officials in colonial Kenya: 'the settlers considered the officials to be transient mercenaries with no stake in Kenya, thinking only of promotion and pension, intent on robbing them of the land they had cleared, ploughed and watered, and eager then to scuttle back to retirement in Britain. The officials saw themselves as conscientious administrators of laws which the settlers apparently believed should not apply to them' (2010: 14). In this vein, Loughran writes of the social tiers which filtered down to the social clubs, with the Muthaiga Club for settlers, and the Nairobi Club for government officers, bankers and businessmen (ibid.).

The Ward case would seem to suggest that these competing agendas continue to mark post-independence relationships between these countries and their former colonies. In effect, the expectation of a homogeneous British position on the Ward tragedy was to be an unfortunate blind spot in the Ward family's interactions with various arms of British institutions. In reality, while sections of British officials genuinely supported the family's quest, other sections appear to have equally actively sabotaged their investigations, in effect prioritizing strategic British interests in Kenya over a British family's tragic loss and grief. This blind spot, however, might equally be understood again with recourse to the logics of whiteness in colonial Kenya. Loughran's lines of cleavages notwithstanding,

David Anderson notes that 'race gave Kenya's white settlers a clear, visible superiority and generated a solidarity that transcended differences in class and social attitudes. Whatever his background, and no matter whether he came to East Africa directly from Europe or via the Natal or Transvaal, every white man who disembarked from a boat at Mombasa became an instant aristocrat' (2005: 78). Part of the problem, then, would seem to be this presumed sense of solidarity which, while seemingly accessible in individual interactions, becomes fractured at institutional levels, in the contact zone between a former empire and its former colony, amidst tricky global politics of the Cold War period, and in a region marked by civil strife (Somalia, Eritrea, Ethiopia, Uganda) and socialist persuasions (Tanzania and Ethiopia).

Fictions of the State

In the official search for the truth behind Julie Ward's death, a medical understanding of death was adopted, with an autopsy as the first step in determining how she died. The first autopsy by Kenya's police pathologist Dr Adel Shaker – an Egyptian Copt who had moved to Kenya to escape religious persecution (Gavron 1991: 74) – noted that, among other things, the remains had been cut using a sharp implement and there was a subsequent attempt to burn them. For him, this pointed towards murder, an opinion he is reported to have verbally expressed to John Ward and the then acting first secretary at the consular division of the British High Commission in Nairobi, John Ferguson, on Wednesday 21 September 1988: 'There is no doubt whatsoever. This is a case of murder' Dr Shaker is reported to have said (Ward 1991: 103). Oddly to Ward, the pathologist further promised to stand by his autopsy report: 'I shall make sure it cannot be tampered with. I will sign it with my Arabic signature. That cannot be copied' (ibid.). Later the same afternoon, when Ward and Ferguson returned to collect the report, an apologetic Dr Shaker reported that all copies had been taken by a policeman; but reiterated that he was certain they were looking at a case of murder. The next day, 22 September 1988, just before a pre-arranged press conference, Ferguson advised Ward that the Kenyan Commissioner of Police, Phillip Kilonzo, considered the press conference most unfortunate, and would prefer that no mention was made of the possibility of murder or foul play, a view the British High Commission in Nairobi supported, and to which Ward conceded (Ward 1991: 111–12). At this point, even though Ward told reporters that he had 'every confidence in the Kenyan police investigation' (Ward 1991: 112), he already had serious concerns about Kilonzo's hesitation to acknowledge foul play.

A few days later, Ward and Ferguson's fears were confirmed when they received the post-mortem report. Ward describes the incident in his book, *The Animals are Innocent*.

The post-mortem report identified the two parts that were examined, the jaw and the lower left leg. Crucial words had been erased and others substituted. With regard to the jaw, Dr Shaker had typed that it had been *cleanly cut* at the level of the 1st bicuspid tooth. Someone had changed *cleanly cut* to read *cracked*. The alteration was obvious. Whoever had done this hadn't even been able to line up the paper in the typewriter properly and cracked appeared half a notch below the rest of the line. It was even possible still to read the words 'cleanly cut' underneath the overtype. With reference to the lower leg, the original report had read *cleanly cut* at the level of the superior tibio fibular joint. Again, someone had changed *cleanly cut* to read *torn*. In this alteration, the falsifier had not been able to fully erase the words 'cleanly cut' and had resorted to xxx-ing out the word 'cut' which could still be clearly read underneath. A little further down the page Dr Shaker had reported a *sharp* wound, 9cm long, in the calf of the leg. The word 'sharp' had been altered to read *blunt*. Once more, the new typing was not level with the rest of the line (Ward 1991: 117; italics in original).

When confronted by Ward, Dr Shaker attributed the alterations to the Kenyan Chief Government Pathologist Dr Jason Kaviti, who admitted to altering the report. Ward demanded that Dr Kaviti sign against the alterations. He also immediately cancelled a scheduled cremation of the remains and had them sent to Britain for a second opinion. The second post-mortem carried out by Professor Austin Gresham of Addenbrooke's Hospital, Cambridge, confirmed Dr Shaker's findings. An additional post-mortem by UK Home Office Pathologist James 'Taffy' Cameron echoed these conclusions.

Apart from the jaw and the leg, the rest of Julie Ward's body appeared to have been reduced to ashes as suggested by the smell of burnt flesh and pieces of bone found in the ashes at the scene of the remains (Ward 1991). According to the investigating police officer assigned to the case by the Kenya Criminal Investigations Department, Supt Muchiri Wanjau, Julie Ward may have been depressed and gone on to commit suicide. Decades later, Wanjau would tell Ward his initial investigations pointed towards murder, involving a major political figure but when he presented these findings to his boss, Director of the Criminal Investigations Department, Noah arap Too, he was instructed to 'look elsewhere' (Ward 2012).

These sets of ideas by state officials suggest various truths regarding the case. The alterations by the state's chief pathologist signalled a specific re-coding of the remains, so as to make them point towards a verdict of wild animals tearing apart the body and not an implement being used by a human agent to dismember it. When questioned about the alterations during the inquest held in Kenya a few months later, Dr Kaviti faulted Dr Shaker's English, arguing that the Egyptian's command of English was wanting and his motive in altering the report was for precision (Ward 1991). Yet Dr Kaviti further admitted that out of hundreds of autopsy reports Dr Shaker had written in the past, this was the first time his 'lack of precision in English' had necessitated editing a report. Dr Kaviti further claimed that he had not physically made the changes to the report, but that he had jointly, with Dr Shaker, asked the typist to change them, with the latter's agreement. In his statement to the police, he explained: 'Mr Ward insisted that I sign against the alterations in the original Post-mortem Form, which I did, not because I had altered it myself, but because I was aware of the alteration after giving my expert opinion on the appearance of the injuries on the specimen I had seen on 15th September 1988' (Kaviti n.d.: 3). Coupled with Supt Muchiri's suicide claim, Dr Kaviti's alterations cast doubt on the cause of death, making an inquest into the death necessary. At this stage, the possibility of Julie Ward having been struck by lightning was suggested by a man named David Michael Rowe, whose interventions would, on hindsight, unmask British state fictions on the tragedy, as I discuss in Chapter 7.

For our purposes then, these framings of Julie Ward's death reveal what I term Kenyan and British state fictions, in reference to official attempts to frame the death in a specific light, to suggest certain truths. These attempts to frame the death – as an act of God, suicide, mauling by wild animals or lightning – signal an interest in placing the case beyond human culpability. In a sense, Kenya and Britain had their own preferred truth(s) about the case, which they sought to validate through these fictive processes.

Eventually, an inquest was held in Nairobi. This first inquest was presided over by Chief Magistrate Joseph Mango and Deputy Chief Prosecutor Alex Etyang, and ran from 9 August to 27 October 1989. It had taken just under a year to convince Kenya and Britain on the necessity of an inquest. During this period, Ward had invested extensive amounts of time, money and effort into investigating his daughter's death, pressuring Kenya and Britain to reject Supt Muchiri's report, dated 6 April 1989, which had concluded that Ward had committed suicide. Ward's lawyer at the inquest, Byron Georgiadis summarized the police's version of the events: 'Julie Ward left through Sand River gate after dismantling her tents but tried to use a shortcut to Nairobi. In the process she got stuck in the dry-river crossing on the Makindu rivulet. She left the safety of her car to wander off with some of her belongings, among them a plastic can containing 20litres of petrol for five days. Then on the sixth day, for whatever reason, she decided to cut herself up before dousing herself up in a petrol fire' (Makali 1966: 25).

Magistrate Mango arrived at a verdict of 'murder by people or persons unknown' despite reports and statements by Kenyan police investigators Supts Muchiri Wanjau and Musimi Rudisi, to the effect that Julie Ward had committed suicide. But Mango advised that he saw no evidence of a cover-up, and would not be referring the case to the Attorney General, as he felt no further investigations were necessary.

For a while, there was no further activity by both Kenyan and British police in relation to the case. But between them, Ward and the Kenyan and British press kept the case alive in the media. Ward's Member of Parliament in the UK 'threatened to raise the matter in the House of Commons' (Ward 2012: 50). Eventually, Foreign Secretary Douglas Hurd became aware of the pressure for a proper investigation. He reportedly had a meeting with President Moi in London in November 1989; among other matters discussed was a request for Scotland Yard to assist with investigations into Julie Ward's murder.

On 1 January 1990, Scotland Yard Supt Ken Thompson flew to Nairobi for a preliminary assessment of the Kenyan police files. On 25 February 1990, Detective Supt Graham Searle and Detective Insp. Dave Shipperlee arrived in Kenya to investigate the murder. A few weeks later, two Maasai Mara game wardens, Peter Kipeen and Jonah Magiroi were arrested for questioning in connection with the murder, on the recommendation of the two detectives, to Ward's initial relief. The two faced a murder trial from January to June 1992. They were acquitted due to lack of convincing evidence against them, but Judge Fidahussein recommended that Simon ole Makallah's role in the murder be investigated further. It was to be another six years before the next trial would take off.

During the six years between the two trials, Ward continued to pressure both the UK and Kenyan Governments to investigate the murder further. In the meantime, in Kenyan politics, demands for multi-party democracy were ongoing, with the opposition party, Forum for Democracy (FORD) emerging as a strong political player, and a threat to the ruling party, Kenya African National Union, under the leadership of Moi.

In April 1992, a man named Valentine Uhuru Kodipo aka Abdul Kadir arap Kigen approached the FORD leadership for refuge, claiming to be a renegade member of a secret militia funded and run by powerful figures in the Kenyan Government. Kodipo claimed to be on the run from the death squad, which wanted him dead for desertion. According to the *Nairobi Law Monthly*, Kodipo was offered refuge by FORD in exchange for intelligence on the ruling party's involvement with this secret militia whose crimes allegedly included the 1992 so-called 'ethnic clashes' which preceded the first multi-party elections, but Kodipo soon felt unsafe in Kenya and narrowly escaped to the UNHCR in Kampala, Uganda, before eventually being granted asylum in Denmark. The Danes were apparently the only country willing to grant him asylum, as several other countries approached, including Canada, declined to host a self-confessed hitman. Kodipo published a detailed confession of his activities as a member of the militia in the 8 July 1995 issue of the investigative magazine, *Indian Ocean Newsletter*. Among his confessions was that he witnessed the murder of Julie Ward at the orders of a high-profile Kenyan political figure. Kodipo's story was picked up by the rest of the Kenyan and British press, and soon a detailed eye-witness account of Julie Ward's murder appeared in the 24 September 1995 edition of the UK's *Daily Mail*. Once again, as media pressure mounted, President Moi, on a visit to Britain later that year, pledged that his government would 'leave no stones unturned' in getting to the bottom of the murder. On 2 March 1996, the then Attorney General Amos Wako ordered a new probe into Julie Ward's murder, to be overseen by Crispo Willis Ongoro, a former Deputy Director of Kenya's CID. The Ongoro Commission was disbanded on 6 May 1997 and followed by the Tole Commission, whose investigations recommended the arrest and charging of Simon ole Makallah, who stood trial for the murder from July 1998 to September 1999, and was acquitted by Judge Daniel K. Aganyanya. Once again, there was a lull in the case, while the Ward family continued to demand answers.

In April 2004, another inquest was held in Ipswich, UK. Meantime, back in Kenya, the Moi regime was finally voted out in 2002. At this point, the official/ state response to the Julie Ward case briefly underwent a radical shift. In 2004, the new Minister for Justice and Constitutional Affairs Kiraitu Murungi was quoted in British media commenting on the case:

> Calling the murder 'one of the great unsolved mysteries' of President Daniel arap Moi's regime, the Kenyan Minister for Justice and Constitutional Affairs, Kiraitu Murungi, acknowledged rumours in Africa that the son of the former president was involved in Miss Ward's murder. Mr Murungi said in a statement read out at the inquest: 'Should any new evidence be unearthed, the government will take all the necessary steps to bring the culprits, irrespective of their status in society, to book' [Barkham 2004a].

Murungi made this statement while on an official visit to the UK, which coincided with the second inquest into Julie Ward's death. He further entered a statement into the proceedings of the UK inquest on 28 April 2004, to the effect that the Julie Ward murder, alongside several other cases was a legacy of the Moi era which the new Kibaki regime intended to resolve. On 3 February 2005, Murungi announced the formation of a new Task Force to review the evidence in the Ward murder, under the leadership of the then Director of Public Prosecutions, Phillip Murgor.

This change of attitude suggested attempts by the new regime to distance itself from what were seen as the sins of the old regime. In this turn of events, party politics feature as part of state fictions, as the new ruling party, National Rainbow Coalition (NARC)'s rhetoric of change included a pledge to get to the bottom of the murder mysteries of the old regime, including the Julie Ward case. Significantly, this was the first instance of official acknowledgement of the speculation that senior political figures may have been involved in the murder, hence the attempts to cover up the truth behind the case.

For a while, John Ward was optimistic and upbeat about the NARC/Kibaki regime's alleged desire for accountability and its willingness to resolve the case.

A few months after the announcement of the Task Force, both Kiraitu Murungi and Phillip Murgor were removed from their offices, and replaced by Martha Karua as minister and Keriako Tobiko as Director of Public Prosecutions, respectively. Murgor was removed from office soon after delivering a *nolle prosequi* in a murder charge against Lord Delamare's great-grandson, Tom Cholmondeley, who had shot dead a Kenya Wildlife Society ranger; and pleaded that he acted in self-defence (I discuss this case in greater detail in Chapter 7).[19] Karua claimed to be unaware of Murungi's pledge to investigate the murder, and the Task Force.

Another four years later, now in possession of new witness statements and DNA evidence, Ward approached the new government. After facing many walls of silence and a back and forth shifting of responsibility between various state dignitaries over who should receive the evidence and act on it, Ward learnt what Kenyans knew all along: that Murungi's promises were a public relations exercise. Seemingly, during its term in office from 2002 to 2007, the Kibaki regime had warmed to key figures of the Moi regime, including the former president himself, as his term in office drew to a close. If, as local publics believed, key political figures in the Moi regime were implicated in Julie Ward's murder, it was optimistic to expect any co-operation from the new government.

Book Structure

This book is divided into eight chapters. Chapter 2 offers a detailed history of Kenya's histories of assassination, and the place of political murders and violence as an old weapon in the practice of state power in Kenya. The chapter draws on the work of Mahmood Mamdani and Peter Ekeh to read the moral dynamics at work in assassination as part of the grammar of statecraft. The chapter provides a backdrop for closer analysis of the texts in the subsequent chapters.

Chapter 3 examines the speculations on the circumstances surrounding Julie Ward's death in Kenya, with particular interest in how circulating discourses in Kenyan and British social imaginaries shaped these speculations. The chapter sketches out the range of ideas that seemed to be mobilized in speculations on the circumstances surrounding Julie Ward's death, particularly the idea of the black peril in British social imaginaries, the notion of the criminal state in Kenya, which is figured as male and violent, and the question of female sexual moralities, which cut across the Kenya–British divide.

---

[19] The court dismissed a murder charge against Cholmondeley because there was insufficient evidence. According to several media reports, Murgor had been removed from office for his handling of the case but, according to him, this was a convenient, well-timed excuse to get rid of him and the real reason for his firing lay in his attempt to go after the powerful, well-connected people behind a tonne of cocaine seized at Mombasa. See Pflanz 2005; *Mail & Guardian* 2005. See also Mayaka-Gekara and Sigei 2013; Lacey 2006.

In Chapter 4, I examine the rumours arising from the Julie Ward case in close detail. In view of the privileging of legal truths in the case, where the Ward family approached the case from the legalistic perspective of a quest for truth and justice through the formal, primarily legal institutions, the rumours on the case would seem to present a provocative critique of this approach and its viability in Kenya, by suggesting that the modern institutions of law and science are prone to manipulation, and as such, unlikely to provide credible legal truths. Drawing on reported rumours and allegations about Julie Ward's death, the chapter reflects on rumour as a medium that contests the legitimacy of hegemonic 'truths' produced through modern institutions in Africa.

Chapter 5 reflects on the narration of the Julie Ward case in the three true crime books. The primary argument of this chapter is that both in life and death, Julie Ward was part of a certain cultural framework which came with certain received knowledge about Africa that mediated both her presence in Africa as a tourist and wildlife photographer, the subsequent search for her killer(s) and the narration of the case in the three books. Yet, some of the Kenyans involved – both the people and the institutional structures – subscribed to a different set of cultural practices, some of which were inscrutable to the British. The chapter explores the epistemological disarticulation that emerged in the interactions between sections of the British and the Kenyan actors in the quest for Julie Ward's killers as a result of the British privileging of categories of knowledge drawn from Western modernity – which are considered to be normative.

Chapter 6 examines the role of wildlife tourism and conservation in contemporary constructions of whiteness in postcolonial Kenya. Using the film *Ivory Hunters*, the Julie Ward case, and the case of Thomas Cholmondeley's killing of two Kenyans between 2005 and 2006 the chapter explores the constructions of whiteness in postcolonial Kenya/Africa. The chapter suggests that Julie Ward's death in Kenya in some ways lay along the transitional terrain between colonial and postcolonial whiteness, and revealed the continued deployment of colonial grammars of whiteness in a postcolonial context, along with a host of tensions and contradictions which made it difficult to construct new, viable grammars of whiteness in contemporary Kenya as they remain concerned with the assertion of white male authority in the postcolonial space.

In Chapter 7, I reflect on the perceptions that Kenyan and British state institutions held sharply polarized positions on the quest for Julie Ward's killers. In this assumed polarization, there seemed to be an unquestioned belief that Britain was sympathetic with, and committed to, John Ward's search for his daughter's killers. The chapter reveals that, in reality, this assumption functioned as a discursive mask behind which ran fault lines of shared interests and complicities between Kenya and Britain in the Julie Ward death – which remained unknown to John Ward for a long time. The last chapter provides a brief overview of the key issues emerging from the study's discussions.

Julie Ward's death traversed various discursive sites, which were laden with specific ideas on race, gender, the postcolonial African state, Western modernity, female sexuality and black male sexuality, among a host of other issues, all of which tinted British and Kenyan narratives on the circumstances surrounding the death. The authors of the three books on the Ward tragedy rely on the metaphoric colonial archive of ideas on Africa, and actively mobilize notions such as the myth of the uncontrollable black male libido and its threat to the vulnerable white woman in understanding the Ward tragedy. While these writers cling to these notions of the black peril, the 'noble savages', Africa as the tourist's wildlife paradise, and the dysfunctional postcolonial state, Kenyan publics read the murder as another symptom of a criminal political elite's brutal deployment of violence to secure immunity for its criminal activities.

However, the two sets of ideas are largely disarticulated, and the British stakeholders in the case were blinded by a rigid polarization of Kenya and Britain, which presumes a superior British moral and technological integrity. These assumptions blind the Ward family to British complicity in the cover-up of the truth in Julie Ward's murder, while at the same time rendering them illiterate in local textualities that remain inaccessible to the instruments of Western modernity, privileged in the quest for truth and justice in the Julie Ward murder. In effect, British dependence on the co-ordinates of empire embodied a return of the repressed in Anglo-American imaginaries and their dealings with Africa, which in turn created blind spots that undermined the quest for truth and justice in the case.

British complicities in the cover-up of the truth behind the case not only underscored the shared interests between Kenya and Britain, but also force us to rethink the tensions between globalization and postcolonial theory, in so far as an implicit hierarchy of access and power remains in place. Julie Ward's presence in Kenya, her death and the subsequent quest for her killers is consistently haunted by neat dichotomies, derived from various master narratives. The book traces these dichotomies, in a bid to outline their configurations and the outcomes of their deployment, while consistently keeping the grey areas of entanglements between these dichotomies in sight. It is in these grey areas that we see the contradictions, blind spots, critiques, complicities and forms of agency that were at play just under the radar of these neat polarities. From these grey terrains, we catch glimpses of the workings of these dichotomies as discursive masks concealing the fault lines that rend the master narratives.

Portrait of an Assassin State   2

> The very situation of the knowledge of Ouko's demise – unsettled, contested, unfin-
> ished – presents an opportunity to interrogate the powers and poetics of knowledge
> production and the nature of knowledge in the setting of this terrible crime [Cohen
> and Odhiambo 2004: xi].

Atieno Odhiambo's 'Hegemonic Enterprises and Instrumentalities of Survival'
sums up Kenya's political history in the twentieth century as

> a rapid march from the creation of the conquest state to its high noon of settler
> ascendancy during the interwar years, to the deep colonial crisis precipitating the
> Mau Mau wars between 1952 and 1956 [followed] by the brief period of mass na-
> tionalisms between 1957 and independence in 1963, which was succeeded by a con-
> tested statehood whose future continues to be uncertain [2002: 225].

Odhiambo identifies four historical themes in this political biography of Kenya: 'state power and who should control that power', 'the tyranny of property
pitting the haves and the have-nots', 'the politics of clan and tribe, pitting insiders against outsiders [translated] into the idiom and practice of ethnic cleans-
ing' and 'the theatre of world citizenship, which links the individual and the
state to an international discourse on democracy ... human rights and international laws against all forms of discrimination' (2002: 225). Each of these
themes was to feature in Julie Ward's murder in some form, from state security
institutions frustrating the family's search for answers, possibly in the interests
of economically (and politically) well-placed individual(s), to the spectre of
'ethnic' militias training in the Mara Game Reserve and the framing of the
case within an international discourse of human rights, as I discuss later in
the book.

Interlaced in Atieno Odhiambo's compact history of Kenya and his four
strands of the country's political biography is a recurrent motif of violence,
whose bloody footprints – to use that patriotic trademark of the Kenyatta and
Moi regimes – reaches back to the British colonial enterprise in Kenya, and
forward to 2015, when Kenya's Vice President, William Samoei arap Ruto is
facing charges relating to the 2007/8 post-election violence in Kenya, which
unfolded along largely ethnic lines that coincided with party loyalties; and saw
over 2000 Kenyans lose their lives and thousands others displaced as alleged

witnesses disappear or turn up dead under mysterious circumstances.[1] In effect then, violence, in various shapes and guises, has been a consistent instrument of state power and its practice in Kenyan history.

This chapter outlines an abbreviated history of Kenya, zooming in on the mobilization of violence broadly and assassination specifically as political instruments of maintaining state order, suppressing dissent or eliminating political threats to the interests of British rule in colonial Kenya and successive regimes of personal rule in postcolonial Kenya. In this respect, David Anderson's remark – 'for white Kenyans, the Mau Mau rebellion was nothing less than an assault upon the racial supremacy that was the foundation of their society [and they] were never going to give up their privileges without a fight' (2005: 86) – might as well be a paraphrase of James Kariuki's (1996) work on the Moi regime's often brutal responses to divergent views as threats to its power. This chapter offers a portrait of Kenya from the vantage point of violence as political instrument across the country's history. This is the socio-political canvas on which the Julie Ward murder was etched. To understand the particular patterns of responses to, inscriptions on and decodings of the Ward murder in Kenyan social imaginaries, it is important to have a sense of the intermeshing histories that preceded the murder, and which also inevitably coloured the trajectories that the quest for truth and justice was to follow subsequently. The patterns of responses to the case – both by state actors, print media and ordinary people – were shaped by distinct combinations of ideas, anxieties and histories that form part of Kenya's biography as a polity. A working sense of Kenyan political histories with keen focus on assassination and violence as political practice is helpful in understanding how a state-manoeuvred cover-up could be possible while the various state structures went through the motions of following proper procedures in resolving the murder mystery, and why both Kenyan print media and ordinary people suspected state complicity and attempts to cover up the murder from the very beginning of the case, as I illustrate later.

This chapter is structured into two main sections. The first section uses Odhiambo and Cohen's idea of a genealogy of assassinations in Kenyan history coupled with Karin Barber's work on popular arts and social imaginaries, to make sense of the construction of assassination as a prominent trope in Kenyan public memory. I am interested in the distillation of what David Cohen and Atieno Odhiambo (2004) call the 'historical ledger' of assassinations and its genealogy in Kenyan social imaginaries. I argue that the exchanges between Kenyan print media and Kenyan publics across Kenyan history have

---

[1] The highly publicized case of Meshack Yebei, reportedly kidnapped in December 2014 and still missing is an example of such recent cases. Yebei was apparently an ICC witness in the 2007/8 post-election violence in Kenya. See *Africa Confidential* 2015.

been instrumental in the conceptualization, construction and circulation of the trope of political assassinations in the social imaginaries. In the context of a repressive, complicit state whose shadow repeatedly features in a series of high-profile murders, a context where both the law and science have a consistent history of inability to deliver truth and justice despite extensive information on the culprits, print media and their interaction with other texts – such as court proceedings, proceedings of commissions of inquiry, everyday conversations, blogs, rumours and speculation – become important nodes in an entangled network of information flows and interpretations, through which people construct the narrative of state-sponsored assassinations as a signature practice in Kenyan statecraft.

The second section of the chapter locates this genealogy of assassinations within a larger history of the workings of state power across Kenyan political history. I explore how violence and assassination as important syllables in the grammar of state power were part of the British colonial endowment to the newly independent Kenyan Government, which, in turn, refined and adapted this brutal inheritance to the needs and greeds of successive post-independence regimes in Kenya to date. I anchor this discussion on four interconnected conceptual nodes: Frantz Fanon's work on the violence of the colonial state, Mahmood Mamdani's citizen–subject dichotomy in the colonial state, Atieno Odhiambo's concept of the ideology of order, and Peter Ekeh's notion of the two publics and their attendant moralities in postcolonial Africa. This exploration of the cultures of violence across Kenyan history allows me to meditate on what can be termed the political morality of violence and assassination as an instrument of state power. Put differently, I suggest that certain permutations of political expediency and negotiations of morality help us understand the disconcerting adaptations that post-independence Kenya makes to the violent state inherited from the British colonial administration.

The Ledger of Kenya's Assassinations

In his novel, *Devil on the Cross* (1982), Kenyan writer Ngugi wa Thiong'o coins the phrase 'taken to Ngong' as short-hand for the phenomenon of political assassinations in Kenyan public memory. If Ngugi's nod to Ngong and political assassinations is so subtle as to be lost on the inattentive reader, then his son, Mukoma wa Ngugi revisits Ngong with more sustained narrative intent in his 2013 novel, *Killing Sahara*. Here, a body found in the Ngong forest (just outside Nairobi), a day before a bomb explosion at the city's Norfolk Hotel, lies at the centre of a thriller that journeys across Kenya, Mexico and the US. Like the body of Kenyan Member of Parliament Josiah Mwangi Kariuki which was similarly found by a Maasai herdsman in the same forest on 11 March 1975 after a nine-day absence and a similar bomb explosion,[2] this body 'has many secrets to tell' (Ngugi 2013: 1). In fact, the younger Ngugi is explicit about his nod to J.M. Kariuki and other political assassinations in Kenyan history when one of the fictional characters in the novel, the African-American detective Ishmael Fofona says:

> I hadn't been in Kenya that long, but I could rattle off names: J. M. Kariuki, a radical
> of this or that, tortured to death, his body discovered by a herdboy. Robert Ouko,
> a well-groomed politician who had allegedly committed suicide in Ngong; first,
> he maimed himself, and then, when he didn't bleed to death, he set himself on
> fire before finally shooting himself in the head. Witnesses for the prosecution and
> defense all died mysteriously, including the herdboy who, again, found the body
> [Ngugi 2013: 2].

For a Kenyan readership, Ishmael Fofona's knowledge of what Atieno Odhiambo and David Cohen term the Kenyan 'genealogy of assassinations and martyr-doms' (2004: 4) signals his fluency in the intricacies of local popular memory in which political and politicized assassinations form an emblematic node.

This node is so firmly embedded in Kenyan social imaginaries that, as Cohen and Odhiambo correctly observe, newspaper commentaries on suspicious deaths are often framed along a recognizable template that recalls previous victims of similarly suspicious murders. In their book, *The Risks of Knowledge: Investigations into the Death of Hon. Minister John Robert Ouko in Kenya, 1990*, David Cohen and Atieno Odhiambo write:

> In its first coverage of Ouko's death, the *Daily Nation* included a prominent arti-
> cle on assassinations in Kenya, and, early in its very first story on Ouko's death,
> the *Weekly Review* drew a comparison between the found corpse of Ouko and the
> mutilated body of J.M. Kariuki. A genealogy of assassinations and martyrdoms has
> been inscribed, perhaps indelibly, into the historical ledger of the Kenya nation,
> and this ledger has enabled powerful and also varied associations for the corpse of
> Robert Ouko [Cohen and Odhiambo 2004: 4–5].

The two historians offer a brief survey of this historical ledger of Kenyan as-sassinations, primarily focusing on the murders of communist pan-Africanist Pio Gama Pinto on 24 February 1965, the suave and ambitious politician Tom Mboya on 5 July 1969, the outspoken cabinet minister J.M. Kariuki on 2 March 1975, Minister of Foreign Affairs Robert Ouko on 16 February 1991, and aca-demic and chairman of the Devolution Committee of the National Constitu-tional Conference Crispin Odhiambo Mbai on 14 September 2003. Like the cir-cumstances surrounding these alleged assassinations and martyrdoms, various

---

[2] See Hornsby 2012 and Loughran 2010 for discussions of the J.M. Kariuki case. See also Kariuki-Machua 2008 for a personal account of the murder from the family's perspective.

victims occupy different spaces in Kenyan public memory of this ledger. While cabinet ministers Tom Mboya, J.M. Kariuki and Robert Ouko – and occasionally clerics Bishop Alexander Muge who was killed on 14 August 1990 in a staged road accident and Fr John Anthony Kaiser who was shot dead on 24 August 1999 – are often cited in newspaper articles on political assassinations in Kenyan history, Julie Ward is often conspicuously absent from most such citations; her story hardly commands the same cross-generational recognizability as Kariuki, Mboya, Ouko, Muge and Kaiser's, despite obvious overlaps and similarities between her murder and those of these men. Although she is absent from Cohen and Odhiambo's ledger, Julie Ward's murder prefigured the Ouko murder in many ways. In fact, this overlapped with Scotland Yard's visit to Kenya to investigate the Ward murder. Another set of Scotland Yard detectives would soon be back to investigate Ouko's murder. A 1996 *Nairobi Law Monthly* report summarizes these overlaps eloquently: 'Ouko's execution was a perfection of Julie's' (*Nairobi Law Monthly* 1996b: 27).

The two historians underline the overlaps between the Kenyan police responses to the two murders, which uncannily mirrored each other, down to the key state actors involved: Chief pathologist Jason Kaviti, who had altered Ward's autopsy two years earlier, examined Ouko's remains – a partly burnt body with a bullet through the head – and arrived at the surprising verdict of suicide; Judge Abdullah Fidahussein, who presided over one of the Ward trials, presided over the trial and acquittal of Jonah Anguka for Ouko's murder; and former CID officer Crispus Ongoro once again presided over a Commission of Inquiry into Ouko's murder (Cohen and Odhiambo 2004: 230–1). Most importantly, both cases featured an elaborate police cover-up. These overlaps between the two cases make Ward's murder very typical of Kenyan assassinations, despite being the only woman on the list, and only the second non-Kenyan and white victim, after Fr John Anthony Kaiser, an American Mill Hill Missionary in charge of the Lolgorian Parish in Ngong, whose dead body was found on 24 August 2000 on the Nairobi–Naivasha highway.

The centrality of assassination in Kenyan historiography and its links to a culture of state violence is powerfully underlined by the Truth, Justice and Reconciliation Commission (TJRC) which was established by an Act of Parliament – the Truth, Justice and Reconciliation Commission Act 6 of 2008 – to examine the historical cleavages of injustice and human rights violations in Kenya; and to contribute towards national unity, reconciliation and healing, particularly following the 2007/8 post-election violence in Kenya. In its report – submitted to the presidency and widely circulated as a public document in May 2013 – the TJRC makes detailed observations on massacres, political assassinations, extra-judicial killings and disappearances, unlawful detention, torture and ill-treatment, and sexual violence, all with state involvement. Under the section on political assassinations, the report comments on the assassinations of Pio

Gama Pinto, J.M. Kariuki, Tom Mboya, Robert Ouko and Crispin Odhiambo Mbai, with brief mention of Fr Anthony John Kaiser. Bishop Muge and Julie Ward are both missing from this version of the ledger.

Julie Ward's position in this register of political and politicized murders is unique: she is a woman, a British citizen, an ordinary tourist and, from the information publicly available so far, she never publicly articulated any opinions that may have been deemed threatening to the sensitive toes of power, unlike the other victims on the ledger. Yet the patterns of her murder, the disposal of her body and state cover-up make her murder typical of Kenyan assassinations, even though her death had less political traction in terms of resonances with local political groupings, compared to victims who preceded or came after her such as Mboya and Ouko, both of whose murders sparked public demonstrations on the streets, anger in parliament[3] and a sense of targeted elimination of the Luo community's political leadership, as James Ogude (2007) illustrates.

Odhiambo and Cohen's idea of a genealogy of assassination implicitly builds on Michel Foucault's concept of genealogy as 'a form of history which can account for the constitution of knowledges, discourses, domains of objects, etc, without having to make reference to a subject which is either transcendental in relation to the field of events or runs in its empty sameness throughout the course of history' (Hacking 1986: 37). Foucault writes of a shift of focus from 'vast unities like "periods" or "centuries" to the phenomena of rupture, of discontinuity [and] incidence of interruptions' (Foucault 2002: 4). His genealogy is rooted in a keen concern with change in 'the mutual relations between systems of truth and modalities of power; [and] the way in which there is a 'political regime' of the production of truth. [Genealogy] looks for accidents, chance, passion, petty malice, surprises, feverish agitation, unsteady victories and power' (ibid.: 224). It is these listed features of genealogies that are interesting to explore, with regards to the patterns, continuities and disruptions in Kenya's high-profile assassinations, and their interface with Julie Ward's murder.

A 1975 book on Pio Gama Pinto rightly describes him as independent Kenya's first (political) martyr (Print Craft 1966). Pinto was shot dead on the driveway to his Nairobi house on 24 February 1965. Two teenagers, Kisilu Mutua, 18, and Chege Thuo, 19, were charged with the murder. Thuo was acquitted, while Mutua was sentenced to death by hanging, but the sentence was subsequently changed to life imprisonment, after appeal (Odinga 1976: 287). Mutua was released in 2000, and 'continued to protest his innocence' (Branch 2012: 46). Daniel Branch cites the US embassy at the time as describing Pio Gama Pinto as Vice President Oginga Odinga's 'brilliant political tactician' (ibid.: 44), while British diplomat Malcolm MacDonald described him as a 'dedicated communist, and the principal brain behind the whole secret organisation of

---

[3] See Kenya National Assembly Record (Hansard) of 23 March 2003 and 15 December 2010.

Mr. Odinga's movement [credited with mobilizing] backbench opposition in parliament to Kenyatta and with leading "other anti-government movements"' (ibid.). This – the first of many political murders to follow – was an attempt to dash Odinga's socialist-leaning politics, deemed a threat to both first-president Kenyatta's government and Anglo-American interests in the region in the context of the Cold War (Cohen and Odhiambo 2004: 4). In his autobiography *Not Yet Uhuru*, Oginga Odinga – independent Kenya's first Vice President, and one of the consistent pro-democracy voices across Kenyan history – writes that during the Pinto murder trial, Chief Justice Sir John Ainley wondered that the "'prime mover of the whole affair" had not been more thoroughly investigated' (Odinga 1976: 287). He further describes an elaborate attempt to hoodwink Kenyans into believing that Pinto was a victim of a Chinese–Soviet conflict (ibid.: 288). Of this case, the TJRC report indicated that Kisilu and Thuo 'were used as scapegoats to divert attention away from the true motive and the more responsible perpetrators of Pinto's assassination' (2013: 24). They would be the first of a long chain of scapegoats who would be tried or found guilty of murders which, while they may have known about or even actively participated in, were not committed on their orders. Magiroi, Kipeen and Makallah, charged with the Ward murder, appear to have their predecessors in Kisilu and Thuo.

Four years after Pinto's death, in 1969, the secretary-general of the ruling party, KANU, and Minister for Economic Planning, Tom Mboya, would be shot dead as he walked into a friend's pharmacy in Nairobi's central business district. In *The Kenyatta Succession* (1980), historians Joseph Karimi and Philip Ochieng describe Mboya as a politician who, owing to his 'legendary efficiency, organisational brilliance, cosmopolitan upbringing and deeply Right-wing world outlook, was the darling of Establishment forces both at home and in the West' and was popularly perceived as the ideal successor to Kenyatta (1980: 16). This placed him squarely in the firing line of a powerful political constituency with close ties to the president, which felt differently about who should succeed the ageing Kenyatta. Karimi and Ochieng note that, ironically, just before his assassination, Mboya had been instrumental in blocking Odinga's rise to power, by first facilitating his removal as Vice President of both the country and the ruling party; then sabotaging the chances of Odinga's opposition party, Kenya People's Union, running for elections. Once Odinga was neutralized, Mboya became a dispensable threat. A man named Nahashon Isaac Njenga Njoroge was charged with Mboya's murder, found guilty, and sentenced to death. Njoroge's question at his arrest – 'why pick on me? Why not the big man?' (Cohen and Odhiambo 2004: 175) – remains an emblematic mnemonic of scapegoating in Kenyan assassinations. Since Pinto's murder, the consistent pattern across these cases has been to charge the 'smaller fish', who are sent through murder trials, often with a questionable guilty verdict or an equally questionable acquittal without a full picture of their involvement emerging. The silence about the 'big man' first introduced to Kenyans by Njenga remains unbroken in each case, beyond rumours which often serve to reinforce the shroud of fear and paranoia that haunts these cases. In view of a rumoured history of indiscreet witnesses dying under questionable circumstances, silence seems wisest for many. In typical Kenyan fashion, the truth of whether or not Njenga was hanged remains unconfirmed. Branch writes that according to intelligence documents which have since been unclassified,

> On the night of 8 November [1969], Njenga was woken by the public hangman, himself a British expatriate officer. Taken aback by the turn of events, Njenga broke down as he was taken from his cell to the scaffold and executed. The hangman was working under explicit orders direct from [Minister Charles] Njonjo. Only the commissioner of prisons, the hangman and Njonjo knew what was taking place. The prison chaplain, who normally attended executions, was not summoned, and the prison doctor was only present because the executioner had personally contacted him. To the British, the indecent speed, secrecy and Njenga's total surprise was 'consistent with the possibility that he had been given assurances that his life would be saved, and that he was summarily dispatched to prevent him opening his mouth' (Branch 2012: 84).

On its part, the TJRC concluded that 'the circumstances surrounding Mboya's assassination – including the political rivalries he provoked, and the failure of the government to investigate fully the assassination – point to the involvement of government officials in the killing and subsequent cover up' (2013: 25).

Another five years later, in 1975, Josiah Mwangi Kariuki, a wealthy businessman and cabinet minister would be murdered. A former Mau Mau detainee, Kariuki retained strong ties and strong opinions on veteran Mau Mau fighters, and regularly spoke out against the Kenyatta government's failure to address growing economic inequality and implement land reforms. This may be what sealed his fate in the eyes of a clique of powerful politicians who had coalesced around the ageing president. Kariuki was last seen in public in the company of the Commander of the General Services Unit, Ben Gethi, a day after a series of bomb explosions rocked Nairobi. He was reported missing for several days, before his body was found by a Maasai herdsman in the Ngong Hills, on the outskirts of the city. The disposal of Kariuki's body and the bungling that would follow attempts to cover up the murder inaugurated a template that would be repeated a decade later, in the handling of Julie Ward and Robert Ouko's remains. Like Ward's, Kariuki's remains were not supposed to have been found, they were supposed to be disposed of by hyenas in the forest. Daniel Branch writes that the bungling happened due to a change of shifts at the police station where, when the Maasai herdsman reported his discovery of a body whose identity he did not immediately register, the police officer on duty was 'unaware of the "situation" and thus sent the body to Nairobi City mortuary' (Branch 2012;

120). In its report on the murder, a Parliamentary Select Committee made up of Kariuki's allies in parliament reported that attempts to 'lose' the body continued in Nairobi City Mortuary, where it was moved around in the mortuary, while the police may have been playing for time 'in the hope that in the confusion caused by the presence in the mortuary of numerous victims of the 1st March 1975 bomb blast, JM's body might be buried as unidentified. There were indications that attempts were being made to get JM's body passed off as that of a "Luo gangster" because of the missing lower teeth' (National Assembly of Kenya 1975: 30). Based on its investigations, the committee suspected that the actual murderer was a policeman named Pius Kibathi Thuo, but he had acted on orders from further above. The report named thirteen prominent political figures adversely, including Kenyatta's brother in-law and Minister of State in the Office of the President, Mbiyu Koinange, and Senior Superintendent of Police, Arthur Wanyoike Thungu. When the MPs delivered their report to President Kenyatta on 3 June 1975, 'the president ordered that Koinange's name and that of the presidential bodyguard, Arthur Wanyoike Thungu, be removed from the list of individuals who deserved more thorough investigation. "When you beat the son, you beat the father"', the president told the committee members. Reluctantly, the MPs did as they were told, and the final draft of the report appeared without mention of Koinange or Thungu. However, earlier versions of the report, with their names included, had already been released to certain journalists and diplomats' (Branch 2012: 116–7). Close to forty years later, the TJRC would find 'sufficient evidence [implicating] Peter Kinyuanji (aka Mark Twist), Pius Kibathi, Ben Gethi, Waruhiu Itote, Ignatius Nderi, Arthur Wanyoike Thungu, John Mutung'u, Silas Mburu Gichua, and Mbiyu Koinange' in the assassination and/or subsequent cover-up (2013: 25). But perhaps the most damning finding in the report was its official observation that 'President Kenyatta deliberately interfered in the independent investigation undertaken by the Parliamentary Select Committee by, among other things, directly removing the following two names from the report because they worked in the Office of the President: Mbiyu Koinange and Arthur Wanyoike Thungu' (2013: 25). This confirmed what had been only rumour since the purging of these names from the official report in 1975.

Killed on February 1990 – just over a year after the Julie Ward murder – Robert Ouko would be the first high-profile murder victim in the Moi government, which had, until now, preferred detentions without trial and torture of elements considered threats to the regime as its strategies of choice. In a salutary nod to the impunity and arrogance of the regime, Kenya's most notorious torture chambers were housed at the 26-storey Nyayo House building prominently located in Nairobi's central business district, with regular pedestrian and motor traffic wrapped around the building on a daily basis. Long before the official acknowledgement of the fact, rumours had flown around the country about the torture chambers in Nyayo House[4] – named after President Moi's nickname, which he acquired upon his rise to presidency, when he assured Kenyans that there would be no radical changes from the Kenyatta regime's policies, as he intended to '*fuata nyayo ya* Kenyatta' (follow the footsteps of Kenyatta). Soon buildings, bus services, songs and suburbs mushroomed, named after Nyayo as he stamped his authority on Kenyan public life.[5] Of this torture capital, the TJRC report noted that

> the Nyayo House basement cells and the 24th, 25th and 26th floors were used for interrogations and torture after the attempted coup of 1982, during the *Mwakenya* crackdown,[6] and the FERA/M crackdown, and [the Commission] further finds … that the use of the Nyayo House basement cells as police cells was never an afterthought but a well meditated plan by the government. The cells at the basement of Nyayo House were designed and built specifically for torture purposes. Indeed, the State established a task force for the specific purpose of interrogation and torture of suspects [TJRC 2012: 30].

Like J.M. Kariuki and Julie Ward before him, Robert Ouko went missing for several days before his partly burnt remains were discovered by yet another herdboy, Paul Shikuku, near his farm in Koru. The official position was that he had committed suicide, an incredible theory which, like the Ward case, had too many loopholes, given the nature of the wounds, including intense burning, a bullet wound through the head and severe bruises to the limbs.[7] The Ouko murder is easily the most-investigated murder in the history of Kenya's assassinations, prompting the Kenya Human Rights Commission to cite it as an example

---

[4] See *We Lived to Tell: The Nyayo House Story* (2003) for survivors' accounts of their experiences in the Nyayo House torture chambers. The torture chambers' location in the basement of the Nyayo House building, located in Nairobi's Central Business District at the intersection of the busy Uhuru Highway and Kenyatta Avenue, a stone's throw from the Parliament Building and with various government ministries in the same building, candidly captures the regime's self-assured impunity and anonymity in its atrocities.

[5] I have explored the Nyayo branding and the cultures of sycophancy it bred, elsewhere (Musila 2009).

[6] *Mwakenya* was, according to the Moi government, a secret political movement that planned to overthrow the government after the failed 1982 coup. The existence of this movement remains unconfirmed. Popular wisdom in Kenya suggests that it was a phantom creation of the Moi state, which needed a legitimate-sounding reason for its assault on people with dissenting views, who would be branded members of the *Mwakenya* movement. See Maina Mutonya's 'Writing Human Rights in Kenya: *Mwakenya* Prison Literature of Wahome Mutahi' (2005). See also Njuguna Mutonya's *Crackdown! A Journalist's Personal Story of Moi Era Purges 1986–1989* (2010) in which he describes his torture experiences at Nyayo House and eventual imprisonment on suspicion of membership of the *Mwakenya* movement. Also Atieno Odhiambo's essay 'Hegemonic Enterprises and Instrumentalities of Survival: Ethnicity and Democracy in Kenya' (2002) for a detailed exploration of the Moi regime's repressive strategies.

[7] See Cohen and Odhiambo (2004: 117–23) for a detailed description of the remains.

of the culture of repeated inquiries with no concrete results: the murder was 'initially investigated by the Scotland Yard team led by Inspector John Troon, then by a Commission sitting in Kisumu under Justice Evans Gicheru, and then, in 2003, a Parliamentary Committee led by the MP for Kisumu Town East Hon. Gor Sunguh was established. None of these produced a conclusive report on the murder' (KHRC 2011: 9). Like Ward's case which featured media accounts by alleged eye-witnesses, on 26 April 1992, an alleged Kenya Special Branch agent named George Wajackoyah, on self-exile in the UK, gave the *Sunday Times* a detailed description of how Ouko was taken from his house, tortured and killed by top Kenyan political figures (Cohen and Odhiambo 2004).

The last three names in the assassination ledger are Anglican Church Bishop of Eldoret, Alexander Muge, Fr Anthony John Kaiser and Dr Crispin Odhiambo. Bishop Muge was killed in a suspicious road accident on 14 August 1990 in Kipkaren, on his way to address a public gathering in Busia, Western Kenya. Muge had been an increasingly vocal critic of the Moi government; and at the height of agitation for multi-party democracy, this automatically made him an 'enemy of the state'. A former Special Branch Intelligence Agent, James Lando Khwatenge testified before the TJRC on the murder in March 2012 that Muge's murder was part of 'Operation *Shika Msumari*' (Muchangi and Mwangi 2012). *Shika Msumari* literally translates to 'Hold the Nail' but was probably euphemistically intended to connote 'nail it' or 'nail them'. Before travelling to Busia, a KANU loyalist and Labour Minister, Peter Okondo, had overzealously warned Muge not to set foot in Busia, in an apparent effort to signal his loyalty to the ruling party by confronting its 'enemies', but Muge defied the order. The clique behind Operation *Shika Msumari* took advantage of this public fall-out to stage the murder as a road accident, with Okondo as their decoy, should the public get suspicious. The driver of the lorry that rammed into Muge's vehicle got a seven-year sentence for reckless driving, but reportedly died after serving five years. Similarly, Fr John Anthony Kaiser had been a vocal critic of the government, particularly following the so-called ethnic clashes of 1991. He had documented the gross violations and complicity of politicians in the tensions between the Maasai and Kisii communities in Trans-Mara district, which also formed the subject of his posthumously published memoir titled *If I Die* (2003). In 1999, Fr Kaiser had 'championed the case of Florence Mpayei, who had alleged she had been raped by Julius Sunkuli, a cabinet minister' (Branch 2012: 243–4). The official police position was that Fr Kaiser suffered from depression and had taken his life in a moment of hopelessness. In his foreword to Fr Kaiser's *If I Die* (2003), the then Apostolic Nuncio to Kenya Giovanni Tonucci writes that the American Embassy and FBI's intervention in investigating the matter had given many the false hope that the truth would come out, but when the FBI Report came, 'we realized that Fr Kaiser had been murdered a second time, this time in his credibility. Those, while continuing to proclaim that they admired Fr. Kaiser and considered him a great American citizen, now try to offer us the image of a sick man, unbalanced, prone to depression, and, of course, with the tendency to commit suicide … With the sterilized language of bureaucratic documents, the Report claimed he died "of a self-inflicted wound"' (2003: 13). Fr Kaiser's murder case illustrates the arbitrariness of the judiciary's role in Kenya's history of violence. In a 2007 inquest into the murder, the court rejected the claims of the joint report by American FBI and Kenya's CID that Fr Kaiser had struggled with depression which may have led to him taking his own life (KHRC 2011: 10).

The murder of Crispin Odhiambo Mbai, according to the TJRC report, may have been linked to his political views on the new constitution, while he chaired the committee on devolution. The committee further found that 'there is sufficient evidence to link Norman Nyaga to the assassination of Dr. Mbai' (TJRC 2013: 26). While Dr Mbai's is the last name in current ledgers, future assassination ledgers are likely to include several new names of witnesses in the ICC case against Uhuru Kenyatta and William Samoei arap Ruto, witnesses who disappeared or were found dead under strange circumstances. One prominent name in this category is Meshack Yebei who was last seen boarding an unknown car in Turbo in December 2014 and disappeared for several days before a body believed to be his was retrieved from River Nyando and taken to a mortuary in the neighbouring town of Kapsabet. This body, like Kariuki's was clearly not supposed to be found. In a strange twist, it would emerge in February 2015 that the body may have been another person's identified as Yusuf Hussein, while Yebei remained missing. At the time of writing this, the two families are waiting for DNA confirmation of the identity of the dead man; Yebei's whereabouts remain unknown. Alongside Yebei, there appears to be a new list of assassinated Kenyans mainly consisting of Muslim clerics considered to hold views sympathetic to the Al-Shabaab militant group in neighbouring Somalia, that has been responsible for much bloodshed in Kenya. Figured as terrorist sympathisers and radical Islamists, these people have been reportedly eliminated by a highly trained elite death squad, with training and intelligence support from a number of international governments invested in the 'war against terror'. A 2014 Al Jazeera documentary titled *Inside Kenya's Death Squads* offers a detailed portrait of these death squads' chilling work.[8]

Read through the lens of Foucault's emphasis on continuities and interruptions in the workings of genealogies, this register of Kenyan assassinations features both recurrent tropes – attempted cover-ups, suicide theories, bodies in the bush, confessions of renegade agents – and discontinuities, such as the manner of killing and the ostensible reasons for the murders. But these patterns were not mechanically interpreted by Kenyan publics.

To understand the centrality of the trope of assassination as a narrative trope

---

[8] See www.youtube.com/watch?v=lUjOdjdH8Uk for the documentary.

in Kenyan public memory, we need to understand the Kenyan socio-political context from the 1960s to the 1990s. Julie Ward's death, in 1988, is located at a pivotal moment both in Kenyan political history, and in the narrative of assassinations in Kenyan social imaginaries. Politically, the late 1980s marked the climax of state paranoia under the Moi government, the genesis of which may be traced back to the very moment of Moi's ascent to power in 1978 – against the wishes of sections of the Kenyatta power clique[9] – and reached its peak with the 1982 attempted coup. The post-1982 years witness increased state repression, and deeper entrenchment of a culture of impunity, thanks to a compromised judiciary and state security machinery. At the same time, this period witnesses increased pressure for multi-party democracy, to which the Moi regime eventually succumbs in 1991. One newspaper claims that Julie Ward may have accidentally stumbled upon a secret militia training camp in the Maasai Mara in September 1989, headed by a clique of influential politicians, who assumed she was a British spy. Intriguingly, militias subsequently feature in the 1991 so-called ethnic violence just before the first multi-party elections,[10] while British Intelligence is subsequently revealed to have been complicit in the cover-up of her murder in the same year. Another alleged eye witness in the Ward murder, Valentine Uhuru Kodipo was to testify to the Kiliku Parliamentary Select Committee on the so-called 'tribal' clashes that he was part of an elite militia group charged with doing the state's 'dirty work' which had included these. Kodipo claims that Julie Ward's case is one in a long history of bloodshed perpetrated by this group. The idea of private armies had come up severally in Parliamentary debates in the early 1990s. Chris Mburu, writing for the *Nairobi Law Monthly* in 1992, cites FORD party leader Oginga Odinga's statement that top politicians 'are training armies in the sprawling Maasai Mara Game Reserve'.[11]

In its report on the culture of impunity in Kenya, the Kenya Human Rights Commission observes that the culture of impunity 'is so entrenched into Kenyan society that human rights violations and grand corruption committed by state and non-state actors remain unresolved'[12] (KHRC 2011: 2). The report

---

[9] As Karimi and Ochieng illustrate in their book, *The Kenyatta Succession* (1980).

[10] See Kagwanja (2003) for an insightful discussion of the so-called ethnic violence. Many reports indicate the attacks were not as spontaneous as the government led Kenyans to believe, but, were in fact orchestrated by armed militias not resident in the affected areas. Significantly, these attacks inaugurated a new culture of election violence in Kenyan politics, which has remained a constant to date.

[11] Chris Mburu, 'Parliamentary Select Committee: Will it name the Real Culprits?' *Nairobi Law Journal* 43 (June 1992): 27.

[12] It must be acknowledged that there have been some changes with the new constitution in Kenya, including the vetting of state officers and exclusion of those who fail the integrity test from pursuing public office. Despite this, the KHRC report on impunity reminds us of President Kibaki's flouting of this law: 'however, these resolutions were vitiated in February 28, 2011 when President Mwai Kibaki appointed Justice Alnashir Visram, Prof. Githu Muigai,

further notes that the problem is not so much a dearth of information about those responsible, but rather, what is lacking is 'a systemic way of dealing with those responsible for the human rights violations and economic crimes' (ibid.: 37). What makes the culture of impunity in Kenya most troubling is that it is embedded in the very institutions and actors charged with upholding the rule of law, as is evident from the above discussion, which underscores repeated complicity of state security apparatuses in murders and their cover-up. Similar patterns would unfold in the Julie Ward case, with active police involvement in undermining attempts to get to the bottom of the murder.

But how do we explain the processes by which the connections and overlaps between these political and politicized murders came to be consolidated in Kenyan public memory into the trope of assassinations, which Kenyan social imaginaries have continued to update for over half a century of murders? Two key platforms in this process are print media and the rumour networks which, in Kenya, especially where suspicious murders are concerned, form a complex circuit of flows of information and perspectives.

Karin Barber's argument that popular arts 'do not merely reflect an already constituted consciousness, giving us a window into something already fully present; they are themselves important means through which consciousness is articulated and communicated' (1987: 4) is equally applicable to newspapers as an important medium in the formulation of the narrative of assassinations in Kenyan social imaginaries. In their coverage of news with a recurrent cross-referencing of a long archive of past coverage and occurrences, newspapers facilitate this consolidation of particular perspectives on the culture of assassination in Kenyan social imaginaries.

The formulation of public perspectives on the Julie Ward murder and similar murders in Kenyan history was mediated through detailed print media coverage of the case and readers' consistent tracking of the twists and turns in the case, without explicitly seeming to influence public opinions on it. This coverage was received by a readership attentive to both ongoing debates about broader political cultures and an ever-growing archive of the state's fatal mischief in the past. Kenyan publics thus located themselves as self-appointed detectives, carefully piecing together the available information and arriving at their own conclusions and suspicions at each turn of the case.

In an essay on media and democratization in the Third World, Vicky Randall underscores the media's role in mobilizing, orchestrating and amplifying

Kioko Kikulumi and William Kirwa to the positions of Chief Justice (CJ), Attorney General (AG), Director of Public Prosecutions (DPP) and Controller of Budget (CoB) respectively without regard to constitutional provisions on leadership and integrity. The appointments were later revoked following a public outcry coupled with the Speaker's and Court rulings that the four appointments were unconstitutional' (KHRC 2011: 12) popular protest (1993: 636). Apart from this well-documented role of print media in Kenyans' struggles for democracy[13] one strand of Kenyan public life that has been variously mediated by newspapers is political and politicized assassinations. There is no Kenyan-authored book on the Ward murder, but it was widely covered in local newspapers and current affairs magazines, including the *Daily Nation*, easily the largest Kenyan newspaper, both in circulation and popularity, *The East African Standard*, *The Weekly Review* and *The Nairobi Law Monthly*, which variously enjoy/ed a competitive and collaborative relationship with each other. In addition to their traditional role of informing the public about current news, Kenyan print media – thanks to a remarkable local culture of avid newspaper consumption – played a second role of framing the debates and mediating a complex flow of perspectives between official sources (British and Kenyan) and public opinion. In the repressive Kenya of the 1980s and 1990s, newspapers were an important node in this network of information flows by reporting and commenting on both the official perspectives on the case, as they unfolded in the Nairobi courtrooms and the unofficial 'public' versions of truths from the streets, bar rooms, family gatherings and other such spaces, forming an intriguing cocktail of court proceedings, rumours, eye-witness reports, informed guesses and anonymous tip-offs by alleged accomplices in the murder. Readerships extended print media reports by decoding the gaps, silences and contradictions and arriving at their own verdicts on this complex case. These verdicts variously filtered their way back to the papers. In light of this location of newspapers in Kenyan public imaginaries at the time, I suggest that for Kenyan publics, the Julie Ward murder mystery animated particular fragments of social memories, which differed significantly from UK newspapers' coverage of the case. Where UK newspapers for a while emphasized protection of the tourism industry as the reason behind attempts to cover up the murder, Kenyan publics read the clues made available by print media reports differently, arriving at the conclusion that the cover-up was to protect a criminal state whose powerful political figures were implicated in the murder.

Vicky Randall observes that 'in circumstances where the mainstream media are subject to extensive political repression, the moment they do criticize authoritarian rule they risk transgressing the hazy boundaries of what is deemed legitimate and becoming *de facto* "alternative" [and "oppositional"]' (1993: 628). This was true of popular perceptions of some newspapers in 1980s Kenya and may, for instance, explain Kenyans' perceptions of the *Daily Nation* as an anti-establishment, and therefore, credible, newspaper, as compared to its two rivals at the time, Lonrho-owned *The East African Standard* and state-owned *Kenya Times*. But Randall cautions that the owners of such papers – in the case of Latin America – were often 'above all businessmen interested in markets and profits,

---

[13] See for instance Loughran (2010).

which now seemed to require some recognition of popular political pressures' (ibid.: 641). This is equally true of the Kenyan press, which increasingly recognized the readerships' desire for robust political coverage of the repressive regime's actions.[14] In this respect, these newspapers were both catalysts and products of popular politicization of Kenyan publics.

This context accentuates Kenyan print media's double role in the Julie Ward story in both archiving the twists and turns and mediating public discourse on the case. In light of the increasingly repressive Moi regime of the 1980s and 1990s, newspapers walked a thin line between capturing the anti-establishment sensibilities of their readerships and being careful not to be banned.[15] In this political climate, the Julie Ward murder got subtly integrated into broader struggles for democracy, while newspapers mediated the inscription of a range of concerns about the political climate of the Moi regime of the late 1980s and the 1990s on the case. Second, print media's coverage of the case underlined the resonances between the Julie Ward murder and similar suspicious murders that preceded and came after, most notably the Tom Mboya and J.M. Kariuki cases before it, and the Robert Ouko murder, just over a year later. This latter role – underscoring resonances and patterns – draws attention to a distinct interweaving of the archival and mediation role of newspapers, not only in the

[14] Vicky Randall writes that initially, many post-independent Anglophone African countries enjoyed a relatively free press which had largely developed in close association with the nationalist movements: 'nationalist leaders like Nkrumah had been able to establish and distribute their own newspapers, recognizing the potential importance of the press as "a collective organizer, a collective instrument of mobilization and a collective educator." But for that very reason, as new national leaders moved after independence to consolidate their position, they grew less tolerant of criticism and the "honeymoon" period was short-lived. At their disposal they had a whole battery of devices to silence such press criticism' (1993: 628). This scenario played out in Kenya too, where, Gerald Loughran writes, 'if Moi's coming proved to be a false dawn in political terms, so it was for the media. Self-censorship was already an accomplished skill of the Kenyan journalist. Gavin Bennett, sub-editor in 1975–8, explained, "You had to understand what would cause a fuss and what wouldn't. You could take a calculated risk if you felt something really important needed to be said. Everyone from the lowest reporter had to know what was acceptable"' (2010: 150).

[15] Gerald Loughran's work suggests that the use of the law to repress freedom of expression, so prevalent across various regimes in independent Kenya, actually traces its roots to colonial Kenya, with the tabling and passing of the Books and Newspapers Bill 27 of 1960 by the then Legislative Council, which called for the deposit of bonds of 500 pounds as 'a security payment of any monetary penalty which may at any time be imposed against any person upon his conviction for any offence relating to the printing and publication of that newspaper' (2010: 37). The Bill 'provided that any police officer could seize any book or newspaper if he suspected it was publishing in contravention of the Act, and could make a search without warrant if he thought delay would defeat the purposes of the Act (2010: 37–38). As Loughran rightly notes, this became a law which 'authoritarian postcolonial governments implemented with enthusiasm … banning titles, searching and seizing with zeal, confiscating and destroying the printing machinery of so-called seditions publications and sending editors to prison' (2010: 38).

traditional sense of newspapers as an archival source to which we can return to retrieve information about past events; but in the distinct role of Kenyan newspapers as active players in the creation, revision and contestation of ever-elusive public memories or what can be termed archives of the present.[16] Put differently, these newspapers' coverage of this (and similar cases) over the years has both *contributed to*, and *counted on*, readers' access to shared popular archives of perceptions of state-linked transgressions.

One of the things an exploration of the Julie Ward murder and its location in Kenyan social imaginaries as mediated by local newspapers and rumour networks reveals is the cross-generational link between newspapers and readerships, which enables interesting patterns of reflection on current happenings with the benefit of a shared archive of previous occurrences, coupled with an equally important cross-referencing of the links between various political events. This invites us to rethink our assumptions about popular memory, especially one archived in people's shared memories, and sustained on print media reports and spoken exchanges and speculations as too ephemeral and unstable to be reliable or informative. Print media coverage of the Julie Ward case across the years not only counted on readers' shared knowledge of similar murders in the past, but they also implicitly presumed readers' familiarity with the repressive political climate of the day. In this respect, Karin Barber's observation that 'audiences make the meaning of the text "whole" by what they bring to it' (2007: 137), is applicable to the print media coverage of the Ward case in Kenya, as both reporters and readerships tapped into an ever-growing archive of similar patterns of state responses to suspicious murders in their reading of Kenyan responses to the murder. For instance, in response to Ward's optimism in 1996, at the launch of the Crispus Ongoro inquiry into his daughter's murder, that the he was dealing with a new Commissioner of Police, Shadrack Kiruki, who would be an improvement on hostile predecessor, Phillip Kilonzo, the *Nairobi Law Monthly* observed: 'Ward could use some skepticism that is current among many observers who view the probe as more self-serving than a final determination by the government to unravel the mysterious murder … Ward is all too unsuspicious of the government's anxiety to clear itself … Yes, Kiruki may not be hostile but if the names floated by [alleged eye witness Valentine Uhuru] Kodipo remain the principal suspects, it may be another case of the same stones that President Moi promised to overturn to get the killers of Dr. Ouko, but found too heavy to shift' (*Nairobi Law Monthly* 1996a: 26). This article presumes readers' familiarity with both the Ouko murder case, and the cliché 'no stones will be left unturned', a recurrent promise by government officials.

---

[16] See for instance *The People*'s 1996 coverage of the Julie Ward death. The article outlines a series of suspicious murders in post-independence Kenya down to the Julie Ward murder, pointing out recurrent tropes between these cases.

In time, the repressive Kenyan state inspired a new newspaper genre, born from one of the core tools associated with state accountability: the commission of inquiry. Gerard Loughran writes that when President Moi ordered a Judicial Commission of inquiry into his Minister of Constitutional Affairs, Charles Njonjo, the *Daily Nation* offered an 'unprecedented verbatim coverage ... the rationale was that people were deeply interested but couldn't be there in person so we had to take the proceedings to them ... [It] paid off handsomely in circulation terms, boosting sales from 130,000 to 154,000' (Loughran 2010: 174). Subsequently, the Commission of Inquiry, and its cousin, the Parliamentary Task Team, became a familiar response to state scandals, most notably the so-called 'ethnic clashes' and the Robert Ouko murder. In a society with this culture of commissions of inquiry which never quite got to the bottom of anything – because their findings often got classified or watered down, if they did not get disbanded mid-inquiry – this new genre of verbatim reportage of proceedings was particularly useful for Kenyans across the country who could follow the proceedings and arrive at their own conclusions. This was particularly important given that, as the Africa Centre for Open Governance (AfriCOG) notes, there was 'an internal rule which prohibited the receiving of evidence prejudicial to the state security and the Head of State' (2007: 7–8). An example here is the Akiwumi Commission of Inquiry into ethnic violence which 'expunged from the record evidence that had been adduced by a witness, Father John Kaiser [ruling that] the evidence made adverse [to] the Head of State must be expunged from the records of those proceedings', while further ordering the media not to report on the expunged evidence (ibid.). As they pieced together fragments of information on the Ward murder mystery, Kenyans read the proceedings, witness accounts and lawyers' interventions, in the many Ouko Commissions of Inquiry, in their daily newspapers verbatim.

From White Man's Country to Uhuru

The deployment of violence as a weapon of statecraft is hardly a post-independence invention in Kenya, though the four post-Uhuru (independence) regimes of Jomo Kenyatta (1963–1978), Daniel Toroitich arap Moi (1978–2002), Mwai Kibaki (2002–2012) and Uhuru Kenyatta (current), have variously sharpened its brutal edge.

The one thread that runs across Frantz Fanon's prophetic book, *The Wretched of the Earth* (1967) is that colonialism is a fundamentally violent experience, and decolonization necessitated revolutionary violence, not only to force the colonizers to cede their ill-acquired power and privileges, but most importantly, as a starting point in healing the psychoses of colonial encounter. Fanon describes the soldier and the policeman as go-betweens, 'the spokesmen of the settler and his rule of oppression [whose] frequent and direct action maintain

contact with the native and advise him by means of rifle-butts and napalm'
(1967: 29). The violence of colonialism in Africa has been extensively explored
in much scholarship on the colonial encounter, with increasing focus on the
logics of empire and its workings. In Kenya, there is a growing body of work that
examines Britain's misadventures in colonial Kenya. One strand of this work has
applied itself to the task of unmasking British brutality in response to the Mau
Mau Land and Freedom Army. Caroline Elkins' *Imperial Reckoning: The Untold
Story of Britain's Gulag in Kenya* (2005) and David Anderson's *Histories of the
Hanged: Britain's Dirty War in Kenya and the End of Empire* (2005), for instance,
offer a compelling exploration of the brutality of British response to Mau Mau,
which resulted in 1,090 Kenyans hanged for suspected Mau Mau crimes. Anderson describes British justice in Kenya as 'a blunt, brutal and unsophisticated
instrument of oppression' (2005: 7), with hangings and extra-judicial killings
as the popular responses in counteracting the Mau Mau movement: 'The British public has always liked a good hanging. They used to flock to the gallows
at London's Tyburn in thousands to watch bodies swing. In Kenya during the
1950s, the white highlanders wanted to do likewise, clamouring for the public
execution of convicted Mau Mau fighters, preferably immediately following
the trial and without the right of appeal, so that Africans could witness for
themselves the dreadful and final rituals of British justice' (2005: 6). Ngugi wa
Thiong'o's novel *A Grain of Wheat*, which reflects on the complexities of the
Mau Mau war, depicts a fictional fulfilment of this morbid fantasy, through the
public hanging of Kihika, an icon of the Mau Mau struggle. While successive
post-independence regimes kept hangings discreet – hence the uncertainty
about Nahashon Njenga's fate – they certainly retained Fanon's policeman and
soldiers as power's spokespersons. One of the ironies of these regimes is that the
hangman's discretion never extended to the spectacular murderers of *adui wa
serikali* (enemies of the state) whose bodies – whether mutilated and discovered
accidentally, or dramatically shot dead in broad daylight, in an articulate gesture
of dispensability – were hyper-visible. These bodies served to deliver a stern
message to would-be transgressives.

According to Crawford Young (1982: 72–73, cited in Odhiambo 1987), the
state is a matrix of institutions through which rule is exercised, with its branches
of governance – legislative, executive, judicial – and its instrumentalities such
as public administration, public enterprises and local government. Within this
understanding, state power is, in principle, moderated by the various institutional structures which guard against abuse. But in practice, the colonial state
amply and regularly demonstrated that it was possible to be legal and lawless,
or, in Jacob Dlamini's words, to 'operate without contradiction both within and
without its own 'legal' bounds' (2014: 15). In his book on the workings of death
squads in apartheid South Africa, Dlamini notes that the apartheid regime 'created bureaucratic procedures that governed everything from the destruction

of communities to the official sanctioning of political murder. [The] killing of political opponents was not [a] desperate measure arrived at when all else failed. It was all of a piece with the bureaucratic and political workings of apartheid' (Dlamini 2014: 14–15). Dlamini's observations are hardly unique to apartheid South Africa. In fact, Mahmood Mamdani insists, apartheid South Africa was far from exceptional; it was a prototypical colonial state, whose practices mirrored those of many colonial states across the continent. Dlamini's observations are equally applicable to the post-independent Kenyan state's deployment of assassination as a response to *adui ya serikali*; and the involvement of state security structures in these murders. Mahmood Mamdani's and Peter Ekeh's work is particularly illuminating in making sense of the logics by which, as Fanon prophesied, the post-independence states in many African countries came to embrace the very tools they objected to in colonial hands.

Mamdani distinguishes colonies of administration from colonies of European settlement which entailed 'the appropriation of land, the destruction of communal autonomy and the defeat and dispersal of tribal populations' (1996: 17). He also makes a case for the ways in which colonial authority in many parts of Africa combined direct and indirect rule: the former in the shape of urban civil power, primarily driven towards the 'exclusion of natives from civil freedoms guaranteed to citizens in civil society', and the latter embodied in rural tribal authority's mandate of 'incorporating natives into a state-enforced customary order' (ibid.: 18). The result was a bifurcated state with two forms of power: 'urban power spoke the language of civil society and civil rights, rural power of community and culture' (ibid.). But this produced a third constituency: 'between the rights-bearing colons and the subject peasantry was a third group: urban-based natives, mainly middle- and working-class persons, who were exempt from the lash of customary law but not from modern, racially discriminatory civil legislation. Neither subject to custom nor exalted as rights-bearing citizens, they languished in a juridical limbo' (ibid.: 19).

As the biographies of many African countries reveal, this middle constituency would become the political elite of the nascent independent states with the fall of empire. For Peter Ekeh, this is part of what precipitated the crisis of public morality that is often described in the diction of Africa's weak institutions, the failure of modernity, the politics of the belly, patronage politics and similar symptomatic tags. Ekeh's work offers a useful conceptual handle in explaining why a constituency that took up arms or pens or both, in protest against colonial parasitism and its violence, would proceed to reproduce the very cultures and institutions it fought against. He also helps us make sense of the crisis of morality that haunts the post-independence state, and manifests in, among other ways, a willingness to commit murder and use state security and judicial structures to cover it up.

In his seminal essay 'Colonialism and the Two Publics in Africa: A Theoretical

Statement',[17] Peter Ekeh distinguishes between the logics of morality in Western and African societies. While the public and private realms have a shared moral foundation in Western societies, in Africa, Ekeh argues, there are two public realms, with distinct moral relations to the private realm: 'the public realm in which primordial groupings, ties and sentiments influence and determine an individual's public behaviour [and which] operates on the same moral impera- tives as the private realm; [and] the public realm which is historically associated with the colonial administration and which has become identified with popular politics in postcolonial Africa' (1975: 92). He notes that this second public realm is based on civic structures such as the police, the civil service and the military, but enjoys no moral linkages with the private realm: 'the civic public of Africa is amoral and lacks the generalized moral imperatives operative in the private realm and in the primordial public' (ibid.).

If we take Simon Gikandi's reminder that 'the men and women who founded … modern African writing [and, one might say, the post-independent Afri- can state] … were, without exception, products of the institutions that colo- nialism had introduced and developed on the continent' (2012: 384), then we already begin to see the ways in which Ekeh's work sheds light on the post- independence African political elite's embrace of troubling aspects of colonial statecraft which they soon re-crafted and re-tooled (to borrow Angela Davis's useful phrasing[18]) to serve their own priorities of the workings of state power. Where Jean-François Bayart notes that 'the public administration, the school, the hospital, the trading-post, the business-place and the mission-station were nurseries in which a "moral subject" was planted and tended, and whose ethical and physical practices were to become constituents of the new public culture, including the bureaucratic regulation of the state, economic activity, religious expression, cultural innovation and political mobilization' (Bayart 2000: 249), Ekeh qualifies this class's relationship to the colonial state, by distinguishing between the African bourgeoisie's anti-colonial ideologies and what he terms postcolonial ideologies of legitimation. Regarding the former, he cautions that anti-colonialism was not always synonymous with opposition to the ideals and principles of the Western institutions; rather, it was often a case of being *anti*- colonial personnel but *pro*-colonial ideals and principles (Ekeh 1975: 101).[19] Among the strategies of anti-colonial struggle was what Ekeh terms 'a necessary but destructive strategy: sabotage of the administrative efforts of the colonizers' (ibid.: 102), a strategy that was hard to reverse in the post-independence context.

---

[17] I am grateful to Phillip Onoride Aghoghovwhia, for drawing my attention to Ekeh's essay.

[18] Angela Davis uses these terms in her discussion of contemporary manifestations of racism, in her public lecture 'Antiracism: Transnational Solidarities' delivered at the Johannesburg Theory Workshop on 10 July 2014, at the Centre for the Book, Cape Town.

[19] Dipesh Chakrabarty (2010) makes the same argument on post-independent India.

Trinidadian novelist, Earl Lovelace offers an excellent example of these logics of sabotage, in the context of descendants of slaves in Port au Spain whom he describes as

> Bluebloods of a resistance lived by their ancestors all through slavery – as Maroons, as Runaways, as Bush Negroes, as Rebels: and when they could not perform in space that escape that would take them away from the scene of their brutalization, they took a stand in the very guts of the slave plantations ... *asserting their human-ness in the most wonderful acts of sabotage they could imagine and perform, making a religion of laziness and neglect and stupidity and waste*: singing hosannahs for flood and hurricane and earthquake, praying for damage and pestilence: *continuing it still after Emancipation, that emancipated them to a more profound idleness and waste ... cultivat[ing] with no less fervour the religion with its trinity of Idleness, Laziness and Waste* [Lovelace 1979: 2–3, emphasis added].

Noting the conventional understanding of citizenship as implying a claim to certain rights, coupled with a willingness to perform certain duties, Ekeh argues that citizenship takes different shapes in the two publics in postcolonial Africa: within the primordial public sphere, the individual 'sees his duties as moral obligations to benefit and sustain the primordial public' they belong to (Ekeh 1975: 106), while the benefits are largely intangible and immaterial, often taking the shape of stability and security in the face of the 'psychic turbulence' that marks their double belonging in the two public spheres. On the other hand, the civic public is understood in terms of material gains accruing from it, with little moral compulsion to invest in it. In this sphere, 'duties ... are de-emphasised while rights are squeezed out of the civic public with the amorality of an artful dodger' (Ekeh 1975: 107). In Kenya, this culture is made manifest in wasteful attitudes towards public property as indicated by the phrase '*Suluhu, mali ya uma*'[20] (Swahili for 'it is nothing, it is public property').

Mahmood Mamdani's colonial dichotomy between citizen and subject in African colonies intersects with Ekeh's ideas in illuminating ways, particularly in relation to how the African political elite navigated what he calls its juridical indeterminacy. This shares certain overlaps with Ekeh's elite's navigations of the psychic turbulence of double belonging. Given Mamdani's assertion that the colonial state was Janus-faced, on the one hand governing a racially defined citizenry with access to a cluster of rights while, on the other hand, ruling over subjects through coercion (Mamdani 1996: 19); and if, as both Fanon (1967) and Ekeh (1975) have argued, the native that takes over power at independence is 'an envious man', more invested in accessing the delights of the settler quarter than in radically revolutionizing the infrastructure of state power, it becomes clear why nationalism – the glorious crystallization of collective hope that Fanon had

---

[20] I am grateful to Oluoch Madiang for feedback on the correct phrasing of this saying.

in mind – becomes 'an empty shell, a crude travesty' (Fanon 1967: 119). Equally, we see how the state run by the post-independence elite reverts to violence soon after the euphoria of independence. In Mamdani's words, the anti-colonial struggle was a struggle of 'the embryonic middle and working classes … for entry into civil society' (Mamdani 1996: 19); or as Bayart puts it, the major players in the colonial institutions – public administration, mission stations, schools, churches – were 'instrumental in creating the foundations of the class which is currently dominant in Africa and in setting in motion the process of primitive accumulation from which that class was to benefit' (Bayart 2000: 249).

President Kenyatta's regime in Kenya variously illustrates Ekeh and Mamdani's portraits of the post-independence elite, and its moral relationship to civic rights and responsibilities. Godwin Murunga describes the Kenyatta state's inauguration of presidential authoritarianism, which included the dismantling of the nationalist coalition of the 1950s and 1960s, amending the constitution to serve private goals and concentrating immense power on the president, who was effectively above the law and reigned over the civil service, the judiciary and the bureaucracy (Murunga 2007: 269). Two examples illustrate Kenyatta's embodiment of Ekeh's ideas on morality and the public–private dichotomy: the first example is the earlier-discussed case of J.M. Kariuki's murder, when Kenyatta ordered the Parliamentary Select Committee to remove Mbiyu Koinange and Arthur Wanyoike Thungu's names from the list of individuals that needed to be interrogated further, because, '[w]hen you beat the son, you beat the father' (Branch 2012). In the choice between the rule of law, the sanctity of life and his power to shield Koinange and Thungu from the law, the president considered his choice to be self-evident. Kenyans would apply the same logic over two decades later, as they speculated on the possible involvement of a well-placed political figure in Julie Ward's brutal murder, as the motive behind the state's attempts to cover up the murder. Interestingly, if Daniel Branch is correct in his claim that J.M. Kariuki was aware of the threats to his life, but he counted on his close relationship to Kenyatta to protect him from attempts on his life (Branch 2012: 106–7), then evidently some sons were more equal than others in the Kenyatta inner circle. A second example of this moral relationship to the civic public sphere is embodied in what Karimi and Ochieng describe as the Kenyatta Family, in reference to a coterie of powerful politicians, not all of whom were related to him by blood or marriage, but who held a shared set of 'financial and other interests' (1980: 15), and most of whom hailed from the Gikuyu nation. Subsequently, each regime in Kenya would feature its own powerful clique, some of whose members would be named as the powers behind certain political assassinations.

The postcolonial state in Africa has often been seen as what Larry Diamond refers to as a 'swollen state' (1987: 567), partly in allusion to its overdeveloped institutions and bureaucracies, which are systematically enlisted in entrenching brutal hegemonies. This was the state of affairs in Kenya during the 1980s and the 1990s, but state repression in postcolonial Kenyan political history goes all the way back to the Kenyatta regime of the 1960s and 1970s. Indeed, it is this regime which had inherited and refined what Atieno Odhiambo (1987: 191) has termed the 'ideology of order' from the British colonial administration. The ideology of order prioritizes political order as a key prerequisite for the effective functioning of the state, while masking a political hegemony that incorporates, excludes or dissolves discordant ideas. Donal Cruise O'Brien's (1972) outline of the ideology of order in America bears striking similarities with the Kenyan political experience. O'Brien sees the ideology of order as entailing the 'entrusting of the management of the state to a bureaucracy; the need for accumulation and concentration of power in the hands of the political elite and not its dispersion into society; and legal lawlessness of the ruling class (O'Brien 1972: 372, quoted in Odhiambo 1987: 189).

The ideology of order in Kenya provides an important backdrop for understanding the place of violence as part of statecraft across Kenyan history. The coercive arms of both the Kenyatta and Moi regimes manifested in a range of disciplinary measures devised to dissuade those who attempted to critically engage with the state, an act that was seen as necessarily insurgent. The oldest of these were detention without trial[21] and political assassination, both important inheritances from the British colonial administration.[22] Odhiambo describes these as powerful ways of performing power and constructing a dramatic grammar that acted as an iconic warning to the rest of the society. In Kenyan parlance popularized by the TV legal drama *Vioja Mahakamani*, this 'warning' came to be described as '*Na iwe funzo kwao na wote wenye nia hiyo*' (Swahili for 'let it be a warning to them, and anyone else of similar inclination').[23]

In his chapter 'Right of Death and Power over Life' in volume one of *The History of Sexuality*, Michel Foucault meditates on what would come to be termed 'biopolitics', but with particular interest in the shifts across history, of the sovereign's power of life and death; or as he puts it, 'the right to take life or let live' (Foucault 1979: 136). Foucault writes that: 'the sovereign exercised his right to life only by exercising his right to kill, or by refraining from killing; he

---

[21] There is a large body of Kenyan prison writing, both fiction, autobiographical fiction and life writing, from this period and its application of detention without trial, including Ngugi wa Thiong'o's *Detained* and Wahome Mutahi's *Three Days on the Cross*. For a discussion of Mutahi's writing see Mutonya (2004).

[22] See David Anderson's *Histories of the Hanged: Britain's Dirty War in Kenya and the End of Empire* (2005) for a discussion of the use of detention without trial by the British administration in colonial Kenya.

[23] I am grateful to Oluoch Madiang, Maina Mutonya, Fred Mbogo and Mutuma Ruteere for their insights on the history of this saying. See also Fredrick Mbogo's 'The "Comical" in the Serious and the "Serious" in the Comical: A Reading of *Vioja Mahakamani*' (2012).

evidenced his power over life only through the death he was capable of requiring' (ibid.). For Foucault, in the West, these workings of power have since been replaced by 'a power to foster life or disallow it to the point of death' (Foucault 1979: 139). While Foucault is looking at the Western state, this understanding of power as 'a right of seizure: of things, time, bodies and ultimately life itself … the privilege to seize hold of life in order to suppress' (1979: 136) in some ways describes the workings of 'legal lawlessness' of colonial authority across much of Africa; with the inevitable continuities of this legacy in post-independent states.

State repression in the Moi era is often understood to have been rooted in the president's insecurity, what James Kariuki has dubbed 'paraMoia',[24] that chiefly contributed to the collapse of the various institutions of governance and the consolidation of state power in the president's person. Moi's rise to power soon after Kenyatta's death was far from smooth. There was an elaborate drama of clandestine plans and counter-plans as various factions sought to secure their interests by influencing the country's political fate in the face of the obvious eventuality of the first president, Kenyatta's death.[25] (I explore this drama in more detail later in the book). According to Karimi and Ochieng, the powerful clique close to the president – the Kenyatta Family – was firmly opposed to the constitutional provision that, in the event of the president's death, the Vice President – Daniel arap Moi at the time – would be acting president for the 90 days within which new elections would be held (1980: 16, 24). Moi had taken over the vice presidency from Joseph Murumbi who had resigned a few months after taking over from the deposed Oginga Odinga. For this powerful clique, one of them was the rightful heir to the Kenyan presidency and, by pushing for a change in the constitution, they set about ensuring the removal of the offending clause that guaranteed Moi's automatic ascendance to the presidency – an increasingly likely eventuality, given Kenyatta's age and frail health. For many scholars, this clique's dogged opposition to Moi's rise to the presidency forms the genesis of the paranoia and repression that would mark the lengthy Moi regime of 1978–2002.

In light of the drama surrounding his rise to power, it was imperative that Moi consolidated his own political base in Kenya, an exercise he read as necessitating the elimination – political or literal – of his 'enemies'. At the onset, he amended the constitution, making Kenya a *de jure* one-party state, where previously this had been *de facto*. The irony of this move was hard to miss, for anyone who had followed the change-the-constitution attempts to block Moi's rise to

[24] See James Kariuki's '"Paramoia": Anatomy of a dictatorship in Kenya' (1996) for a detailed discussion of the repressive Moi regime. See also Angelique Haugerud's *The Culture of Politics in Modern Kenya* (1995), on Kenyan political culture during the Moi regime.

[25] See Karimi and Ochieng's *The Kenyatta Succession* (1980) for an excellent discussion of the political drama behind Moi's rise to presidency.

presidency. Gradually, he strengthened the presidency and the party (Kenya African National Union) while simultaneously reducing parliament and the judiciary to rubber-stamp institutions. Through various constitutional amendments, in 1986 and 1988, Moi further strengthened his power at the expense of the judiciary, the most telling of these being the power to hire and fire judges, the Attorney General and the Controller Auditor-General (Karimi and Ochieng 1980). This assured him of the liberty to act against his 'enemies' with a fair amount of impunity, and without much legal restraint (ibid.). By the late 1980s, Kenya was a typical example of what Robert Jackson and Carl Rosberg call personal rule: a regime marked by 'conspiracy, factional politics and clientelism, corruption, purges and rehabilitations, and succession manoeuvres' (2003: 28).

When located on the arc of post-independence Kenyan history, Julie Ward's murder happens at an important point: in global politics, this was at the cusp of the end of the Cold War, with Kenya as an important ally to Britain, in a region marked by a turbulent mix of socialist persuasions and civil war. Locally, resistance to the Moi autocracy was at its peak, with consistent demands for multi-party democracy. In fact, Julie Ward's murder precedes the unbanning of multi-party politics by just over two years, but it would be another decade and a half before KANU and Moi would be dislodged from power.[26] This political context may have influenced British and Kenyan responses to the murder.

Bayart writes that incumbent power holders across Africa countered pro-democracy agitation of the 1980s and 1990s with dexterity and brutality, largely because they had certain resources at their disposal: security forces which they could both use and abuse and financial resources accumulated though plunder and rent-seeking, an important combination which could afford them the support of some key political opponents, the creation of small parties to split the opposition vote and 'strategies of tension' in the shape of engineered agitation (Bayart 2000: 224–5).

Odhiambo explores Moi's abuse of the state's security apparatuses to manage demands for multi-party democracy, by forming a special intelligence unit which arrested and tortured hundreds of people in the 1980s: 'In 1986, the state detained more lecturers and students, business people and ordinary peasants for allegedly belonging to an underground revolutionary movement, *Mwakenya*. They were subjected to untold cruelties: physical assault, water torture, and

---

[26] Atieno Odhiambo lists the forces that confronted the authoritarian single-party regime of Daniel arap Moi as 'the original radical tradition of dissent sustained by Oginga Odinga; [the] active pulpit opposition maintained by Reverend Henry Okullu since 1974 and joined by mainline Protestant and Catholic churches in the mid-1980s; [a] tradition of protest sustained by groups of intellectuals and students at university campuses since the 1960s; a group of reformist-constitutional lawyers; [the] urban crowd' and the donor community's shift towards conditionality, with emphasis on accountability and good governance as prerequisites for aid (2002: 227).

mental abuse in the basement of Nyayo House, an administrative and security building at the heart of downtown Nairobi; summary ... trials and judgements in the courts; and harsh prison sentences averaging five years for people like Dr Adhu Awiti. Some ... died at Nyayo House, including Mbaraka Karanja. The unbroken ones were shunted to detention' (2002: 229). Njuguna Mutonya's *Crackdown! A Journalist's Personal Story of Moi Era Purges (1986–1989)* is a chilling description of his imprisonment and torture at the notorious Nyayo House torture chambers.

Moi eventually conceded to the amendment of the constitution, legalizing multi-party politics in 1991, but not before cautioning the country that it risked facing ethnic clashes. This was a self-fulfilling prophesy, thanks to an elite paramilitary army that unleashed terror on communities considered to harbour political sympathies for the opposition parties.

In recent years, these assassinations have made their way into fictional imaginaries of Kenya in ways that prompt me to read political assassination as a recognizable trope in Kenyan fiction. While the idea of assassinations featured briefly, and often subtly, in earlier fiction and cultural productions – such as the music of Benga musician D.O. Misiani which allegorises political assassination, and Ngugi wa Thiong'o's novel, *Devil on the Cross* which mentions 'being taken to Ngong' as short-hand for assassination – it is instructive that explicit explorations of political assassinations in Kenyan fiction have largely emerged in the new millennium, coinciding with the demise of the Moi regime.

In closing, I briefly explore three different fictional appropriations of actual assassinations by three novelists: Mukoma wa Ngugi's appropriation of the 1975 murder of cabinet minister J.M. Kariuki in his novel, *Killing Sahara* (2013), Sam Okello's fictionalized reconstruction of the 1991 murder of Dr Robert Ouko in his novel, *The Night Bob Died* (2005), and Yvonne Adhiambo Owuor's re-imagining of the assassination of Tom Mboya in her 2014 novel, *Dust*. In their appropriations of specific political murders in Kenya, these novelists use fictional imaginaries to archive these historical brutalities, while imagining and offering different commentaries on contemporary structures of power abuse that spill beyond local political greed to implicate an international network of stakeholders. I am particularly intrigued by the ways in which Ngugi projects the assassination motif – which has hitherto been a highly localized trope in Kenyan imaginaries – onto a transnational canvas marked by capitalist and political greed, playing out across a network of global metropolitan spaces, variously connected to Kenya. I read these fictionalized re-imaginings of Kenyan political murders as both a recognizable narrative trope for Kenyan publics, and an analytic unit in making sense of the complicities of transnational networks of capitalist power in African political and economic crises. I am also interested in the narrative textures that emerge in these three texts, and the ways in which the three authors' distinct perspectives are variously marked by particular moral perspectives, ranging from the sharp binary of good and evil in Okello's novel, to the moral ambiguity of Ngugi's novel.

A striking element of most of the assassinations and political murders in Kenyan history is that the victims' moral fibre comes up for contestation, with the pro-victim side often underscoring the victims' moral and ethical excellence while the state – which invariably finds itself trying to motivate for anything but murder – often makes much of the victim's supposed immorality. In the Julie Ward murder for instance, the state was at pains to paint her as a promiscuous woman who changed sexual partners too often and probably rendered herself vulnerable to attacks by one of her partners, or committed suicide out of depression following a fight with a partner. A similar dynamic emerged in the Robert Ouko case, where reportedly there were attempts to frame the murder as a crime of passion in a love triangle with either his PA's husband, Nakuru District Commissioner, Jonah Anguka or his neighbour, friend and Minister of Internal Security, Hezekiah Oyugi.

In Kenyan social imaginaries though, Ouko has been sanitized and rendered a moral hero and innocent victim of state brutality and the violent paranoias of powerful politicians close to the Moi regime. Ouko's murder, in Kenyan popular opinion, was the result of his courageous attempts to reveal the rot of corruption that implicated a powerful minister. In his novel *The Night Bob Died*, Sam Okello deeply invests in this sanitization project. He closely approximates the popular version of the circumstances surrounding Robert Ouko's murder. The novel features Bob Ooko as a fictionalized version of Ouko. Right from its opening chapter – which figures Ooko arriving at the pearly gates of heaven, and being preceded by a blinding light – he is depicted in religious iconography associated with light and purity.

The Night Bob Died repeatedly reiterates Ooko's moral uprightness and deep commitment to the country and its people. His distress over corruption in 1990s Kenya is so deep that, as his driver notes, it mirrors his grief at the death of first president, Kenyatta (named Johnstone Kamau, in the novel):

> Bob narrowed his eyes. Sargeant had seen that reaction once before. It was during the death of the founding father of the nation, the late President Johnstone Kamau. Was whatever was in Bob's mind something that rose to the level of the late president's death? Could it possibly be as grim as that morning was? [Okello 2005: 14]

Bob's driver, Sargeant, has a close relationship with the minister, and deep admiration for his sense of integrity. As a representative of ordinary people, his endorsement of Ooko, after having 'watched him over the years' and concluding that 'Bob was the most honest official in the Darapmio administration' (Okello 2005: 16), is part of this novel's moral endorsement.

Okello's novel is a thinly veiled reconstruction of the rumoured circumstances surrounding Robert Ouko's murder. It is also a strongly opinionated book, not only in its highly affirming depiction of the Robert Ouko figure (Bob Ooko), but equally in its clear contempt and indictment of cabinet ministers Nick Boit, Ezekaya and Darapmio (thinly veiled references to prominent politicians, whose names featured prominently in the many investigations into Ouko's murder).

Okello's book references the notion of private militias and hit men, through the figure of Bozo, a contact of Nick Boit's hired to kill Bob Ooko to prevent him from circulating a report on corruption in Kenya which names the president and the two ministers adversely: 'Nick knew how lethal Bozo could be. This was the man he'd relied on in the past to knock off his political and business opponents. Together, they'd killed more than three-dozen people and the CID didn't even know it. Or did they?' (Okello 2005: 18). This portrait of the hitman Bozo mirrors similar real-life figures who were to come out to the Kenyan media in the late 1990s, with damning depictions of themselves as members of elite killing squads, tasked with dealing with political and economic 'enemies' of the state. Among these were Valentine Kodipo and Big Mo, both of whom claimed to have witnessed the murder of Julie Ward, under instructions from 'a prominent politician', while George Wajackoyah claimed to have been a member of the Special Branch Unit and made allegations about key political figures involved in the Ouko murder.

At play in Okello's book is a moral grid which clearly distinguishes between good and evil, with Bob Ooko epitomizing good, while Ezekaya, Boit, Bozo and the president, Darapmio, embody the forces of evil and corruption, out to sabotage development in the country. At the centre of the actual Robert Ouko murder was a multi-million dollar development project to revive a molasses plant in Kisumu on one hand and, on the other, popular belief that the US wanted to back him for presidency, in an explicit gesture of contempt and faithlessness in the Moi government. Okello's book reconstructs and fleshes out these two sets of narratives, emphasizing the idea that, indeed, these were the reasons behind his murder.

Notably, Okello's fictional portrait of the fall-out over the molasses project in Kisumu signals overlaps with both John le Carré's and Mukoma Ngugi's portraits of transnational capitalist interests (I discuss le Carré's *The Constant Gardener* later in the book). In a candid critique of international consultancies, the novel depicts international trade networks and the new scramble for African businesses and resources, unfolding in the boardrooms of the US and Europe. Through the figure of Marina (who bears close resemblance to Marianne Brinner, a Swiss air-hostess and business-woman who was reportedly part of the negotiations with Ouko over the Kisumu Molasses plant), and an Italian business consultant, we have a glimpse of the deep cynicism that attends international consultancies seeking business in Africa as they choose to work with the best-connected political figures in the partner countries, and not the best qualified or even those most committed to the projects' success. In the novel, Dr Raghi quickly dismisses Marina's desire to work with Ooko by telling her: 'Bob is too straight, he is too clean. His type never make it in Africa ...Your man is Nick ... He's a cabinet minister [and] the president's cousin. [In] any Third World country, the President's relative is always the go-to-guy. He's always the President's eyes and ears' (Okello 2005: 80–81).

Turning to the second novel, *Killing Sahara*, I find Mukoma wa Ngugi's deployment of the Ngong assassination motif particularly intriguing at two levels. First is the way in which he draws connections between four key but very distinct nodes in Kenyan politics: the J.M. Kariuki assassination in 1975, the 1975 bombings that rocked Nairobi a day before Kariuki's disappearance, the 1998 Nairobi suicide bombing and the 2007/8 post-election violence. In Ngugi's re-imagining of these three brutal moments in Kenyan history, all three moments are variously linked to a powerful fictitious international organization called the International Democracy and Security Council (IDESC).

IDESC in the novel is made up of seven board members, all powerful deputies in major international development organizations. The Council is a product of humanitarians' disillusionment with corruption and poor governance in postcolonial countries, which repeatedly sabotage development and change. In response to this scenario, the Council devises a decisive solution: they engineer dramatic chaos in target countries, bring them to their knees, then build a new, clean crop of leaders. As one board member describes it: 'Our goal is to eradicate all of them, the sitting government, the opposition – leave the country without leadership, scoop out the cancer, and then let a new leadership emerge from the people themselves, with a gentle guiding hand from IDESC' (Ngugi 2013: 211).

The two detectives in the novel, Ishmael Fofona and O, had set out to find out who the dead man in Ngong forest was, what story he had to tell, and whether there was any connection to a bomb attack on the Norfolk Hotel in Nairobi a day earlier. What they discover is that the man was a board member of IDESC who had developed cold feet about the organization's next plan of action: to take advantage of the fragile situation in Kenya following the 2007/8 post-election violence and, at the right time, take out all the politicians, both in the ruling party and the opposition, by blowing up the Kenyatta International Conference Centre building in which an important peace-brokering meeting was to take place. As one member, Mpande, explains it 'ours was not to create the circumstances, it was to take advantage of them. At the right time, take out the opposition and the ruling party, then offer interim stewardship that comes with economic assistance, security and nurturing of leadership by forward-looking youth' (Ngugi 2013: 211).

The second striking aspect of Ngugi's use of the Ngong assassination motif in his novel is the moral ambiguity he introduces to what has hitherto been remembered in Kenyan popular imaginaries as a clear-cut moral narrative of the evil of the state and the innocence of the victims. In fact, most of the assassination victims in Kenyan popular memory are often selectively remembered as martyrs and heroes, carefully sanitized of any prior complicity with the state that eventually murders them. Contrary to popular perceptions, which were quick to sanitize many of the assassination victims and turn them into instant martyrs, some of them had more ambiguous relationships to the hegemonic political powers that eventually eliminated them. So, Kenyans selectively remember J.M. Kariuki not as an ultra-wealthy politician who, for better or worse, benefited from his proximity to power in the newly independent Kenyatta state, but as a victim of a cannibalistic Kenyatta state that kills its own when they speak out against the economic status quo. Kariuki enjoyed, and benefited from, a close relationship to the Kenyatta political elite, a patronage that, according to Charles Hornsby, was in part instrumental to his acquisition of prime land in 1965 as reward for his contributions to the anti-colonial struggle, but under circumstances that were questionable (2012: 118–9). Similarly, Tom Mboya is correctly remembered and celebrated for his role in the Kennedy airlifts which afforded many Kenyan students higher education in the US, and often deemed the embodiment of a progressive modern Kenya that died with his assassination; but Kenyan popular memory carefully overlooks Mboya's complicity in undermining fellow Nyanza politician Jaramogi Oginga Odinga's socialist political vision for the country, in the face of the emergent Kenyan plutocracy of the 1960s and 1970s. In true spirit of contradictions of popular memory, sections of Kenyan politics which see a deliberate exclusion of the Luo nation from the political centre, read both Mboya and Odinga alongside each other, again with little acknowledgement of the tensions between the two. The important fact becomes their respective exclusion from the nation's political centre. A similar editing of history once again emerges with Robert Ouko's murder, as his close relationship to the regime that would later deem him a threat is downplayed in favour of a narrative of martyrdom and targeted elimination of Luo leadership.

Our third novel, Yvonne Owuor's *Dust*, is an ambitious exploration of Kenyan history from British colonial occupation to the post-election violence of 2007/8. What holds together the narrative is the murder of the fictional Moses Ebewesit Odidi Oganda, shot dead on the streets of Nairobi. Oganda's murder is explicitly linked to the suspicious murders of several prominent Kenyans in the country's history, most notably Tom Mboya, whose assassination is regularly alluded to in the novel. As Oganda's body is airlifted from Nairobi to his home in Northern Kenya, the narrator notes: 'the dying had started long ago. Long before the murder of prophets named Pio, Argwings, Ronald, Kungu, Josiah, Ouko, Mbae. The others, the "disappeared unknown." National doors slammed over vaults of secrets, threat loomed' (Owuor 2013: 28). Owuor traces the country's history of assassination to the murders of both supporters of British colonial rule and suspected Mau Mau members, whose variously mutilated bodies are given quick secret burials in the middle of the night, with blood-soaked sacks as the only coffins they are afforded. The trope of assassination haunts the first independent republic under Kenyatta, when the euphoria and hope of independence swiftly gives way to a frightened silence as 'the seizing of lives began [and] bodies started showing up mutilated and truly dead' (ibid.: 30).

Like *Killing Sahara*, *Dust* uses an assassination on the streets of Nairobi to comment on an elaborate network of betrayal, corruption and greed which drives a lethal wedge between two good friends and business partners Odidi Oganda and Jeremiah Musali. The two college friends set up an engineering firm for which they receive a tender to build a dam for a hydroelectric power project that promises to create sufficient electricity to supply the country's needs at an affordable price. However, a well-placed politician has other ideas: he bribes them to silt the dam, causing artificial downstream flooding and rendering the project impossible, after which he imports and supplies expensive power generators for the country's citizens. Odidi Oganda refuses to co-operate and is devastated when his friend accepts the bribe and does as instructed. When he writes a detailed report on this plan, he finds all doors closed on his face: nobody in the country's media houses will touch his report. After a downward spiral into alcoholism one night he turns up at his friend's house, but his friend calls the police on him, on the assumption – deliberate or accidental – that he is a burglar. Odidi Oganda is shot dead while trying to escape the armed policemen who then proceed to plant weapons on him and give a press conference on their battle with armed robbers who they managed to overpower. Owuor's novel is a remarkable depiction of the bloody bedrock of murder as a political weapon across Kenyan history. It further underscores the connections between moral ambiguity in Kenyan political culture and the casual disposal of lives as a response to anybody that threatens politicians' personal interests.

Overall then, while these novels do not engage directly with the Julie Ward murder, they are instructive in reminding us of the broader canvas of political and politicized assassination as part of Kenyan statecraft across the country's history. The three novels offer distinct interpretations of particular high-profile assassinations in Kenyan political history, in ways that signal not only the increasing embedding of assassination as a narrative trope in fictional imaginaries of Kenya, but also the moral reconfigurations of these actual historical assassinations. An important reminder that these novels underscore is that the narrative slant of retellings of Kenyan assassinations is very much dependent on the subject positions of those telling the story as different narrators invest particular kinds of interests in these murders, which in turn determine what they choose to emphasize and what gets downplayed. These shifting patterns of accent form our core focus in the next chapter in relation to the Julie Ward murder.

In her study, *Intimate Empire: Reading Women's Autobiography*, Gillian Whitlock finds Raymond Williams' notion of residual elements of cultural processes (Williams 1977: 122) instructive in understanding the continued valence of white settler imaginaries in readings of contemporary Kenya. As she writes,

> Certain experiences, meanings and values which are no longer expressed or substantially verified in terms of the dominant culture are nevertheless lived and practiced on the basis of the residue – cultural as well as social – of some previous social and cultural formation [Whitlock 2000: 117].

Whitlock's observation speaks to this chapter's interest in the influence of social memories in shaping speculations on Julie Ward's murder. Indeed, as she rightly points out, 'values and meanings, tropes and allegories which were part of the hegemony of settler culture re-emerge ... in interpreting [incidents like] the Ward affair' (ibid.).

This chapter reflects on how circulating discourses in Kenyan and British social imaginaries shaped the speculations on the circumstances surrounding Julie Ward's death. Drawing on John Ward's speculations as laid out in his book *The Animals are Innocent: The Search for Julie's Killers*, Jeremy Gavron's speculations in *Darkness in Eden: The Murder of Julie Ward*, and the claims of alleged eye-witnesses in Kenya, the chapter suggests that Julie Ward's death was interpreted through the lens of ideas constructed across Kenya's post/colonial history, which have over time crystallized into popular wisdom regarding the multiple intersections between sex/uality, race, gender and state power in Kenyan and British social imaginaries. By excavating the subterranean discourses that underpinned the various speculations, the chapter suggests that Julie Ward's death took place in a discursive landscape marked by deeply layered and intermeshed contours of British and Kenyan social memories which tinted speculations on the circumstances surrounding the death.

Julie Ward's murder and the subsequent quest for her killers was a much publicized affair, which convened a range of publics, to borrow from Michael Warner's (2002) useful concept, both through formal institutions such as the media and the courtrooms, and the more informal discursive spaces created by rumours and books about the death. If we take Warner's argument that texts (and by extension, events) can only address publics – and thus create them – when 'a previously existing discourse is supposed and a responding discourse [can be] postulated' (2002: 90); and if we consider Mikhail Bakhtin's reminder that

> any concrete discourse (utterance) finds the object at which it was directed already as it were overlain with qualifications, open to dispute, charged with value, already enveloped in an obscuring mist – or, on the contrary, by the 'light' of alien words that have already been spoken about it … entangled, shot through with shared thoughts, points of view, alien value judgements and accents [1981: 276]

then Julie Ward's death was preceded by certain discourses in Kenyan and British social imaginaries that provided important 'handles' in understanding the murder. Therefore, an understanding of social imaginaries and their attendant social memories offers insights into the interpretative patterns that emerged in the Julie Ward mystery, and the prominence of sex/uality in these speculations, as mapped along overlapping tropes of inter-racial rape, female sexual moralities and criminal state power across British and Kenyan imaginaries. It also becomes instructive in making sense of the intertextual dialogues that unfolded in the relationship between Julie Ward's death and other deaths in Kenyan history, most significantly the ledger of assassinations discussed in the previous chapter, and the murders of two Kenyan women, Monica Njeri and Judy Angaine, allegedly by their partners.

Shadows of the 'Black Peril'

Although a finding of murder in the inquest into Julie Ward's death was able to resolve the contested question of the manner of death, both science and law have, at the time of writing this, been unable to determine the identity/identities of the killer(s) and the motive(s) behind the murder. This gap inspired many speculations on the circumstances surrounding the death by, among others, John Ward and Jeremy Gavron.

In their respective books, *The Animals are Innocent* and *Darkness in Eden*, Ward and Gavron speculate that Julie Ward's death started out as rape by the game rangers in the Maasai Mara, who then proceeded to kill her in order to cover up their crime. What is interesting in both Ward's and Gavron's speculation is the prominence of rape as the initial motive that led to Julie Ward's death. At one level, rape is a plausible speculation in light of global patriarchy that takes various shapes in different contexts, perhaps most prominently in the shape of sexual violence against women's bodies – the ultimate brutality in the arsenal of what Carole Sheffield (1998) terms sexual terrorism. She describes sexual terrorism as a pervasive culture of fear-mongering that targets women through the threat of rape, battering, harassment and other forms of sexual violence (1998: 272). The logics of sexual terrorism demand that women 'take responsibility for the fact that [they] may be attacked at any time and modify [their] behavior accordingly' as Pumla Dineo Gqola writes (2006: 9). Although Gqola is writing about gendered violence in South Africa, her observations resonate across the world in the shape of the unwritten women's handbook to safety that trains women to avoid poorly-lit and deserted spaces, dress conservatively, and generally reduce the chances of 'provoking' male sexual aggression.

This unwritten handbook featured prominently in both the Julie Ward inquest in Kenya and the two murder trials, as the court debated whether Julie Ward had 'irresponsibly' driven off the main tracks in the game reserve, then decided to walk across the reserve to seek help when her jeep got stuck in the gully, at which point she got attacked by wild animals, or whether she had had several sexual partners and therefore, by some bizarre logic, precipitated her death as the official Scotland Yard and Kenyan police version of events speculated. While the one version emphasized the risk of attack by wild animals, the grammar of female vulnerability was evident here – and therefore female responsibility to follow the handbook of safety. It was the same handbook on women obviating the risks of men's sexual violence that was now being applied to taking precautions against attack by dangerous wildlife.

But Ward's and Gavron's speculations on rape are striking not because rape was an unlikely hypothesis here, but because of the particular logics of rape into which the two authors tapped. These logics become even more curious in view of the absence of evidence pointing towards rape.[1] Why would rape come to occupy such a central position in Gavron and Ward's speculations? One possible clue to understanding this lingering conviction about rape as the key motive lies in the colonial archive of ideas on the nexus between race, gender and sexuality.

In *White Hero, Black Beast: Racism, Sexism and the Mask of Masculinity*, Paul Hoch argues that Western civilization historically constructed many forms of sexuality as immoral, with the devil, dark villain or black beast being figured as the receptacle of all the sexual taboos and desires, thereby embodying all the forbidden possibilities of sexual desire (1979: 45). These ideas resulted in classifications along binaries such as human/animal, spiritual/carnal, higher/lower, white/black. For Hoch, inter-racial struggles in the nineteenth century were a test of virility in which the struggle between Europe and Africa represented an assertion of virility whose ultimate statement of control lay in the control of the other group's women (ibid.: 47). Hoch's argument spotlights the junction

---

[1] Only her left leg, skull, jaws and spinal column were recovered. The rest of her body appeared to have been burnt to ashes. This situation brings to mind the narrative in Lewis Nkosi's *Mating Birds* (1987), a first person narrative by Ndi Sibiya, a prisoner facing a death sentence for accusations of raping a white woman, Veronica Slater. The novel remains unclear as to whether the two had consensual sex as Sibiya claims or if Sibiya raped Veronica as she claims, just as it remains unclear whether Julie Ward was raped before being murdered. See also Lucy Graham's incisive essay, "'Bathing Area – For Whites Only": Reading Prohibitive Signs and "Black Peril" in Lewis Nkosi's *Mating Birds*' (2006).

between race, gender and nation, and in particular, women's bodies as embodiments of the nation and its attendant anxieties.

Many scholars have observed that the colonial experience was grounded in a sexualized discourse, not only in its grammar of rape, penetration and the feminization of the new frontiers – what David Dunn describes as 'a moment of penetration into a suggestively feminine locale'(1988: 9)[2] – but also in what David Attwell (2005: 3) has described as its preoccupation with 'policing intimacy', which in apartheid South Africa became institutionalized through the Immorality Act that forbade sexual contact across racial boundaries. While majority of the colonial administrations across Africa did not formalize this policing of cross-racial intimacy through explicit laws, their control of native populations was nonetheless equally shot through with sexual anxieties which traced their roots back to an older archive of myths about Africa(ns) specifically, and black people in general. Among these were myths of black sexuality as aberrant, uncontrolled, contaminating yet intriguing. Long before the colonial project took root in Africa, the myth of the black rapist had claimed countless lives both through lynching and legal prosecution in the United States where it would be 'methodically conjured up whenever recurrent waves of violence and terror against the Black community have required convincing justifications' (Davis 1982: 173). In the case of colonial contexts, Ann Stoler writes that 'the tropics provided a site for European pornographic fantasies long before conquest was under way, with lurid descriptions of sexual licence, promiscuity, gynaecological aberrations, and general perversions marking the Otherness of the colonized for metropolitan consumption' (2010: 179).

With colonial occupation, these myths and fantasies bred a range of ambivalent anxieties that indexed black sexuality as both desirable and repulsing. These anxieties took the shape of the black and yellow perils, ostensibly concerned about the perceived threat of black men to white femininity, and the accompanying terror of miscegenation. The logics underpinning these 'perils' in colonial imaginaries are better appreciated in relation to the place of the white woman in white male colonial imaginaries. Gareth Cornwell suggests that what was at stake in these perils was 'the integrity of the white female body, which had been mythologized by a frontier society as the last and most intimate frontier of all' (1996: 441). Fears of the black and yellow perils were particularly intense in colonial spaces, where the white woman's body was a powerful embodiment of the nation-body. As Cecily Devereux persuasively argues, there was an analogy between the settler colony and the white woman as sites for racial renewal: 'Both white women and the settler colonies were represented in imperial rhetoric as at once innately pure and inherently purifying. Degenerating Anglo-Saxondom was to be rescued and restored equally in the womb of the imperial mother and

---

[2] See also Ashcroft et al. (1998) and McClintock (1995).

in the bosom of the "daughter" nations' (1999: 15–16). This casting of the white woman as the regenerating 'mother-of-the-empire' was primarily articulated in tones of moral purity, where 'the moral condition of the nation … was believed to derive from the moral standards of women' (Nead 1988: 92, cited in Devereux 1999: 11).[3] Ann Stoler highlights the moral asymmetries of the colonies, where men were assumed to me more morally vulnerable, and therefore dependent on women's moral vigilance to insulate them from cultural and sexual contact with the colonized: 'male colonizers positioned European women as the bearers of a redefined colonial morality [and] moral laxity would be eliminated through the example and vigilance of women whose status was defined by their sexual restraint, and dedication to their homes and to their men' (Stoler 1989: 649).

For Stoler then, black peril referred to sexual threats, but also connoted 'fears of insurgence and perceived non-acquiescence to colonial control more generally' as rape accusations were often based on perceived transgressions of social space; and tended to coincide with internal tensions within European communities and the quest for consensus (2010: 188). Notably, she writes, 'the threat of native rebellion produced a "solidarity that found sustenance in the threat of racial destruction"' (ibid.: 188, quoting Kennedy 1987: 138).[4] David Anderson makes similar observations on white solidarity in the face of the Mau Mau movement in 1950s Kenya (2005: 84).

The symbolic construction of the nation on women's bodies is far from a British peculiarity, since in most societies, 'women bear the symbolic weight of nationalism; their bodies are the contested sites on which national identities are erected and national unity is forged' (Samuelson 2007: 2). Haunted by the potential threat of political upheaval – both real and imagined – the racialized moral panics of the 'black' and 'yellow perils' seemed inevitable. In this

---

[3] Stoler further notes that 'European women in these colonies experienced the cleavages of racial dominance and internal social distinctions very differently than men precisely because of their ambiguous positions, as both subordinates in colonial hierarchies and as active agents of imperial culture in their own right. Concomitantly, the majority of European women who left for the colonies in the late 19th and early 20th centuries confronted profoundly rigid restrictions on their domestic, economic and political options, more limiting than those of metropolitan Europe at the time and sharply contrasting the opportunities open to colonial men' (1989: 634).

[4] Ann Stoler's work on the regulation of sexual relations in some French, British and Dutch colonies suggests that the policing of cross-racial sex was not always a straightforward matter. On the contrary, it was variously encouraged and discouraged, depending on its expedience to the interests of capital and the development of permanent colonial settlements in the colonies. So, concubinage arrangements with Asian women were encouraged because 'Asian women provided for the daily needs of the lower-level European staff without imposing the emotional and financial obligations that European family life would demand [and] men would be more likely to remain if they established families with local roots; [effectively] permit[ing] permanent settlement and rapid growth by a cheaper means than the importation of European women' (Stoler 2010: 183, 181).

way, these 'perils' in the colonial imaginary represented a metaphor which not only expressed sexual anxieties rooted in an age-old demonization of sexuality and the accompanying ambivalent attitude towards a mythologized black sexuality but, as Cornwell's work shows, the 'perils' were also rooted in real political concerns, as cross-racial relationships worked to dismantle the myth of white supremacy and its requisite exclusionary boundaries embodied by the white woman's body and exclusive white male access to it (1996: 443–4). 'Black peril' anxieties additionally went hand in hand with extensive policing of white women on the fringes of white society, particularly poor and mentally unstable women – categories which were often considered synonymous, as Will Jackson's work on understandings of mental instability in colonial Kenya shows: 'simply for European women to be unmarried, independent and occupying less than salubrious circumstances was enough to raise the spectre of sexual contamination and racial disrepair. Bearing "the reproductive destinies of their race," poor white women were far more problematic than poor white men. [For] women and girls, to neglect the crucial female role of guarding racial reproduction – the most vital, tender point at which colonial boundaries were breached – was to find oneself irredeemably beyond the bounds of social solidarity and racial self-defence' (Jackson 2011a: 86–87).

The intermeshing of race and class exclusion in the colonial project is remarkable in the ways it underlines the artifice of white supremacy and the labours of social engineering that went into maintaining what was euphemistically coded as 'white prestige'. Put differently, as Will Jackson's (2011a) work shows, poor whites represented vulnerability for white society because their social position was believed to make them agreeable to 'inappropriate' forms of cross-racial contact, at great risk to the myth of white exceptionalism. One Kenyan settler puts it succinctly: 'if the natives are to be raised [it] is no good trying to do it by lowering the European in their eyes' (cited in Jackson 2011b: 348). J.M. Coetzee underlines a similar logic in *White Writing*: 'the degeneration of the white colonist in Africa was no peripheral matter to his masters in Europe, in that it threatened one of the arguments by which expansive imperialism justified itself: that those deserve to inherit the earth who make best use of it' (1988: 3). Elsewhere, Stoler illustrates how the asymmetrical gender demographics in the colonies underlines anxieties about white poverty as a product of the unholy alliance between capital and the colonial bureaucracy, where companies were hesitant to pay white employees higher wages, yet they remained concerned about the risks of white poverty: poor whites lowered the tone of racial superiority but companies were unwilling to pay white employees higher salaries. In view of the belief that white women would make expensive economic and affective demands on white men, 'concubinage was tolerated precisely because "poor whites" were not. Government and plantation administrators argued that white prestige would be imperiled if European men became impoverished in attempting to maintain middle-class lifestyles and European wives' (Stoler 2010: 184–5). The same logic appears to have been at work in the implicit endorsement of local women's prostitution, which in turn was not without its own contradictions, as Anne McClintock has noted in her review of Luise White's study of sex work in colonial Nairobi: 'prostitution may very well have confirmed colonial fantasies about white men's privileged access to the bodies of black women, but it also confused racial segregation and gendered distribution of money: in the bodies of the prostitutes, the liquid assets and body fluids of black men and white men mixed promiscuously' (McClintock 1991: 98). Overall, fixation on the black peril in white supremacist contexts was motivated by the need to protect and affirm hegemonic white male authority and supremacy through exclusive access to white women, as boundary-markers and symbols of morality.

Although seemingly steeped in an outdated colonial context, these ideas on sex, gender and race seem to have resurfaced as important points of reference for both John Ward and Gavron, in imagining the circumstances surrounding Julie Ward's death. Indeed, as Whitlock observes, Julie Ward's death in Kenya caused 'the long history of ideas and associations which are released by the association of *lustful* black men and *defenseless white women* to be set loose once again' (2000: 114). Ward and Gavron's speculations bear eloquent witness to the re-activation of Williams' residual elements as important fragments in shaping social imaginaries on contemporary experiences. In *The Animals are Innocent*, Ward speculates:

> I believe she [Julie Ward] spent the night at Makari Outpost. I think, also, she wasn't molested that first evening. But perhaps the rangers then became reluctant to let this smiling friendly girl out of their control. Three months posted to the Makari Outpost must be one of the most boring jobs the ranger service has to offer. Fed up with each other's company, the presence and conversation of a young woman must have made a welcome break from their dreary routine … Muff [Julie Ward] would have sensed the situation getting dangerous. Their banter would have become more personal, more sexually aggressive. The dry gulch behind the huts at Makari is littered with empty beer bottles. *A few drinks and these rangers would soon have lost their thin veneer of civilization. If Muff had been a tough, hard woman, she would probably have 'kept them in their place' and survived. But she was not* … I am sure that, one terrible night, Muff was raped. I pray it was only once, but reluctantly, my mind cannot avoid the worst scenario. Once the act was committed, she was doomed. They could never set her free for fear she would identify them [1991: 381, emphasis added].

Ward's theory largely draws on the grammars of the 'black peril' in the colonial archives on black male sexuality. He identifies the rangers as the murderers, whose 'thin veneer of civilisation' once dissolved by alcohol, unleashes an uncontrollable, aggressive lust. But if Ward couches his speculation with isolation, boredom and alcohol, in Gavron's rendition, these qualifying factors are stripped by his conviction that Julie Ward's body represented the classical object of uncontrollable black lust, and that the rangers merely acted true to type. Gavron writes:

> Although her camera was missing and still not recovered, some money had been found in the fire in which her body had been burned. *To the men who killed her, Julie's body must have been her most attractive possession. It may be that Julie's killers had initially intended to rescue her, and that at some point temptation had simply grown stronger than common sense* ... Julie's rescuers had turned into her assailants and raped her ... For several days, Julie must have been held and perhaps further abused [1991: 183; emphasis added].

Considering that the money Gavron refers to was a few Kenyan 10 cent coins, while the missing camera was a fairly pricy Olympus model which could fetch a handsome amount anywhere, Gavron's thesis that the killers' uncontrollable sexual urges overwhelm common sense, their initial mission of rescuing the stranded tourist, and any desire for her material possessions is striking. Ward and Gavron draw on the afore-discussed colonial repertoire of ideas, in which Julie Ward epitomizes the white woman's vulnerable femininity, desirability and purity pitted against the black man's purportedly uncontrollable lust.

But if Ward and Gavron's speculations are scripted onto an absent body, the world of fiction seems to reconstruct the violated body in a novel set in Kenya, which features a white woman murdered in the Kenyan wilds, with her body showing medical evidence of sexual violation. A remarkable illustration of the continued validation of the 'black peril' discourses in British social imaginaries, John le Carré's *The Constant Gardener* is published thirteen years after Julie Ward's death.

Le Carré's *The Constant Gardener* is a fictional narrative set in the 1990s during the Moi regime, which is marked by what a character in the novel describes as terminal government corruption, a breakdown in public infrastructure and police brutality (2001: 52). The novel tells the story of the murder of a young diplomat's wife, Tessa Quayle. After the murder and disposal of her body in a deserted spot by the shores of Lake Turkana in Northern Kenya, the British High Commission in Nairobi attempts to frame her close African friend Dr Arnold Bluhm for the murder. However, her husband, Justin Quayle launches a private investigation and discovers that his wife may have been killed because she had put together a report about the fatal use of poor Kenyan tuberculosis patients for trials of a new TB drug, Dypraxa, by a British multinational corporation, Bell, Barker & Benjamin, otherwise known as the House of ThreeBees. Tessa attempts to pressure the British High Commission and the Foreign Office into stopping the company from continuing these drug trials and doctoring fatal side-effects in the interests of fast-tracking the trials in order to introduce the drug to the market before their competitors. All along, the novel reveals, the British Government is complicit in the drug trials, Tessa's murder and subsequently, Justin and Arnold's murder.

In the novel, scandalized suspicion haunts Tessa's friendship with Arnold Bluhm, the handsome African doctor working for the Médicins de l'Univers, a non-governmental humanitarian organization providing healthcare in Kenya.[5] Before her death, the grapevine in the British expatriate community is full of rumours about Tessa Quayle and the possibility that she is having an extra-marital relationship with Arnold, owing to their close working relationship and friendship. These rumours reach their peak when it emerges that Tessa was last seen with Arnold at a guest house Turkana, Northern Kenya; before her murder. Arnold too goes missing for days after the murder, before his mutilated body is discovered in the same deserted area.

In the novel, the British find a convenient and convincing scapegoat in Arnold Bluhm, as the 'archetypal black killer'. But what remains most instructive in this narrative is that in the face of scandalized rumours in the British community about Arnold's close friendship with Tessa Quayle – which is assumed to be sexual – the narrative redeems Arnold by de-closeting his homosexual orientation. Implicitly, both the fictional community and the narrator are keen to firmly clip the possibility of a cross-racial sexual relationship between the two: Arnold's homosexuality assures Tessa's virtuous faithfulness to both her husband and the race. Yet Arnold's de-closeting is also abbreviated to a photograph in the novel, and less than a few minutes of screen-time in the film version, suggesting both an opportunistic use of homosexuality as narrative tool, and the possibility that the narrative is as anxious about queer sexuality as it is about a cross-racial relationship.

It is significant that in both the novel – published in 2001 – and the film version of the same title released in 2005, the idea of inter-racial sexual relationship remains a source of significant anxiety. Like the narrative's struggle to contain Arnold – both metaphorically by making him gay, and literally, by killing him off soon after the 'black peril' statement is made, freeing up narrative space for a heroic Justin Quayle to emerge – this anxiety about inter-racial sex underlines the continued policing of cross-racial intimacy in the postcolonial context, through the scripting of the white woman as vulnerable to black lust and violence.

Like the Julie Ward case, rape looms large in *The Constant Gardener*. In fact, it is actualized, as the novel paints images of gang rape in a horrible instantiation of the 'black peril': 'Tessa had had recent intercourse … we suspect rape. It's only a vaginal swab they've taken at this stage and peeked through the microscope

---

[5] This organization's name reminds one of the organization, *Médicins sans Frontiers* which operates in Kenya, among other countries.

… but they still think it may be more than one person's sperm. Maybe a whole cocktail … [The murder] was random. Unplanned. A blood feast, African style' (2001: 91, 96). This extract from *The Constant Gardener* could easily be a re-phrasing of Ward's fears about his daughter's horrible ordeal, particularly his speculation: 'I am sure that, one terrible night, Muff was raped. I pray it was only once, but reluctantly, my mind cannot avoid the worst scenario' (1991: 381).

A few days after Tessa's murder, Arnold Bluhm's mutilated body is found hanging from a tree. The cinematic portrayal of Arnold's murdered body offers important pointers to the undertones of the 'black peril' and the iconography of lynching in the text, especially when read alongside Billie Holiday's haunting rendition of Abel Meeropol's poem on lynching in the South, 'Southern Trees'.[6] The lines 'Southern trees bear a strange fruit … black bodies swinging in the Southern breeze' might as well be describing Arnold's gruesome body, hanging from a tree, mutilated in the ultimate racist fantasy of ostensibly mutilating the prototypical 'black rapist', but actually, the real fantasy at play here is the fantasy of mutilating transgressive black men. In our case, the transgression here is a medical doctor who dared confront white men's deadly exploitation of black women's vulnerable bodies for capital interests, a black man who dared recruit a white woman to work with him against white male capital. To be sure, Arnold's murderers would know he was gay and had no sexual interest in Tessa Quayle, but the film still opts to depict his murder in the iconography of lynching. The decision to imagine Arnold's murder using an iconography that recalls lynch-ing in the American South points to a disturbing transplanting of not just a distinctly American manifestation of 'black peril' anxieties through lynching to contemporary Kenya, but the uncritical return of the Euro-American un-conscious to what I call the 'strange fruit' iconography in a 2005 film, and its equally uncritical reiteration on a geo-cultural and temporal landscape that did not have the same historical manifestation of 'black peril' discourses. To be sure, settler Kenya nursed its own feverish 'black peril' panics, and responded to a number of such cases with jail terms and occasionally, flogging, such as the examples David Anderson (2010) describes in his essay on 'black peril' in Kenya. But lynching was never part of the equation. The murder of Arnold Bluhm in *The Constant Gardener*, and the retrieval of lynching iconography, says more about the yoking of unease towards queer sexuality and inter-racial relation-ships, than it does about the professional hit men who do the pharmaceutical industry's dirty work of murdering Tessa, Arnold and Justin in the novel. If we

---

[6] According to David Margolick, 'lynchings – during which blacks were murdered with un-speakable brutality, often in a carnival-like atmosphere and then, with the acquiescence if not complicity of local authorities, hung from trees for all to see – were rampant in the South fol-lowing the Civil War and for many years thereafter. According to figures kept by the Tuskegee Institute … between 1889 and 1940, 3833 people were lynched; ninety percent of them were murdered in the south and four-fifths of them were black' (Margolick 2001: 36–37).

read these anxieties of 'black peril' rape alongside the anxieties of rape over Julie Ward's murder, *The Constant Gardener* grants itself the fantasy of lynching as the worst punishment for 'black peril' transgressions, then attempts to reverse these fatal results by making Arnold innocent.

The Constant Gardener's flirtation with 'strange fruit' is a troubling narrative sleight of hand which is evidently not endorsed by the narrative's moral focalizers – Justin Quayle and Tessa Quayle – but nonetheless remains disturbing in the ways it retrieves a particular archive of racial attitudes barely submerged in Euro-American social psyches. The first glimpse of this slant emerges when Belgian newspapers, followed by the British press, 'accuse Tessa and Bluhm of "a passionate liaison"' (le Carré 2001: 65). Soon, Arnold Bluhm – an adopted Congolese son of a wealthy Belgian family – is depicted as the murder suspect.

> A Belgian daily ran a front-page story accusing Tessa and Bluhm of a 'passionate liaison' … The British Sundays had a field day; overnight Bluhm had become a figure of loathing for Fleet Street to snipe at as it wished … From now on, he was Bluhm the seducer, Bluhm the adulterer, Bluhm the maniac. A page-three feature about murderous doctors down the ages was accompanied by lookalike photographs of Bluhm and O.J. Simpson … Bluhm, if you were that kind of reader, was your archetypal black killer. He had ensnared a white man's wife, cut her throat, decapitated the driver and run off into the bush to seek new prey or do whatever those salon blacks do when they revert to type [ibid.].

The novel's allusion to the real-life O.J. Simpson case is notable here, not only in the ways it gestures at a contemporary case which was equally framed by an old history of black peril discourses and the accompanying race, sexuality and gender tensions, but also in the way it underscores the narrative's immersion in an American imaginary on cross-racial relationships that will later be embodied by the lynching imagery.[7] Yet, as with the O.J. Simpson case, where the victim – Nicole Brown Simpson – was a white woman perceived as a sexually promiscuous woman who therefore commanded limited empathy (cited in Gates 1997: 113), Tessa Quayle's brutal murder too attracts lukewarm empathy in the novel.

Another equally troubling scene in the novel which references a distinctly Southern racial topography is when Tessa Quayle loses her baby soon after birth at the fictional Uhuru Hospital in Nairobi – evidently alluding to Kenyatta National Hospital. Tessa opts to have her baby at this poorly resourced public hospital in solidarity with the poor women among whom she works, but the narrative appears to punish this transgression by having her lose her baby. While at the hospital, Tessa meets Wanza Kalulu, a sickly new mother, and one

---

7 See Morrison and Lacour's *Birth of a Nation'hood* (1997) for a detailed discussion of the O.J. Simpson case.

of the patients subjected to the illegal medical trials of the new drug, Dypraxa, by the pharmaceutical company, ThreeBees, which Tessa is investigating. At the hospital, soon after losing her child, we see Tessa nursing Wanza Kalulu's child, in a fictional subversion of the figure of the wet nurse, who, historically, was conventionally a black woman feeding a white child.

> She is cradling the child to her left breast, her right breast free and waiting. Her upper body is slender and translucent. Her breasts, even in the aftermath of child-birth, are as light and flawless as [Sandy] has often imagined them. The child is black. Blue-black against the marble whiteness of her skin. One tiny black hand has found the breast that is feeding it, and is working it with eerie confidence while Tessa watches [le Carré 2001: 73].

Initially, this sight disturbs Sandy Woodrow, one of the British diplomats in the novel who visits Tessa in hospital. Sandy has heard the rumours of Tessa and Arnold's friendship, and wonders whether the child is theirs, before she explains that she is actually feeding the other woman's child. Once again, the novel plays with, and subverts, the iconography of race relations in the American South while interlacing it with anxieties about cross-racial relationships.

Ward, Gavron and le Carré's seamless retrieval of 'black peril' ideas suggests their embeddedness in British social imaginaries on Africa(ns), and their con-tinued availability as useful grammars which are easily teleported across time and space in understanding contemporary experiences. Through these portable tropes of race and gender discourses, Ward, Gavron and le Carré illustrate the continued valence of what Maughan-Brown (1985) terms 'psycho-sexual myth-making', which he traces in colonial settler fiction on Kenya. This fiction per-sistently rehashed myths of brutal African sexuality by drawing a link between sex, violence and blackness (ibid.: 124) and often lingering on the rape of white women by Mau Mau 'terrorists'.[8] If, as John Pape (1990: 702) points out, the attribution of an ungovernable libido to black men harks back to the tenets of Social Darwinism, which was an important ideological ingredient underpinning colonial conquest, then it is in this unquestioning retrieval of ideas associated with colonial epistemic archives that these writers illustrate Williams' notion of residual elements of cultural formations.

But Stoler remarks on the irony of European men's investment in 'black peril' discourses: 'although novels and memoirs position European women as

---

[8] As Duder (1991) persuasively argues, popular literature of the genre called the 'Kenya nov-el' played a central role in constructing and circulating certain ideas about colonial Kenya for Anglo-American readerships, including notions of interracial rape. Robert Ruark for instance was a prominent 'Kenya writer' whose work set in Kenya was engrossed with the question of sexual violation of white women by black men. See for instance his novel, *Uhuru*, which vividly explores the fears of the threat of black men to white womenfolk during the emergency period in colonial Kenya.

categorically absent from the sexual fantasies of European men, these very men imagined their women to be desired and seductive figures to others. Within this frame, European women needed protection from the "primitive" sexual urges aroused by the sight of them' (Stoler 2010: 187). Her irony here inadvertently underscores a second unstated irony: that, in practice, there was a more serious crisis of the 'white peril', in form of white male sexual predation on women of colour and, broadly, the shadows of white terror over black life. For bell hooks [*sic*], whiteness historically featured in black imagination in the US as a representation of terror, the terrifying and the terrorizing (hooks 1995: 39). Similarly, Richard Dyer highlights the contradictions that attach to associations of white with light and goodness, and black with darkness and danger: 'socialized to believe the fantasy that whiteness represents goodness and all that is benign and non-threatening, many white people assume this is the way black people conceptualize whiteness. They do not imagine that the way whiteness makes its presence felt in black life, most often as terrorizing imposition, a power that wounds, hurts, tortures, is a reality that disrupts the fantasy of whiteness as representing goodness' (Dyer cited in hooks 1995: 37). As scholarship on both colonialism and slavery shows, one of the ways this terror has manifested in white supremacist regimes of colonialism, and before that, slavery, is in the ruthless shape of 'white perils', as rape and sexual coercion formed part of these regimes of terror for women of colour. In their work – both fiction and academic – writers such as bell hooks, James Baldwin, Toni Morrison, Gloria Naylor, Angela Davis, Pumla Dineo Gqola and Gabeba Baderoon highlight the brutal prevalence of 'white peril' in such diverse contexts as the American South during slavery, at the peak of the civil rights movement in the US, and in apartheid South Africa. Toni Morrison's *Beloved* and James Baldwin's *Go Tell it on the Mountain* for instance feature some of the most vicious depictions of white rape of black women, in fiction. Equally, Angela Davis highlights the institutionalization of rape under slavery and beyond as a cornerstone of racism, an illustration of economic power, or property rights over black women's bodies, and as a weapon of control (1982: 175). For her, this brutal culture would subsequently feature in the Vietnam War, where US soldiers were systematically encouraged to use rape as a weapon of war (1982: 177).

Decades later, a similar pattern emerged in Kenya when over 2,000 Maasai and Samburu women accused the British Army of mass rape of women, girls and boys between the 1970s and the 1980s. The British Army Training Unit in Kenya (BATUK) hosts about 3,000 British soldiers who train in the region surrounding Nanyuki, annually. In 2003, reports of mass rapes committed by British soldiers over three decades came to light, first from the predominantly Maasai Dol Dol range, then subsequently from other areas. The case was difficult to prosecute due to the dearth of legally admissible corroborating evidence, thanks to a combination of the stigma of rape, illiteracy among many victims which made it impossible to accurately determine dates and time, and some degree of deceit by sex workers from elsewhere, who purportedly tried to pass off children born from transactional sex with tourists in Mombasa, as children born of rape by the soldiers. Although the case was eventually rejected for lack of evidence, lawyer Martyn Day who investigated the case believes several hundreds of the cases were genuine. Martyn Day and Jill Patterson Leigh's investigations revealed that the British Army was alerted to many of the rape cases in Dol Dol shortly after they happened. There were records of minuted meetings between local chiefs, government officials and the British Army officers, along with chiefs' letters dating back to 1977 pleading with the British Army officers to intervene in the mass rapes of Maasai women, but Day and Leigh found no evidence of the British Army's investigations of these claims, nor any charges or punishment brought against any soldiers. In effect, all the complainants ended up being classified as opportunistic sex workers. More recently, in 2015, an allegedly leaked UN Report made serious allegations of sexual violation of displaced children in war-torn Central African Republic in 2014 by French peacekeeping troops.[9] If we recall Gabeba Baderoon's work on slavery in South Africa, particularly the ways in which a demographic gender imbalance within the white community rendered both enslaved women and free Khoisan women's bodies sexually available to white men and subject to sexual violence with impunity (2014: 84), and considering that colonial rape laws were race-specific, as 'sexual abuse of black women was not classified as rape and therefore was not legally actionable, nor did rapes committed by white men lead to prosecution' (Stoler 2010: 188),[10] then these legacies might explain the British Army officials' dismissive response to reports of British soldiers' sexual assault of Maasai women as early as 1977, long before these cases came to acquire such publicity in 2003. Here, we see the construction of certain categories of women as 'unrapeable', to borrow from Pumla Dineo Gqola's (2015) work on

---

[9] See Sandra Laville 'UN Aid worker suspended for leaking report on child abuse by French troops' *The Guardian* 29 April 2015, www.theguardian.com/world/2015/apr/29/un-aid-work-er-suspended-leaking-report-child-abuse-french-troops-car, accessed 10 May 2015.

[10] A variant of this logic has been noted in the rape of Dalit women in India by men of a higher caste: 'Much of the caste-based sexual violence emerges out of a feudal sense of entitlement among some upper-caste men. "You have not really experienced the land until you have experienced the Dalit women" is a popular saying among the landowning Jats, a politically powerful group ... Though upper-caste men are rarely imprisoned for raping Dalits, they have a widely accepted defense at their disposal, should they ever need one: They would never touch a lower-caste woman for fear of being 'polluted.' In one famous 1995 case, a Dalit woman's allegations of gang rape were dismissed by a judge who claimed that 'an upper-caste man could not have defiled himself by raping a lower-caste woman' (Fontanella-Khan 2014). In effect, the Dalit women find themselves in an impossible paradox of being considered untouchable, contaminating, yet sexually available to the upper castes, should these men so desire to transgress caste boundaries.

the historical intersections of rape. The discussion on 'white peril' here does not exempt black men from sexual violence, especially against black women. As Angela Davis' work on the myth of the black rapist (1982) and on the blind spot on intra-racial rape in blues music (1999) suggests, in contexts where false rape charges were habitually brought against black men as justification for lynching, to 'acknowledge abuse perpetrated by the abused' became difficult (1999: 36).

The Criminal State

Perhaps apart from the dramatic and mysterious nature of Julie Ward's death, the one feature that drew both local and international attention to the case was the Kenyan official /state response to the finding of Julie Ward's remains and subsequent search for her killers. For the local publics, the Julie Ward murder mystery animated different fragments of social memories contained in Kenyan social imaginaries, which yielded conclusions that differed significantly from Ward and Gavron's speculations. Where Ward and Gavron were convinced that the Maasai Mara game rangers were behind the murder, local suspicion point-ed towards high-ranking political figures. Further, although rape still featured prominently in the local grapevine and the alleged 'eye-witness' accounts, the idea of rape took different trajectories, which seemed more preoccupied with what Achille Mbembe (1992) has in a different context described as 'the phallus of power'.[11] These narratives directed the idea of rape towards a critique of the abuse and brutality of state power. Where Ward and Gavron saw a case of black men losing their 'thin veneer of civilization' and succumbing to uncontrollable lust for the young white woman's body, local imaginaries saw a political elite's deployment of violence – including sexual violence – as part of its performance of power. Julie Ward's brutal death was one more episode in a long logbook of the political elite's trail of violence.

As highlighted in our discussion on the historical ledger of assassinations in Kenya, the idea of state-commissioned murder occupies a prime position in Kenyan social imaginaries; this is, in part, thanks to the Kenyan press's role in archiving these murders and underlining patterns and overlaps between the different murders. Outside the media, the idea of state assassination has been absorbed into popular culture as illustrated not only by the fiction discussed in the previous chapter, but also the music of Benga musician D.O. Misiani,[12] all of

---

[11] I use the phrase here in Mbembe's sense, to refer to an economy of pleasure associated with political power in the African state, which includes sexual indulgence. But, beyond this 'taste for lecherous living', the sexual indulgence is also an important site for the performance of power, sometimes through sexual violence.

[12] See Ogude's "The Cat that Ended up Eating the Homestead Chicken': Murder, Memory and Misiani's Dissident Music' (2007) for a discussion of D.O. Misiani's music and its commentary on state-commissioned assassinations.

which closely approximate dominant motifs of the idea of state-commissioned assassinations.

The notion of silencing inconvenient people has been such a recurrent phenomenon in Kenya that certain elements have solidified into recognizable tropes which the popular imaginaries have come to read as tell-tale signs of state involvement. Among these tropes is mysterious disappearance, sometimes announced on the state-owned KBC radio as was the case with Moi's Minister for Foreign Affairs, Dr Robert Ouko in 1991, before his body was 'found' in the bushes. Julie Ward also went missing for six days before her remains were 'found', while Kenyatta's cabinet minister, J.M. Kariuki went missing for six days before his remains were 'discovered' in the Ngong Hills. A second motif in these deaths is the mutilated and burnt body, which popular imaginaries have come to interpret as an attempt to destroy evidence. As well as Julie Ward, both J.M. Kariuki and Robert Ouko's bodies were mutilated, while Ward's and Ouko's bodies were burnt. In addition, the mutilated remains of Ward, Ouko and Kariuki were disposed of in forests and bushes – Maasai Mara, Koru and Ngong respectively – seemingly in an attempt to make the bodies disappear completely by getting them eaten by wild animals;[13] but when the remains were eventually discovered, then the official state position turned to wild animal attacks as the cause of death.

Another trope is the suicide theory, usually put forward by the police and the chief state pathologist. This theory was raised in the murders of Julie Ward, Fr John Anthony Kaiser and Robert Ouko. Subsequently, the state set up commissions of inquiry and parliamentary select committees to investigate the death. These were eventually disbanded and re-commissioned in an endless cycle, while their findings remained either mysterious or unreliable. An example of this is the Gicheru Commission of inquiry into the Robert Ouko murder, which appears to have been set up in response to public pressure demanding answers on the circumstances surrounding Ouko's death. But 'when it became clear that the Commission was moving in an uncomfortable direction [i.e. likely to implicate political heavyweights] it was disbanded' (AfriCOG 2007: 24).

Finally we have Scotland Yard – and in one case, the FBI – often called in to counter accusations of partial self-investigation by the guilty state. Scotland Yard has not been known to get to the bottom of any murder in Kenya and the three Scotland Yard detectives sent to Kenya to investigate Julie Ward's death remained true to this tradition. Scotland Yard detectives investigated Julie Ward's murder, and two years later, Robert Ouko's murder, while the FBI investigated Fr John Anthony Kaiser's murder. In the Ouko case, detective John

---

[13] Some versions of the story claim Ouko's body was dropped by a helicopter which intended to drop it into the nearby River Nyando, but missed their mark as the body ended up some distance away, on dry land. See Cohen and Odhiambo (2004).

Troon's report was never publicly revealed, while in the Ward case, Detectives Shipperlee and Searle surprisingly recommended the arrest and charge of two junior game rangers in the Maasai Mara, while overlooking obvious pointers towards the chief game ranger, who appeared to know more about the case than he was willing to reveal. Similarly, the FBI's finding of suicide due to depression in Fr John Anthony Kaiser's case was so unbelievable it was rejected by the Nairobi courts.

These tropes have come to form a recognizable lexicon in the grammar of the state's murder mysteries, usually punctuated by the statement, 'no stones will be left unturned in the search for the killers'[14]; in Kenyan imaginaries, this is understood to mean no stone will be left unturned in the fabrication of cover-ups.[15]

In light of this context then, for the Kenyan publics following the case, official attempts to frame Julie Ward's death as an act of God – suicide, mauling by wild animals or lightning – revealed state interest in placing the case beyond human culpability; a fact that was variously read as suspicious, and suggestive of attempts to conceal the truths behind the case.

The state's insistence on acts of God or suicide as the causes of death is often accompanied by elaborate, but poorly executed, cover-ups. The cover-up has become an all too legible symptom and consequence of state involvement for Kenyan social imaginaries. The cover-up in the Julie Ward case took the form of layers of inactions: delays in searching for the missing tourist, investigating the circumstances surrounding her death, the inquest as a delaying tactic; actions, such as altering the post-mortem report; and bungling, by a wide array of individuals, authorities and institutions – all forming a complex web in which the sheer volume of people involved points to the frightening depth of impunity at play. Given the large number of people who had to know about either the circumstances surrounding Julie Ward's murder or the circumstances surrounding the disposal of her body, and given the subsequent number of people and institutions entangled in ensuring the truth remained unknown, the success of this initiative, in so far as ensuring that twenty-six years on, the killers remain at large, is phenomenal. Like the continuing mystery regarding previous and subsequent murders, it is a salutary nod to the power and impunity of the culprits.

Given our interest in the workings of narrative, the rhetoric of protecting

---

[14] Cohen and Odhiambo's chapter titled 'No Stone Unturned' offers a meticulous record of President Moi's repeated pleas to leave 'no stones unturned' to find the truth about the Ouko murder (2004: 158–72), even as a plethora of Commissions of Inquiry and Parliamentary Select Committees and the Scotland Yard investigated and variously released reports or got suspended mid-inquiry, by the president. Moi had made a similar pledge to 'leave no stone unturned' in exposing Julie Ward's murderers in 1995. See 'Julie Ward Murder: Starting all over Again'. (*Nairobi Law Monthly* 1996a: 21).

[15] I am grateful to Florence Sipalla for drawing my attention to this fragment of Kenyan social imaginaries.

Kenya's tourism industry as the reason behind the cover-up of this murder is a powerful illustration of the levels of deceit at work in the case. This tourism motive was, interestingly, tabled by one of the Scotland Yard investigators, Detective Supt Searle, during the murder trial of Mara Game Wardens Magiroi and Kipeen. As Judge Fidahussein cites in his judgement on the case, Searle 'considered alteration of postmortem report by Dr Kaviti was an attempt to cover up the investigation. When pressed why such attempt was made, Mr. Searle thought that "this was an attempt to remove suspicion of murder in order to protect the Tourist Industry of this country"' (Fidahussein 1992: 68–69). Searle's observations were picked up by print media in the UK, some of which wholly bought into this logic. One such editorial commentary in *The Guardian* went beyond reporting this view to chastise the developed world, and Americans particularly, for their double standards in issuing travel advisories whenever there were such incidents in Kenya's game reserves, while overlooking their own much higher crime rates: 'The idea that Kenya's crime rate makes travel by Western visitors too dangerous is an absurdity. [It] is far safer – and culturally much more interesting – to travel to Kenya and visit its glorious national parks. Unlike America, the only killings you are likely to witness will be by big cats against defenceless antelope' (*The Guardian* 1992: 22).

In the same trial against Magiroi and Kipeen, Kenyan defence lawyer for the accused, James Orengo, described the Kenyan police investigations as having been compromised by 'by willful neglect, cover up and sometimes extreme carelessness' (Fidahussein 1992: 69). Presiding Judge Abdullah Fidahussein not only shared this view, but also commented on Supt Searle's speculation on the tourism industry: 'To say that there was no cover up is to shut eye [*sic*] to the obvious. We do not know why such exercise of cover up was carried out. One may accept the charitable opinion of Mr Searle that this was done to protect the Tourist Industry in this country'(ibid.). The Judge's description of Searle's tourism industry argument as charitable would seem to suggest an inclination towards a less charitable motive behind the cover-up. Subsequent revelation of British complicity in the cover-up was to shed a different kind of light on Supt Searle's charitable interpretation, as potentially part of the cover-up itself.

In his judgement, Judge Fidahussein further observes that although there were four or five game rangers' huts near Sand River Gate, Maasai Mara at the time of the murder, these huts were never forensically examined at any time, nor were the identities of these rangers properly established (1992: 108). In fact, 'most of them were apparently moved from the Sand River Gate after Mr Ward actively involved himself into [*sic*] the investigation: who was responsible to have these rangers removed?' (1992: 108). The redeployment of these rangers, including the Chief Game Warden, Simon ole Makallah, who would later be charged with the murder, coheres with the forging of Julie Ward's signature in one of the reserve's exit gate registers to suggest that Ward had left the reserve.

Although Julie Ward appeared to have been, until her death, an ordinary tourist in Kenya, lacking the political stature of many of her predecessors on the Kenyan ledger of assassinations, her death and the state responses to it mirrored earlier and subsequent deaths in Kenyan history, over which the shadow of a suspect state hovered. Parallels such as her disappearance, attempts to destroy the remains by burning, official insistence on wild animals, suicide or lightning, and the doctored post-mortem report, all seemed to situate Ward's death, alongside other murders, at the doorstep of well-placed political elites.

It must be emphasized, though, that the process of linking Julie Ward's death to other deaths in Kenyan history was far from mechanical. In addition to the tell-tale similarities between this death and previous deaths, other important factors included the lack of credibility of the various state institutions, which could have offered alternative truths – including the judiciary and the police. In this environment, where both law and science had failed to produce credible truths, the local social imaginaries fell back on social memories of similar incidents in Kenyan history. (I discuss the failure of science and law in greater detail in Chapter 4). Convinced by these parallels with other suspicious deaths in Kenyan history and similar attempts by the state to cover up the truth, local imaginaries cast Julie Ward as a political threat to criminal elements in the state. Among these were claims that the murder started out as rape by a prominent politician, as I also discuss in the next chapter.

The claims of rape in these allegations open yet another angle on the question of sexual violence, most troublingly, shifting the sexual violence from the prototypical 'black peril' imagined by Ward and Gavron, to a black man's inversion of the historical 'white peril' in the shape of powerful black men's sexual assault on black and white women's bodies simply because they could, with impunity. These allegations underscore a concern with a predatory black elite's impunity that recalls white impunity in the contexts of slavery depicted in the writings of James Baldwin and Toni Morrison. Discussing these allegations with a Kenyan colleague, when I expressed my disbelief at this version of the Ward murder, my colleague commented: 'power corrupts and perhaps it is the little things that bring out the worst reactions from the powerful. Being used to having their way almost all the time, not having your way may easily provoke a "know people" response, Nancy Baraza-style.'[16] My colleague's comment here underscores the

---

[16] Personal communication. 'Know people' is a phrase that made its way into the Kenyan street dictionary when the then Deputy Chief Justice Nancy Baraza refused to undergo a mandatory security check when entering the upmarket Village Market Mall, in Nairobi, and allegedly threatened to shoot the security lady Rebecca Kerubo Kemunto, for daring to subject a person of her stature to the routine search. Part of Ms Baraza's fury was that Kemunto did not recognize her, so, she instructed her to 'know important people' in future, meaning she must familiarize herself with the Kenyan elite and be appropriately revering towards them. The incident sparked major public furore resulting in Baraza's suspension and subsequent

ways in which allegations about the involvement of a powerful political figure in the murder were also forms of commentary on Kenyan cultures of statecraft and power. For such publics then, the Ward murder was yet another instance of the unnecessary excesses of power; just as, on hindsight, the murders of the key politicians in the Kenyan assassination ledger were excessive responses to minor political threats that had been blown out of proportion.

The Sex Question in the Julie Ward Case

So far, from our discussion above, Julie Ward appears to have been portrayed through two tropes, both of which emphasized her victimhood – as an innocent Madonna and as a martyr. In their speculation, Ward and Gavron portray Julie Ward in strokes of what Diane Roberts has described as 'the Victorian mantle of white womanhood – frail, delicate, sexually pure' (2005: 33), which sustains the idea of the defenceless white woman at the mercy of lustful black men. In the Kenyan social imaginaries, Julie Ward is elevated to a status bordering on martyrdom, as yet another victim of a violent and criminal political elite, who either dies collecting incriminating evidence of this elite's crimes, or is yet another victim of this elite's brutal exercise of power, simply because they can.

There was a third portrayal of Julie Ward, which framed her as a woman of loose sexual mores. This perception was produced across the Kenya–Britain divide. It is this perception that highlights the continuities in the ideas held in British and Kenyan social imaginaries on race, gender and sexuality. In this third version, the cross-cultural dialogues and overlaps of the values held by the various popular archives become evident.

In his 1992 judgement of the Julie Ward murder trial against Peter Kipeen and Jonah Magiroi, Judge Abdullah Fidahussein wrote:

> There can be no doubt that Julie was charming and affectionate girl [*sic*] … She was probably too trusting and unconcerned about her personal safety. Although not of low moral character, her liberal attitude towards sex may not sit well with those of older generation. I do not wish to be too critical in not eliminating the possibility that *her easy ways may have contributed to her predicament, resulting in her murder and grisly disposal of her flesh* [*sic*; Fidahussein 1992, emphasis added].

In this extract, Judge Fidahussein draws links between Julie Ward's death and what he describes as her 'liberal attitude towards sex … [and] easy ways'. Despite his cautious note that Julie Ward was not of low moral character, Judge Fidahussein nonetheless considers her sexual mores to have been an influential

resignation, when a judicial committee appointed to investigate her conduct in this incident recommended her removal from office. See East African Centre for Law and Justice 2012 for a detailed discussion of the case.

factor which contributed to her murder, although his judgement stops short of explaining exactly what he considered to be 'her easy ways' and how these 'may have contributed to her predicament'.

The notion that Julie Ward was a woman of loose morals probably had its roots in the friendships she formed with various men in the course of her trip although, in most cases, there is no available information that she had sexual relationships with them. As noted from the itinerary of her trip to Kenya, she met and interacted with various men and women on her way from England to Maasai Mara. Among these were Dave Tree the Hobo Trans-Africa Expeditions truck driver, Paul Weld Dixon and his wife her hosts in Lang'ata, Doug Morey in Lang'ata whose cottage she rented, Glen Burns her companion on the journey to the Mara, David Weston a balloon pilot whose acquaintance she made in the Mara, and Steven Watson who towed her jeep when it got stuck there.

It is probably in view of these interactions that Judge Fidahussein described Julie Ward as having 'easy ways'. Similar sentiments had been expressed three years earlier at the inquest into her death, held in August 1989. During the inquest, the state prosecutor Alex Etyang had described Julie Ward as 'a twenty-eight-year-old, adventurous woman, with three men in her life at the Maasai Mara who were close friends' (1994: 144–5). Describing Etyang's line of argument, Gavron reports:

> One of his [Etyang's] key defences was that Julie had died because she was a woman of little education and loose character. 'She left school at the age of seventeen years' Etyang said. 'This might be considered a relatively young age for a girl to leave school'. Julie's time in Kenya, Etyang suggested, was spent moving from one man to another. … Julie was taken to the Dixons by a man called David Tree … She then met Glen Burns … Later she met David Weston, the balloon pilot who 'fancied her, got her into conversation, bought her a beer or so, had cocktails with her … And finally there was Stephen Watson, 'the man who slept with Julie at the Maasai Mara' [ibid.: 144].

In these two sets of sentiments – Judge Fidahussein's and Etyang's – Julie Ward is portrayed as a woman with multiple partners. The idea of her as a woman with multiple partners was further echoed by the Kenyan police in the course of their investigations into her death. Although Etyang's argument above reveals the sentiments of the investigating officers charged with the case, this thinking was more candidly captured by Police pathologist Dr Adel Shaker's testimony at the second inquest into Julie Ward's death, held in England:

> [Police Commissioner] Kilonzo was satisfied with the report from [Chief Government Pathologist] Kaviti and other police officers that the animals had mauled the body. Inside Kilonzo's offices, the officers made jokes and suggested that Ward was

a prostitute, that she had been sleeping around with different men in the game reserve and that she had been depressed leading to suicide [Nation Team 2007: 3].

These three sets of statements from official quarters in Kenya are striking for the ways in which they signal a specific regime of ideas on female sexual morality which was at play in the Kenyan official approach to the investigations into Julie Ward's death. From these statements, there seemed to be an underlying criminalization of Julie Ward's sexuality, with undertones of blame for the fate that befell her. In fact, from publicly available information, she may have been sexually involved with only two of the men she met between February and September 1988: Dave Tree and Stephen Watson. It goes without saying that if she had been a man, this would have been considered unremarkable, once again underlining the Kenyan police and judicial forces' investment in the myth of the sexually pure woman, and the attendant overlaps with the earlier-discussed colonial notion of women as custodians of morality. These attempts to link her sexual interactions to her fate, and implicitly limit public empathy towards her brutal fate bring to mind sections of responses to the murder of Nicole Brown Simpson who, bell hooks observes, was 'a woman that many people, white and black, felt was like a whore. Precisely by being a sexually promiscuous woman, by being a woman who used drugs, by being a white woman with a black man, she had already fallen from grace in many people's eyes – there was no way to redeem her' (hooks cited in Gates 1997: 115). Although Julie Ward's biography differs significantly from Simpson's, we witness the same logic of apportioning of empathy proportional to a woman's sexual purity, which is considered proportional to her grievability.

To a certain degree, the official focus on Julie Ward's sexual behaviour as a contributing factor in her death spoke to similar cases in Kenyan history, most notably the 1980 murder of Monica Njeri, a commercial sex worker in Mombasa and the 1978 murder of army captain Judy Angaine in Nairobi. Njeri plied her trade in the tourist town of Mombasa, a hub of activity known in Kenyan lore for a vibrant sex economy involving local men and women, and primarily white tourists.[17] She was killed by an apprentice American Navy fireman, 19-year-old Frank Sundstrom, who was part of an American Navy crew that had docked at Mombasa.[18] Sundstrom had allegedly tried to steal back the money he had paid her while she slept, but she caught him red-handed. In the ensuing struggle, he

[17] See Omondi's paper 'Gender and the Political Economy of Sex Tourism in Kenya's Coastal Resorts' (2003) and Kibicho's essay 'Tourism and the Sex Trade: Role Male Sex Workers Play in Malindi, Kenya' (2003).
[18] Former American ambassador to Rwanda and the Central African Republic, Robert Gribbin who was posted to Mombasa in the late 1970s gives an account of these two murders in 'Moments in U.S. Diplomatic History: Port of Call Girls' (2013) available from http://adst.org/2013/06/port-of-call-girls, accessed 18 February 2015.

allegedly broke a beer bottle and repeatedly stabbed her until she died. After pleading guilty, the charge was reduced to manslaughter and Frank was set free on the condition of a US $70, two-year 'good behavior' bond (Omondi 2003: 14).[19] This bizarrely lenient sentence sparked much public uproar in Kenya and even came up for discussion in parliament. Tellingly though, it would appear that it was the racial overtones in the case that had provoked this response, as seen by calls for the removal of racist white judges in the Kenyan bar. The sentence had been passed by a white Judge Harris. The intersections between race and gender in the case remained largely unacknowledged.

In the second case, Capt. Judy Angaine was found dead in a bathtub in her house. The chief suspect was her boyfriend, Major David Kisila, who was tried for the murder. During the trial, State Counsel William Mbaya argued that Major Kisila had a motive of jealousy, to murder Judy Angaine, as Kisila 'had reason to believe Capt. Angaine was seeing other men – including Mr Ngei, Mr Nyagah and Mr Lithimbi' (Ngotho 2004a: 3). Countering this argument, Kisila's defence lawyer Byron Georgiadis – who was to subsequently represent the Ward family in the inquest into Julie Ward's murder – argued that 'though his client may have had a love-related motive to kill Capt. Angaine, he was not the only one with a similar motive' (ibid.). In view of Angaine's history of potentially multiple sexual partners, including Ministers Paul Ngei and Jeremiah Nyagah, and the father of her child, John Lithimbi, with whom she had exchanged Valentine's Day cards only a month and a half earlier (ibid.),[20] the defence argued, each of these three men had the shared motive of jealousy. Kisila was acquitted of the murder charge in the case which remains unsolved four decades later. The case was serialized in the *Daily Nation*. Public response to the judgement was unremarkable.

In these two cases, Njeri and Angaine's sexual practices seemed to have lowered perceptions of their victimhood. The foregrounding of the two women's sexual relations echoes the outlined emphasis on Julie Ward's sexuality. This lingering on the murdered women's sexuality in the three cases suggests that the Kenyan legal apparatuses in these cases operated with great awareness of popular moral economies regarding female sexuality in Kenya. Far from being a stable, laid down set of rules though, this moral economy is a constantly negotiated code of conduct, constructed from popular wisdom that is gleaned from various social practices, institutions and experiences. In Kenya, popular wisdom on morality is distilled from a range of institutions including religious doctrine and an array of customary practices, all of which are firmly conservative regarding sexuality in general, and female sexuality in particular. In light of these hegemonic assumptions regarding female sexual practices as

---

[19] See also Nation Reporter 1980: 1–2.
[20] See also Kimondo, 'Judy: Blood Clues Found', *Daily Nation*, 10 June 1978: 1, 4.

normatively monogamous and grounded in exclusive fidelity to one partner, the three women's sexual practices would seem to have been important mitigating factors in their families' failure to find justice.

What is striking in these three cases is the subtle incrimination of the murdered women for the social crime of 'rendering themselves vulnerable' to violent murder by contravening their men's/society's rules on female sexual etiquette. Read differently then, these verdicts seemed to legitimize, or at the very least 'understand' femicide as a matter-of-course punishment for contravention of this gendered sexual moral code. This line of thought is consistent with the logics of charging women with responsibility for their own safety in patriarchal societies that subject women to sexual harassment and violence.

Beyond a patriarchal judicial system which echoed similar responses to other women's murders though, the lingering on Julie Ward's sexual practices could be further traced to yet another set of social memories, constructed from colonial practices in Kenya and postcolonial popular knowledge on tourist culture in Kenya. It is this fragment of social memories shared across Kenyan and British social imaginaries that underlined both the porous boundaries between the two and their dialogic engagements on race, gender and female sexuality.

A useful entry point into this set of social memories is provided by David Barritt in his article on the Julie Ward murder, titled 'Lion girl's last sex-crazed night' and which appeared in the British *Sunday Mirror* on 7 November 1988. Describing the article, Gavron writes:

> It pictured Julie Ward as a buxom, scantily clad, sexually overdeveloped nymph who had slept her way through Africa. The implication was that Julie had played with the primitive sexual emotions of Africans and therefore contributed towards her bloody end [1991: 103].

Although they remain anchored in the 'black peril' discourses which assign Africans 'primitive sexual emotions', Barritt's sentiments are nonetheless interesting in their allusion to the notion of the tourist in search of adventure, often captured in the popular phrase 'sun, sand and sex'.

The persistent portrayal of Julie Ward as a sexually adventurous tourist, despite the lack of evidence to this effect can be understood through what Tony Bennett calls 'reading formations'. Bennett defines reading formations as 'intersecting discourses that productively activate a given body of texts and relations between them in a given way', resulting in new formations of meaning (1983: 5). In attempts to piece together the circumstances surrounding Julie Ward's death, the above outlined movements and interactions between her and her male acquaintances were 'productively activated' by existing ideas in Kenyan and British social imaginaries on indulgence and adventure as definitive practices in tourist cultures.

In the Kenyan context, ideas of adventurous tourist cultures find further resonance with three sets of ideas: the historic construction of the country as an eroticized Edenic garden, a vibrant sex-tourism economy especially along the coast and the colonial reputation of the country as what a character in le Carré's *The Constant Gardener* describes as 'an adventure playground for derelict upper-class swingers' (2001: 125). Within the context of the Julie Ward case, these three sets of ideas can be understood in line with Rose Omondi's (2003: 9) argument that the assurance of anonymity releases tourists from the restraint that polices behaviour in their home environment, creating fertile ground for adventure, pleasure-seeking and living out fantasies with little inhibition.

In Kenyan popular imaginaries, the area stretching from Nairobi to Maasai Mara is a distinctly tourist terrain, predominantly featuring the Maasai community – a cultural tourist attraction in themselves – and private game ranches and lodges. The lingering focus on Julie Ward's sexuality in these instances was anchored in popular wisdom on white tourists' sexual practices in Kenya, wisdom that partly owes its roots to the 'Happy Valley' culture in colonial Kenya, which was comprised of a hedonistic culture of safaris, hunter-playboys and heavy indulgence in sex, drugs and alcohol.[21] In an allusive manner therefore, the references to Julie Ward's alleged sexual escapades in Maasai Mara and her subsequent murder appeared to evoke the case of the unsolved murder of Happy Valley's Lord Errol, a renowned ladies' man. This murder mystery was a glamorous cocktail of sexual adventures, alcohol, drugs and violence, as vividly explored in James Fox's *White Mischief* (1983). To a certain degree then, portrayals of Julie Ward as a woman of loose morals would seem to have been anchored in circulating discourses about tourist practices and their indulgence in sexual adventure.

Despite this though, Kenyan officialdom's keenness to portray Julie Ward as a 'loose tourist' further alerts us to a second dynamic that seemed to be at play in the case: attempts to manipulate local public opinion on the matter. To some degree, this mission was accomplished, as the local grapevines revelled in Julie Ward's alleged promiscuity. One of the more widespread strands of rumours was that Julie Ward had been having a relationship with an influential politician who had her killed for being unfaithful. A second variant of this rumour suggests that she was a British intelligence agent masquerading as a tourist, who used her sex-appeal to access important state secrets, held by the son of the influential politician, by getting into a relationship with him, but he soon discovered her real identity and had her killed.[22]

The idea of Julie Ward as a temptress who uses her body to manipulate information out of a powerful man echoes old mythology – both Christian and traditional African – that constructs women as tricksters and men as sexually

---

[21] See James Fox's *White Mischief* (1983) for an informative reconstruction of Happy Valley culture.
[22] Personal communications with various Kenyans, who insisted on anonymity.

vulnerable to women. The Biblical equivalent of this is the story of Samson and Delilah. The Luo community in Western Kenya has a similar narrative about a beautiful woman from the Kipsigis community, who baited a famous Luo warrior Lwanda Magere with her sexual charm, and persuaded him to share the secret of his strength, leading to the defeat of the Luo in war.

While imaginings of a sexually abused Julie Ward emphasize her vulnerability to sexual violation, it is this victimized woman who is sympathetically portrayed in both Kenyan and British imaginaries, suggesting an implicit affirmation of the notion of female vulnerability. The narratives that portray Julie Ward as a promiscuous and sexually manipulative woman, read from a less conservative moral episteme, grant her some degree of agency that momentarily places her in a position of power over her body and the men in question. However, given the conservative moral lenses that celebrate female sexual purity which British and Kenyan imaginaries appeared to embrace, these rumours portrayed Julie Ward as a scheming woman who had been punished for presuming to take advantage of a man's natural sexual desires. In this instance, both the legal institutions and the popular imaginaries were drawing on specific cultural productions of female sexuality, and elevating them to legitimate principles on human nature and indeed the very concept of life, by suggesting that the worth of a life lies in its owner's 'morality'.

Beyond her sexuality however, Julie Ward's whiteness played an interesting role, further complicating local responses. While her death has since found its way into the list of unresolved mystery murders which – at least so goes popular wisdom – the state had a hand in, Julie Ward's death did not inspire as much emotional identification as other murders, including Tom Mboya's before her, and Robert Ouko's after her. Several factors account for this. On the face of it, these two were both men and they commanded influential positions in the local political landscape, which were seen to have played a role in their death. Beyond this, however, Julie Ward as a white British woman in a patriarchal society with a politically invisible white minority failed to command significant local identification. Indeed, it cannot be overemphasized that the attention the case received both formally and informally in Kenya and internationally was mainly the result of her father's persistent effort, and willingness to spend time and money in the quest for his daughter's killers. Yet, at the same time, as a white woman, she commanded more empathy than a black woman would have commanded both in Kenya and internationally, thanks to an older history of racialized valuing of lives. Writer and academic Njabulo Ndebele unpacks this history: 'We are all familiar with the global sanctity of the white body. Wherever the white body is violated in the world, severe retribution follows somehow for the perpetrators if they are non-white, regardless of the social status of the white body. The white body is inviolable and that inviolability is in direct proportion to the global vulnerability of the black body' (Ndebele, cited in Coetzee 2013: 66).

In a country heavily mapped along ethnic lines, which in a very real sense determine the distribution networks for most (national) resources – including justice and sympathy – Julie Ward as a white non-Kenyan fell outside these distribution networks. In the public imaginaries, Julie Ward largely inspired local passions in so far as her death could be laid at the doorstep of the incumbent Moi regime, a position which served to progress the populist politics of the day more than the search for the truth behind her death.

The subsequent murder of the American priest Fr John Kaiser in 2000 proves this point persuasively. Fr Kaiser's murder is believed to have been sanctioned by certain elements in the country's political elite, allegedly because he was in possession of incriminating evidence regarding the so-called ethnic clashes in the Rift Valley Province, and a rape case which supposedly implicated a powerful local politician. In Fr Kaiser's case too, a compassionate local identification was lacking, beyond political condemnation of the government. In contrast, other murder victims such as Robert Ouko, J.M. Kariuki, Bishop Alexander Muge and Tom Mboya have continued to receive attention with frequent calls for new investigations to bring their killers to book. For instance, the Ouko and Mboya murders fed into an already existing Luo ethnic politic of a conspiracy to deny Luos an opportunity to lead the country, by eliminating prominent Luos. But as a woman and a member of a minority race in Kenya, Julie Ward's murder failed to inspire such sentiment. While the Ouko and Mboya murders are the subject of various scholarly studies, music and fiction by Kenyans – as indicated by Cohen and Odhiambo's book-length study of the Ouko murder, *The Risks of Knowledge*, the music of D.O. Misiani, Sam Okello's novel *The Night Bob Died*, and Stephen Omamo's *The Men do not Eat Wings* – both Julie Ward's and Fr Kaiser's deaths have only managed the occasional anecdotal mention by Kenyan scholars; and to my knowledge, the only book-length text on Fr Kaiser is his own posthumously published, premonitory memoir-cum-report *If I Die*.

What stands out from our discussion on the patterns of speculations about Julie Ward's death is the lingering on her body and her sexuality across the various constituencies. It is in this that we begin to see the interpenetration of social imaginaries which appeared to be anchored on circulating discourses about the female body. Julie Ward's body became a site for the articulation of a broad spectrum of ideas including critiques of the workings of officialdom in the Moi era, female sexual moralities, race relations and a voyeuristic gaze at the body of power.

The political climate and the prevalent anti-establishment ethos in the late 1980s and 1990s in Moi's Kenya gave certain theories greater purchase in local imaginaries. The credibility of these circulating theories about Julie Ward's death was rated not so much by the supporting evidence – though this too was relevant – but by the extent to which they were founded on and confirmed social truths about the incumbent establishment and the practice of power within the Moi regime. Through the rumours and these alleged 'eye-witness' accounts – which were circulated in the media and further circulated in everyday conversations in Kenya – people were able to filter through available information about the death and weave their own interpretations, which provided a forum to comment on state power. In this, the extant social memories provided important ingredients in weaving credible scenarios.

Far from displaying mechanical or linear processes of retrieval of social memories, the speculations on Julie Ward's death firmly emphasized the intertextual relationships that existed between Julie Ward's death and other deaths in Kenyan history, which in turn reveals the interpenetrating contours of social memories across otherwise distinct constituencies. Interestingly, where the British and Kenyan constituencies held sharply differing views on race, when it came to gender, there seemed to be a shared pool of patriarchal attitudes from which the various constituencies drew. Whether in voyeuristically revelling in Julie Ward's so-called sexual escapades, or in attempting to preserve her virtue by persistently desexualizing her, as John Ward and Jeremy Gavron did, the various constituencies all appeared to subscribe to the same conservative moral economy that prized female sexual purity.

As early as 1991, Ward describes the rumours and allegations about a powerful man behind his daughter's murder:

> Throughout the two-and-a-half-year investigation, two other accusations have constantly surfaced, always anonymously. One concerns the son of a very highly placed government official. Rumours of his alleged previous record of rape continue to reach my ears, as do his frequent releases from custody once the police realise who they have picked up. His association with the Masai Mara and Keekorok are constantly mentioned. I have received more than a dozen unsigned messages and anonymous telephone calls naming the man who, the informants claim, is responsible for Julie's murder. During his short time in Nairobi, [Scotland Yard detective] Graham received a couple of these calls too. No one has presented a shred of hard evidence to support these allegations and, more meaningfully for Kenya, none of the informants has sought to claim the reward. Possibly the information comes from people with a political axe to grind. Like Graham, I must dismiss such accusations – until provided with some proof [1991: 386].

This early in the case, Ward concedes that the involvement of such a figure would explain why the Kenyan authorities went to such trouble and expense to orchestrate the cover-up. As he ponders 'would they really do all that just to save a couple of murdering park rangers who they would obviously be better rid of? This kind of protection is only afforded to someone with great influence' (ibid.). Despite this line of thought, Ward seems to have stuck to his resolve to 'dismiss such accusations until provided with some proof'. It would be another twenty years, before he publicly acknowledged these rumours and took them seriously, in a 2012 publication.

Although on the surface the rumours and allegations on Julie Ward's death appeared to be primarily interested in incriminating what was perceived to be criminal political elite, as discussed in Chapter 3, at another level, these rumours were also a commentary on the limits of privileging legal truths produced in modern state institutions, especially in a context such as Kenya in the 1980s, where these institutions were largely compromised. But even in a context where these institutions are not compromised, Patricia Williams' comment on the O.J. Simpson trial and its verdict resonates: 'trials don't establish absolute truth; that's a theological enterprise' (cited in Gates 1997: 120).

This chapter reflects on rumours as a critique of legal truths. I suggest that while the Julie Ward case was formally prosecuted within the Kenyan and British legal systems, a parallel prosecution was unfolding among the various publics constituted by the case, which appropriated available information from various sources, and reached their own verdicts. I borrow this idea of parallel publics from Cohen and Odhiambo (1992) who, in their discussion of the 1987 S.M. Otieno burial saga in Kenya, argue that the case constituted various publics who followed the case closely and had their own views on it. The Ward case however differs on the basis of the radical contestation of the legal investigation, and the sharply alternative readings that emerged. While the S.M. Otieno court case enjoyed popular legitimacy, even among people who disagreed with the eventual verdict,[1] in the Ward case, the inquest and the two trials were all haunted by suspicion by Kenyan publics that saw these court procedures as yet another layer of cover-up tactics. These parallel courts had radically different senses of what constituted evidence, in which logic and credibility along with a range of social truths and assumptions became the central principles as opposed to the conventional understanding of evidence as corroborated facts in the formal legal systems.

For various publics – both Kenyan and British – Dr Kaviti's alterations of a legal document written by a colleague – especially one who had repeatedly expressed his belief that he was looking at a case of murder[2] – became suspect. The various sets of official 'truths' lacked coherence, making them suspect, in a case where logic and credibility were indispensable. The autopsy report – whether one believed Dr Shaker's version or Dr Kaviti's revised one – shed further doubts on the investigating police officer Supt Muchiri's conclusion of suicide. Given that the autopsy revealed attempts to burn the remains *after* decapitation, the suicide theory lost credibility, while the incineration of the remains complicated the notion of an attack by wild animals. In this environment of suspect and suspicious state truths, Kenyan publics following the case

---

[1] S.M. Otieno was a prominent Nairobi lawyer whose death was followed by a lengthy legal battle between his Nairobi-based wife and his Nyanza-based clan, over where he would be buried. Despite his wife, Wambui Waiyaki-Otieno's insistence that Otieno had verbally expressed a wish to be buried in Nairobi, his clan, the Umira-Kager lodged a legal claim for their right to bury Otieno in his ancestral land in Nyanza Province. The case raised complex debates on the tensions between 'tradition' and 'modernity', customary and common law, with Wambui Waiyaki-Otieno underlining Otieno's profile as a modern, urban man, no longer subject to clan protocols. In the end an intricate distinction between a home and a house became important in solving the matter. The court ruled in favour of the Umira-Kager clan. See Cohen and Odhiambo's *Burying SM: The Politics of Knowledge and the Sociology of Power in Africa* (1992).

[2] Procedurally, Paul Dixon – Julie Ward's host while she was in Nairobi – was called upon to officially identify the remains before the post-mortem, as a family representative. Dr Shaker verbally noted that the evidence on the body parts made it a 'case of murder' (Ward 1991; Gavron 1994).

actively sought, created and circulated their own versions of the truth behind the tragedy through the grapevine, some of which made their way into local print media and back.

Hearsay and rumour become reliable sources of truth(s) in as far as they 'can resolve some of the confusions that are contained in experience' (White 2000: 34). These are fluid texts that must be read using interpretative tools that transcend conventional notions of veracity. In using rumour as a source of social truths, I am interested in local constructions of meaning regarding Julie Ward's death and how the case became a repository of people's fears, anxieties and social truths, while simultaneously enabling them to subvert and critique both a repressive local regime and logocentric assumptions of the modern epistemologies of science and the law. As Luise White (1998: 39) notes regarding hearsay, such texts 'allow people to appropriate them and map out experience and negotiate realities'. The rumours about the Julie Ward case are part of the way in which people were able to filter through the available information about the death, and weave their own interpretations and analyses, which provided a forum to comment on various socio-political concerns in Kenya, and even imagine with a fair amount of detail, exactly what happened, who was involved and what the motivation for the murder was. Notably, the rumoured narratives are a lot more adventurous in their speculations on the truth behind the death and in a sense appear to fill in the gaps in the three books, and the courtroom truths by arriving at conclusive truths. For Kenyans, the various rumours regarding the murder provided material with which to map out the circumstances surrounding it, which in turn could be used as a fairly reliable index of the levels of brutality and violence of the Moi regime, among other things. In effect, the insertion of these stories into social discourse provided openings into debates regarding issues ranging from the incumbent establishment to the place of race and gender in Kenya.

While truth is conventionally taken to be logocentric and hinged on a provable veracity, rumour as a genre gains its legitimacy from precisely the suspect nature of officially produced truths. Within systems of institutionalized domination, such as Kenya was in the 1960s–1990s, people learn to enact inscrutable forms of resistance. In his study, *Domination and the Arts of Resistance: Hidden Transcripts* (1990), James Scott observes that people who occupy subordinate positions in oppressive societies often have an extensive social existence outside the immediate control of the dominant group. These 'sequestered settings', he notes, provide a healthy breeding ground for critiques of domination. Scott's argument here is in line with Raymond Williams' (1977: 125) assertion that no form of domination/oppression is ever so complete as to encompass all the possible forms of expression. This book takes Scott's ideas as an entry point in understanding the competing versions of truth in these narratives. It is framed within the interaction between what Scott calls 'public transcripts' – that is open interactions between the dominant and the subordinate – and 'hidden transcripts' – a term he defines as 'discourse that takes place offstage, beyond the observation of the power holders, and which tend to confirm, inflect, qualify or contradict the public transcript' (1990: 16). This framework informs my reading of the various interpretations of Julie Ward's death, with particular interest in the forms of subversion that emerge across the various narratives.

Mapping the Julie Ward Grapevine

I find Mbembe's (1992) concept of the vulgarity of power in the postcolony particularly illuminating in reading grapevine interventions on the Julie Ward case. Mbembe persuasively delineates power relations in the postcolony as being based on performance and fetishization. In this, the very body of the '*commandement*'[3] becomes a site for the production and performance of power (1992: 7). To affirm itself, the *commandement* produces a whole series of signs and images of itself, which are then circulated and reproduced by the subjects, as manifestations of state power. Mbembe's ideas on the performance of power and the fetishization of the *commandement* in the postcolony are quite appropriate in mapping out the media–state relationship in the postcolony. As an opinion-shaping institution, the media mediates between reality and its representation. This is an important process in the performance of power for, as Mbembe (1992) observes, the postcolony operates on an economy of signs, which are used to encode and mediate reality.[4]

While Mbembe's ideas on performance and fetishization eloquently outline power relations in post-independence Africa, they also paint a vision of passive victimhood in his idea of 'a logic of conviviality … and the dynamics of domesticity and familiarity' (1992: 11). True, as he notes, the binaries of oppressor/oppressed and subjection/resistance may be too facile to yield a feasible framework for understanding power relations in the postcolony. But in much the same way, a 'mutual zombification between the oppressor and the oppressed' that does not dig beneath the surface of ambivalence to unearth its promises is equally frugal. Ordinary people's engagement with state power, while seemingly complicit, is in itself an expression of agency. They may be active participants in their oppression and they make certain choices whose limitations perhaps lie in the unambitious temporariness and the ambivalences inherent in these short-term solutions – but even these are informed by an instinct for survival.

---

[3] The ability of an individual to acquire or exercise authority in a group according to competence, popularity, or as an elected or imposed leader.

[4] Mbembe's reflections on the postcolony have received extensive engagement and critique by various scholars.

Within a hegemonic power structure, revolutionary action does not quite take the shape of an upward thrust of the masses that Fanon (1967) had in mind for the nationalist revolution. As Neil Lazarus (1993) finds in his attempt to understand the missing link between the revolutionary action of the masses during the struggles for independence and their lethargy in the face of the betrayal of the national ideals, perhaps the governed at times suffer from what the elite may see as plain lack of ambition. Yet even this seemingly unambitious stance, this indolence in the face of oppression, is in itself an expression of agency, for they learn to find little pockets of freedom for the pursuit of their own aspirations, and articulation of their fears, desires and ambitions. This act of finding sites of freedom must be understood in light of the structures in place, which then necessitate a search for alternative ways of articulating these marginalized discourses.

Therefore, bearing in mind Mamdani's (1996) cautionary note that all acts of resistance must be understood within the structural frame of the space in question, while it may appear to be a collusive act, ordinary people's actions are in the real sense strong expressions of agency within a proscribed structure. For Strinati (1995: 160), subordinated groups accept the ideas, values and leadership of the dominant group often because they have a reason of their own: it is a pragmatic reading of the overwhelming raw power controlled by the dominant groups. As such, yielding to Mbembe's intimate tyranny that links the ruler to the ruled is a highly suggestive act of reclaiming agency, by pursuing self-preservation. It is a survival gesture reminiscent of the Ethiopian proverb cited by James Scott (1985): 'When the great lord passes, the wise peasant bows deeply and silently farts.' In some ways, Kenyan rumours on the Julie Ward case operated within this logic of 'silent farts' at the emperor's nudity.

DiFonzo and Bordia's observation that rumours arise when information is not available or when information sources are not trusted (2007: 30) holds true in the Julie Ward case. As earlier noted, official attempts to frame Julie Ward's death as an act of God, suicide, attacks by wild animals or lightning were read as suspicious, suggesting a state with its own preferred truth(s), and grapevines across the country sought to make sense of the official interest in placing Ward's death beyond human culpability. As official investigations into Julie Ward's death were going on in Kenyan and British courtrooms, the case captured the popular imagination across Kenya, resulting in parallel 'trials' in informal discursive terrains. Through interpretations of media reports, hearsay, court verdicts and state officials' comments, available information and the accompanying silences were woven into verdicts which found their way into the yellow press and mainstream media, and back again to the spaces of allegation and speculation.

Much scholarship emphasizes that rumour is a highly ephemeral medium, in large part thanks to its traditional association with oral cultures.[5] However, rumours about Julie Ward's death have found their way into the printed page over the years, largely through newspaper reports – both local and international – and anonymous calls and notes addressed to her father, John Ward, who later wrote about them in *The Animals are Innocent: The Search for Julie's Killers* (1991). This chapter mainly relies on these written (i.e. rephrased and 'translated') records of the rumours on the case, contained in the Kenyan print media of the 1990s.

As outlined in Chapter 2, the rumours on Julie Ward's death were embedded in, and indeed a response to, the socio-political climate of the time, during the repressive Moi regime of the 1980s and 1990s. In this socio-political climate, the relationship between the state and the citizenry was one of mutual paranoia. On the citizenry's part, this was accompanied by a general suspicion of both the state institutions and state-owned media as tools of propaganda, and independent media as (self-)censored. The process by which the Julie Ward death was absorbed into social discourse as an avenue for discussing a whole range of social, political concerns can be seen to illustrate what Cohen and Odhiambo have called the production of culture,[6] in a slightly different context. The Julie Ward murder provided a forum for engaging with issues of race, power and even sexuality through the rumours and allegations.

For Atieno Odhiambo (1987) rumour-mongering is one of the informal oppositional institutions in Kenya which grant the ordinary *mwananchi* (citizen) a democratic space to express various forms of socio-political consciousness. Odhiambo historicizes these forms as alternative avenues that grow in the vacuum left by the criminalization of organized oppositional politics (what one might call an institutionally recognized public sphere) on the one hand, and the conscription of state institutions in the service of a select political agenda, on the other. In a sense, one sees in rumours an active process of interpreting, decoding and encoding socio-political discourses in Kenya. In such contexts, where formal media are either co-opted or censored, other informal spaces emerge as local variants of what Habermas calls the public sphere. Odhiambo's argument here resonates with Henry Louis Gates jr's commentary on the appeal

---

[5] See Patricia Turner's *I Heard it through the Grapevine: Rumor in African-American Culture* (1993) and Luise White's *Speaking With Vampires: Rumor and History in Colonial Africa* (2000) for insightful explorations of rumour and its logics.

[6] The two historians discuss this with reference to the saga of burying S.M. Otieno. In their text, they argue that the case resulted in a complex process of re-writing culture through the insertion, adaptation and even alteration of various Luo customs to suit the two contending sides' cases – the Umira Kager clan and the widow, Wambui Otieno. In the larger Kenyan context, the case provoked debates all over the country, regarding issues such as death, the place of widows in the burial process and notions of home. See Cohen and Odhiambo *Burying SM: The Politics of Knowledge and the Sociology of Power in Africa* (1992).

of rumours in the African-American community as a product of 'a history in which the official story was a poor guide to anything that mattered much, and in which rumors sometimes verge on the truth' (1998: 106). Gates jr echoes Patricia Turner's view that rumours encode anxieties: they 'flourish where 'official' news has proved untrustworthy' (ibid.).

I find Keguro Macharia's comments on blogging in Kenya equally useful in making sense of the work of rumours in Kenyan social imaginaries. He talks of Kenyans' blogging as entailing 'the relationship between temporality – when something is published, edited, revised, deleted – and circulation, through re-blogging, as a link, as a forward. And even this is an inadequate way to describe how blogspots circulate – the value they accrete over time and space. [The] conversations we pursued on blogs, in comments, in private emails, on newly-established newsgroups, and, when we could, over the phone and Skype, were practical attempts at world-building, even if those worlds were only populated by two or three of us' (Macharia 2013: 120–21). Although Macharia is here commenting on queer blogging in Kenya, his description of these exchanges and the processing and circulation of ideas from diverse sources and perspectives is an equally accurate description of the workings of Kenyan social imaginaries beyond the cybersphere. Indeed, 'Kenyan truth is as invented as it is real and is marked by innovation and play' (Wainaina and Macharia 2011: 153).

In fact, this culture of conversations, explorations, revisions and analyses can be traced back to the repressive 1970s and 1980s Kenya where, Atieno Odhiambo (1987) reminds us, the criminalization of various platforms of critical engagement with social and political issues pushed Kenyans to alternative spaces of debate including funerals, commuter taxi-*matatus*, weddings, soccer stadia and pubs as places where people could exchange views and opinions on matters of public interest. This explains why, even with increasing democratization of both politics and the media, Kenyan public discourse continues to unfold in these networks, which have now been expanded to include blogspots, mailing lists, social media and online discussion forums. An apt illustration of the continued appeal of rumour in a slightly more democratic Kenya is the March 2012 issue of the *Nairobi Law Monthly*, whose cover story was John Ward's allegation that *Mr B.* was the man behind his daughter's murder. While this story circulated across the lively Kenyan cyberworld, rumours flew around in Nairobi that the print edition of the journal – which at the time was printed in Dubai – had been impounded at Jomo Kenyatta International Airport, hence the delay in hitting the shelves in Nairobi. Another version claimed that somebody had bought the entire batch, to keep them from circulating. Both rumours turned out to be untrue as the delay was apparently due to logistical hiccups. That these rumours would fly around, regarding one of the most damning reports on the Ward murder is unsurprising as they revealed a lot about Kenyan publics' astonishment at the publisher's audacity to run the highly volatile story.

Seemingly, too, despite the evident loosening up of media freedom in Kenya in the new millennium, Kenyans still retained their doubts about the reach of this freedom and the political elite's tolerance for it.

In 1970s and 1980s Kenya, various institutions mediated public discourse, ranging from the arts and the media institutions to the yellow press, to alternative spaces such as football matches, bars and political rallies. Where Haugerud (1995) sees the *baraza* (a semi-official public deliberation meeting) as a forum predominantly used in the performance of power, Odhiambo (1987) broadens this platform to include *matatus* (public minibuses), churches, soccer and rugby matches, *harambees* (fundraisers), funerals and bars as spaces which constitute the public sphere, spaces where parallel court trials were run to deliberate on the Julie Ward case. In these spaces, rumour, or what Stephen Ellis (1989) terms 'pavement radio' (following the francophone *Radio Trottoir*), occupies an authoritative position, to a certain degree substituting the prohibited formal media as a legitimate source of information (Odhiambo 1987). Such alternative spaces are also sites of establishing interaction across the rural/urban, literacy, class and generational divides. In these interactive zones, rumours diffuse rapidly as people mirror the *jua kali* artisan's eclecticism in actively drawing on various information archives including formal media, personal opinion, public memory and social imaginaries, to further re-interpret, update, revise and reinforce variants of orally-transmitted narratives in a dynamic but chaotic web of circulation.[7]

The 1980s and 1990s in Kenya was also a period when the Kenyan press was at the forefront of the struggle for democracy. However, it was still a fairly censored space. In addition to the repressive Newspapers Act which ensured government surveillance of all publications, George Ogola (2006) notes, there were numerous libel suits and defamation fines which made many small publications fold, while some publications were banned altogether. This approach by the state was ingenious in encouraging self-censorship by the media. Notably, Ogola writes, most of these publications were edited by human rights lawyers and journalists who were political activists, among them Njehu Gatabaki (*Finance*), Pius Nyamora (*Society*), Bedan Mbugua (*Beyond*) and Gitobu Imanyara (*Nairobi Law Monthly*). Mbugua and Imanyara were regularly harassed under the Moi regime, and served prison sentences thanks to their outspoken views and their publications.

Bearing in mind this environment of bans, libel suits and prison sentences for media publishers that strayed from the state's self-portrait, in such a case with scant legally admissible evidence to legitimize speculation and rumours

---

[7] *Jua kali*, Swahili for 'harsh sun', is a Kenyan idiom referring to the informal sector that mainly makes use of metal, wood and cloth, and whose workers often work with limited resources under open-sided shades, exposed to the elements.

as the Ward case was, it is possible that the media practised extra caution in its reportage of the allegations, often signposting them as rumours. Despite this, the reported rumours remain relevant to our purposes not only because of their consistency and the recurrence of specific motifs, but also in the way such rumours tease out questions about the epistemological embeddedness of notions of truth and legitimacy of information. In this sense, while the possibility of fictionalization – for whatever range of reasons – attaches to the process of reporting the Julie Ward rumours, it may also serve to underscore rumour's elasticity as a constantly morphing medium, which remains elusive and multivalent even in the face of the seeming power of writing to pin down meaning. It is arguable that the shapes taken on in the press by the reported 'grapevine narratives' yield insights into the ways in which rumour articulates a critique of state institutions and official rationality. Notable too, is the way in which these rumours conversed with Kenyan popular memory.

According to James Scott, domination experienced systematically over a period of time by a group of people results in hidden transcripts that bear the marks of collective scripting, in so far as they express shared sentiments, and as such become collective cultural products which, though varied in expression, nevertheless remain repositories of shared social truths (1990: 12). It is this fluidity of hidden transcripts as highly valent and mobile texts that enables them to archive a whole range of interpretations of experiences (ibid.: 8–9). In our case, one can map out specific motifs in the various rumours regarding Julie Ward's murder. One ubiquitous feature in all these rumours is that influential political figures were involved, implying that they had something to hide. At this point, the rumours take up various shades regarding what exactly they had to hide. Again, all the versions suggest activities that would destroy the establishment's political credibility, both in Kenya and internationally. The existence of these motifs reflects the dominant socio-political concerns of the local population, while at the same time reinforcing the place of such marginalized discourses as rumour as important sites for negotiating social truths, meaning and popular knowledges.

After Julie Ward's death, there were anonymous calls and notes addressed to her father. In addition to the reports cited in this chapter's opening, there was a second set of allegations that took the form of accounts by people who claimed to have witnessed the murder. Among these was Uhuru Valentine Kodipo, who claimed to be a renegade of 'an elite gang which carried out political torture and murder missions in the country' (*The People* 1996: 4). According to Kodipo, Julie Ward

> may have sealed her fate after stumbling across one of the secret training camps used by the death squads hidden in the Maasai Mara Game reserve … Everyone in the group was whipping her with hippo hide whips and shouting questions at her

about her movements and what she knew about them. They thought she had been spying on them [ibid.].

As part of his work, Kodipo claims to have been sent on spy duty in Tanzania in 1983, after the failed 1982 coup in Kenya. This coup is often considered to have been the tipping point of President Moi's paranoia, which would cast a shadow of heavy repression over Kenya for the next two decades. The coup, by some members of Kenya's air force, was unsuccessful, and several alleged masterminds escaped to neighbouring Tanzania as political exiles. For Kenyans familiar with the events surrounding the 1982 coup, this facet of Kodipo's story was striking in its approximation of the arrest of the alleged coup masterminds in Tanzania. They are reported to have been kidnapped at gunpoint by a joint Kenya–Tanzania paramilitary team and brought back to Kenya to be executed for treason (Citizens for Justice, 2003). This piece of evidence doubtless lent further validity to Kodipo's claims in the eyes of the public, despite the state's insistence that Kodipo was a fraud on the grounds that the state archives had no record of his military service. Predictably, this denial held no water for Kenyans following the case as, being in an unofficial army, Kodipo's records would naturally not be available in the official military files. Kodipo further 'recalls how he was appointed commander of a military unit after leading a team which massacred hundreds of Somalis in north-eastern Kenya in the early 1980s' (Stern 1996: 23). Kodipo might be referring here to the Bulla Karatasi Massacre of November 1980 or the Wagalla Massacre of February 1984, both of which remain among the bloodiest unresolved horrors of independent Kenya, where state security forces, apparently addressing problems of insecurity in the region, committed horrific acts of torture, looting, rape and murders in the region.[8]

A second alleged 'eye witness' was Big Muhammad a.k.a. Big Mo, a Kenyan exile in London, who also claimed to be a paramilitary renegade: 'I have either witnessed or been part of terrible evil things in Kenya. I was just doing what I was trained to do: KILL for the state. I was trained in Israel and Libya ... I am a really dangerous man. A vicious killing machine' (wa Njenga 2004a: 2). Big Mo claims to have witnessed Julie Ward being gang-raped and killed by three unnamed politically powerful individuals from the Moi regime. According to him, the murder started out as a rape:

> After the rape, they discovered that in her possession she had sensitive information which suggested she was no ordinary tourist. They concluded that she was a British secret agent on a mission in Kenya and that assumption sealed her fate. Julie Ward was then forced to drive her jeep miles from where she was staying in an effort to make it appear that she had gotten lost. She was then blindfolded and dragged into

---

[8] See the Truth, Justice and Reconciliation Report (2013) for detailed descriptions of these atrocities.

a thicket where she was butchered ... They wanted the murder to appear as if Ms Ward had been attacked by wild animals but they quickly realised that they had left hair, fabrics, semen and saliva on her body which could be used for DNA profiling. That was why they set the body on fire [ibid.].

Both Kodipo's and Big Mo's narratives contain the ideas of a paramilitary arm which carried out the state's dirty work, of Julie Ward's murder starting out as a rape, and of Julie Ward being a spy. The three tropes point towards the notion of state power being wielded by corrupt and violent political elite. Julie Ward's murder is thus scripted as the elimination of a woman who – either knowingly or inadvertently – knew too much or posed the risk of exposure for the powerful agents involved.

Long before Kodipo and Mo came into the picture, Kenyans had heard rumours about paramilitary units. One of the earliest references to an elite paramilitary unit affiliated to the official state security units but operating independently of these, and above the law, was the so-called Ngoroko militia in the late 1970s. Karimi and Ochieng give a detailed account of the formation, training and financing of the Ngoroko militia, which was ostensibly an anti-stock-theft unit, but whose elaborate training, primarily parallel to other official military and policing units, pointed towards a less noble agenda. According to the two historians, the political figures behind this elite team made it seem like the official Kenya Police Stock Theft Unit, but the team was called The Rift Valley Operation Team. Members of this later team called each other 'Ngoroko' – cattle rustlers – as an insiders' code:

It was a useful password because the men were – consciously or not – made to resemble the paramilitary General Service Unit in practically all ways in their outward appearance. The 'Ngoroko' uniform for instance, was identical in colour, texture and shape to that of the GSU, and the only way one could be distinguished from the other was that the 'Ngoroko' wore black berets, whereas the GSU ones are red. Was it anticipated that one day the 'Ngoroko' force would be used in disguise as GSU men? If that was the case, and if the day should arrive then, particularly at night, the Mungai group would recognise themselves through the code name 'Ngoroko' [Karimi and Ochieng, 1980: 143].

Apparently having failed to push through a change to the constitution that would ensure Deputy President Moi did not ascend to presidency in the event of President Kenyatta's death, a clique of powerful politicians – the Family, as Karimi and Ochieng describe them – allegedly set about implementing Plan B: an elite, well-trained military unit that would eliminate all the major politicians within two days of Kenyatta's death. This army, the Ngoroko, was allegedly trained and resourced by diverting resources intended for actual police and army forces, including uniforms, training opportunities and weapons from allied countries such as Israel, to the unit (Karimi and Ochieng 1980: 165–7). According to the two historians, there was a long list of people to be eliminated upon Kenyatta's death, with conservative estimates standing at 300 names. The plan was to assassinate them 'in such a way that the public attention was not attracted towards a "secret army," in such a way, moreover, that the victims themselves took all the blame for their own death' (ibid.). The alleged plan is outlined in detail in *The Kenyatta Succession*:

> According to Government sources, the 15 [prime targets, including Vice President Moi and several key ministers] would have been killed just before the death of the President was announced, an announcement that would have been delayed until the complete elimination of the arch-enemies of the 'Ngoroko' organisers. Most of the 15 were Kenyatta's appointees and all were quite close to him in one way or another. So, on the death of the Old Man it would be easy to summon them to State House, Nakuru, under the pretext that the President was critically ill and would like to see them at his last hour. The three most wanted of the 15 – Moi, Minister of Finance and Economic Planning, Mwai Kibaki and Attorney General Charles Njonjo – would be conducted to the room containing Kenyatta's dead body; then some 'Ngoroko' men armed with sub-machine-guns with silencers, who would already be standing at strategic spots, would leap from their hiding places and shoot all three with their lethal weapons. The assassination would not attract any outside attention because of the silencers and since under no circumstances would the bodyguards of the victims be allowed anywhere near the President's suite. Having killed the three most wanted enemies, the dead bodies would be removed to another room. Then the rest of the 15 would be killed in similar fashion. The 'Ngoroko' chiefs would then pump bullets into the dead body of the President so as to make believe that it was the 15 who had earlier showered the President with bullets. An announcement would follow to the effect that the Presidential Guards had caught the 15 – led by Moi – in the act of murdering Kenyatta. The announcement would say that the guards had (in the manner of Macbeth), in their 'fury' at the 'treachery' opened fire on the 15 and killed them all. The bodies of those shot dead at State House would then be removed to the 'Ngoroko' base near Lanet, where they would be dumped into a tank containing some sulphuric acid – a highly corrosive chemical – which would consume the bodies. The announcement concerning the 'attack' on the Old Man would be followed by a curfew ordering all Kenyans to remain at home. During the curfew the [over 1000] 'Ngoroko' operatives would be dispatched to all the parts of the Republic with copies of the lists of those to be done in. They would raid homes in the guise that they were GSU men on a law-and-order mission. If there was any immediate opposition, then the submachine-guns with silencers would be used to get rid of such possible nuisances as guards, watchmen, house servants and dogs. In cases where house security was tight they would attack from a distance, using the 60mm rockets … It was estimated that the entire exercise

would take no more than two days, during which the organisers of the 'Ngoroko' would move with lightning speed to install themselves in positions of authority [Karimi and Ochieng 1980: 168–9].

This shocking plan, which reads like a thriller novel, was supposedly hinged on the ageing president, who was in frail health, passing away at the Nakuru State House. As it turned out, the president died at his Mombasa residence – his preferred home – and reportedly, the pro-Moi sections of government imme-diately summoned Moi to Nairobi where he was safely sworn in as president (ibid.). I have cited this description of the 'Ngoroko' and their *modus operandi* in detail because of the parallels with subsequent private militias in Kenyan history, most remarkably, the paramilitary unit which Kodipo claims to have been part of, which was allegedly trained at the official GSU compounds, and more recently, the elite hit-squad allegedly carrying out targeted assassinations of Muslim leaders perceived to be radicalizing Muslims and supporting the Al-Shabaab movement in the East African region.[9] Israeli training also features in both Kodipo's and Big Mo's versions of their stories, as does the idea of a secret army governed by a powerful politician and operating outside the law while seemingly impersonating official security units. The unit's uniform too, as per Kodipo's description, bears a close resemblance to official GSU uniforms, with the exception of the jersey which was a different colour, a fact the government latched on to discredit his allegations.[10] Significantly, Kodipo claimed that his unit was under the Moi presidency and answerable directly to the then minister in the office of the president. This facet of Kodipo's story is remarkably ironic in its approximation of the 'Ngoroko' who were allegedly out to sabotage a Moi presidency upon Kenyatta's passing.

A notable motif in the Ward rumours, allegations and speculations, is the notion of the involvement of powerful politicians or what in Kenyan parlance is termed a 'Big Politician'. The idea of the involvement of 'a powerful politician' or 'the son of a highly placed politician' in Julie Ward's murder remained a recurrent motif in local rumours, most of which seeped into both local and international dailies, with minor differences in the details, including those quoted below.

> Sources indicate that evidence might be adduced to the effect that *the son of a power-ful Rift Valley [Province] politician* had been booked at the Mara Lodge at the same time Julie was there. But his name mysteriously disappeared from the guest list immediately Julie was reported missing. Evidence might also be adduced that the powerful politician summoned one of the witnesses to his office twice to discuss the modalities of a cover-up in the Julie mystery [Ngotho 2004b: 4; emphasis added].

---

[9] See Al Jazeera documentary *Inside Kenya's Death Squads* (2014).
[10] This detailed denial was published in the *Kenya Times* newspaper of 28 September 1995: 7.

Rumours have flourished, including persistent claims that *one of the sons of former president, Daniel arap Moi, was implicated in the murder* and dismemberment of Julie Ward before her body was burned in the savannah [Barkham 2004c: 1: emphasis added].

The Kenyan minister for justice and constitutional affairs, Kiraitu Murungi, acknowledged rumours in Africa that the son of the former president was involved in Miss Ward's murder [Barkham 2004a: 1; *emphasis added].*

Kodipo reportedly claimed that among the figures present at Ward's murder scene were 'a senior political officer [accompanied] by two men, Israelis who clearly had strong connection with Israeli security; [a] close confidant of the President [and] one of Kenya's most senior policemen' (Stern 1996: 23).

The Big Politician is a common figure of political lore in Kenyan social imaginaries, and can be traced back to the repressive one-party state during the Moi regime and further back to the Kenyatta regime. Often deeply rooted in patronage relations, the Big Politician was believed to command so much power as to border on the untouchable, enjoying comprehensive immunity guaranteed by his uninhibited access to state institutions and resources. This figure – who was invariably male – embodies the blatant personalization of state power during the Moi regime and the culture of self-censorship bred by the regime's violent impunity. In Kenya, the Big Politician is a unique variant of Bayart's (1993) 'Big Man', as a signifier of economic and political power. This figure was invariably singled out in corruption scandals, political torture at the infamous Nyayo House basement torture chambers, the so-called ethnic clashes and suspicious murders in Kenyan history.

It is thanks to such a profile that for decades, the Big Politician remained nameless in the rumours and allegations about Julie Ward's death. His access to all these resources further explains why the Big Politician could credibly be said to have his name removed from the Mara Lodge guestbook, summon the witnesses to discuss the modalities of the cover-up and even assure the silence or elimination of any witnesses who dared to break the code of silence, as Big Mo alleged. The identities of the three influential men in Kodipo's allegations remain officially unconfirmed; though Kodipo identifies them by name in his article in the *Indian Ocean Newsletter.*

In a detailed article published in the March 2012 issue of the *Nairobi Law Monthly,* John Ward finally named one of the 'Big Men' figures allegedly behind his daughter's murder; a well-known, politically connected man. Ward's sources and evidence for this serious accusation are in themselves part of the cocktail of rumours, allegations, speculations and alleged eye-witness accounts that form the roots of the Kenyan grapevine. In addition to Kodipo's claims, Ward cites a Swiss film crew staying at the Mara in the same week his daughter was there, and leaving a few days after the finding of the remains. The crew reported going to clear their bill at the Chief Game Warden, Simon Makallah's office, where they found him 'sitting head in hands. He said he had been summoned to a meeting with President Moi' (Ward 2012: 32). His second source is a Mombasa-based second-hand clothes dealer who regularly visited the Mara to sell clothes to the women in the surrounding villages. On one of his visits to the Mara, in the days soon after the murder, Ward reports that this lady approached him, 'pressed a tightly folded note' into his hand and walked away. When he opened it later, it read 'The man who killed your daughter is *Mr B.*'[11] (Ward 2012: 34). The lady had included a Post Office box number for Mombasa, and Ward contacted her to explain why she made this claim. The lady claimed she had heard the allegations all over the park and the adjacent villages, from women who included the wives of game rangers in the park (ibid.). Ward handed over this note to Scotland Yard.

The journey of this particular rumour, seemingly from the game wardens, to their wives in the surrounding villages, and back into the game reserve via a Mombasa-based second-hand clothes seller, to John Ward, and over to Scotland Yard is an absorbing portrait of how rumour networks operate. Alongside alleged eye-witness reports, anonymous notes, phone calls and letters would feature prominently in the case. Once back in the UK, Ward writes that received another hand-written letter from Kenya, with no return address. The writer claimed to have been employed at Keekorok Lodge in September 1988. One afternoon, while waiting for transport at the Lodge's entrance to Sekenani Gate – she lived in a neighbouring village – she 'witnessed three men dragging a white woman from a Land Rover, into the [neighbouring] Government Guest House' which was 'kept exclusively for use by visiting Heads of State and VIPs' (Ward 2012: 35). Ward passed the letter on to British Police.

Certain patterns are notable so far. First, the alleged eye-witnesses and apparent renegades of secret armies tended to be men. Second, these two notes, which in a sense allowed Ward to plug into rumours that appeared to be common-knowledge to everyone in Mara, except him, despite his regular visits, while investigating his daughter's death, were from Kenyan women. Two decades on, Supt Wanjau, the CID officer assigned to the case would take Ward into his confidence, and inform Ward that within the first ten days of his investigations in the Mara, his findings had pointed towards *Mr B.*, but when he reported this to his boss, CID Director Noah arap Too, he was instructed to 'look somewhere else' (Ward 2012: 42). In fact, Wanjau claimed, from the very start, his boss had sent him to the game reserve with instructions to 'relax', 'go slow', 'this is priority for Moi' (ibid.). When Wanjau returned to the reserve for further investigations, he reportedly found that all his resources had been withdrawn,

---

[11] Ward names this man throughout his article, but I opt to anonymise him as *Mr B.* in this book. The article is in public circulation.

in a clear attempt to paralyse his investigations. It was in this state that on one of his visits to the Mara, Ward found Wanjau catching a nap under a tree, in Ward's assessment, being lazy and disinterested in the case. Two decades later, Ward would understand Wanjau's frustrations.

In building his case against *Mr B.* in his article, Ward himself becomes part of the Kenyan parallel courts and rumour networks. Two instances illustrate how Ward soon found himself actively joining the dots between pieces of information. In the one instance, Ward writes of driving from the Mara via the Oloololo Gate towards Kilgoris in early 1989, a few months after the murder of his daughter. After passing several small farms and villages, Ward noticed an impressive modern farm which was evidently well-maintained and well-resourced, compared to the neighbouring parcels of farms.

> Out of curiosity, I asked the Serena driver who owned the farm? 'It belongs to *Mr B.*,' the driver replied. About two years later, I had reason to visit Kilgoris and once more, the driver took the same route from Serena Lodge. On passing the same farm, I noticed that it appeared nearly derelict. The previously neat fencing was sagging and damaged and the place appeared to be deserted and generally in a state of disrepair. Uncertain whether it was the same farm I had seen, I inquired whether that was *Mr B.*'s farm. The driver confirmed, adding: 'He doesn't come here anymore.' I asked: 'Since when?' 'About two years,' the driver replied [Ward 2012: 35–36].

It remains unclear whether there was a clear connection between the dereliction Ward observed on *Mr B.*'s farm and the fact that it had reportedly started two years earlier, coinciding with the murder in the Mara. But the driver in this instance would seem to belong in the same league as Toundi and his cohorts in Ferdinand Oyono's portrait of interactions between African domestic labourers and French colonial administrators in Cameroon in his novel, *Houseboy*. These are figures who the polito-economic elites would hardly ever notice, but whose eyes and ears place these elites' lives under close scrutiny. The same dynamic played out in the Robert Ouko murder case, when the minister's house help became a key witness to his movements, moods and interactions on the days preceding his murder. A second insight from Ward's description of *Mr B.*'s farm is the manner in which Ward appears to read its very adjacency to the Mara, coupled with its dereliction soon after the murder as lending some credence to the rumours about his alleged involvement. Ward reports a second incident that further pointed towards *Mr B.* This followed after another anonymous informant approached the British High Commission and reportedly demanded Ward's contact details. After threatening to contact Ward publicly at the High Court where the Simon ole Makallah trial was ongoing, Rufus Drabble, the Press Attaché at the High Commission finally passed on the contact details to Ward who met him.

This informant was articulate and well dressed. He had no restraint confirming his identity. The man said he used to work for *Mr B.* and produced several photographs he took with *Mr B.* ... Clearly, the man knew *Mr B.* well and the photographs showed they were relaxed in each other's company. The informer started his story with the bland statement that *Mr B.* was responsible for Julie's murder. He said that on September 6, 1988, *Mr B.* and his farm manager, together with two bodyguards and a driver, had left the farm. *Mr B.*'s group used a short wheelbase Landrover on their way to another farm belonging to *Mr B.*. Their route took them through the Maasai Mara, using the Oloololo Gate to enter, and the Sekanani Gate to exit. On 6th September, Julie had left the Serena Lodge and would have travelled on the same road. [There is only one road] ... The informer said Julie was taking photographs when *Mr B.*'s vehicle stopped. At first a joking conversation and banter took place. He said the banter turned nasty and the situation became aggressive. The informant said Julie was raped by *Mr B.* At this point, there was a gap in Mr X's story. Specifically, as to what happened next and where Julie was taken. The informant's story continued, that later in the day, believing that Julie would report *Mr B.*'s assault, he instructed his bodyguards to kill her. The informant provided the names of the bodyguards and their locations. He also provided the name of the driver and the other witnesses to the rape [Ward 2012: 37].

Mr B. was scandalized at Ward's article in the *Nairobi Law Monthly*, and firmly denied the accusations in an article published soon after in *the Star*, a Nairobi newspaper. The article quotes *Mr B.* as saying

'I am totally shocked to hear this,' [*Mr B.*] told *the Star* yesterday. 'I had no relationship with the said lady (Julie) and I even didn't know her. I never did such a thing and it has never crossed my mind to do it.' ... [*Mr B.*] said people were out to taint his good name just because he was the son of [a prominent politician] and described the claims as total malice. He said it was impossible for a man of his calibre to commit such an heinous act, especially in the presence of other men. 'In the [B.] family I have had a clean record. I have never been involved in any scandalous deals and that is why this is directed to me,' he said adding, 'but time will tell my innocence' [Koross 2012].

Whatever the merits of the case against *Mr B.*, in the current Kenyan political environment, it is unlikely that he would be prosecuted, if there was enough evidence and the theories could be tested. As Daniel Branch reminds us in a different context, the culture of impunity in Kenyan public discourse means that 'the government's control over the police, judiciary and electoral system ensured that there was no possibility of punishment for major crimes, even if they attracted considerable attention and censure in the press' (Branch 2012: 21).

In view of the status of the Big Politician as an almost legendary figure in Kenyan social imaginaries, enjoying self-reinforcing anonymity and impunity, one begins to understand why Ward's dismissive attitude towards the rumours and anonymous allegations about big men's involvement in his daughter's murder on grounds of lack of evidence may have been ill-advised. Ward failed to appreciate the grip of the political elite on the formal institutions and channels which he privileged in his quest for truth and justice. Here, we are reminded of Nahashon Njenga's plea, regarding the murder of Tom Mboya: 'Why pick on me? Why not the big man?' (Cohen and Odhiambo 2004: 175).[12] It is notable that even at this point – faced with execution and with little more to lose – Njenga could not dare identify the 'Big Man' by name. For us, the Njenga incident gestures at the futility of legal truths, as truths whose hegemony is contestable on the basis of their openness to manipulation by, among others, those in power[13] and, broadly, the question of the lack of independence of the judiciary in Kenya.[14]

The rumours on Julie Ward's death, and particularly their fascination with the involvement of political elites, provided a remarkable albeit cynical admonition against the privileging of so-called rational/legal truths in the case. To a certain degree, the rumours were also a critique of the legacies of modernity in Africa. If one considers Frederick Cooper's (2002: 156) argument that the post-independent African state was built on 'a set of institutions – bureaucracies, militaries, post offices and (initially) legislatures – set up by colonial regimes', then in their critiques of the Kenyan state institutions as ill-suited to the Ward family's quest for truth and justice, the rumours were also critiques of postcolonial manifestations of colonial modernity's selective distribution of the privileges of modernity.

The Paradoxes of Modernity in Africa

Urban theorist Jennifer Robinson points out that 'accounts of modernity have commonly described the modern era or modern people as having a sense of historical time and space, and as drawing on a rationalist understanding of events to inform inventiveness and progress' (2006: 13). Yet, the experience of modernity and by extension, urbanization in Africa, is often understood to have been deeply marked by ambivalence, as signalled by the 'resistance to [and] selective appropriation of, modernity' (Macamo 2005a: 3). Following

---

[12] See also *The People*, 15–21 March 1996.

[13] Kenya was to witness a similar scenario in the murder of Dr Crispin Odhiambo Mbai, the then chairman of the Devolution Committee of the National Constitutional Conference, on 14 September 2003. In the case, three suspects confessed to the murder, insisting that they were hired by a top Kenyan politician to kill Dr Mbai because he was 'bothering him'. See 'What Was the Motive for the Don's Murder?' *Sunday Standard*, 28 September 2003.

[14] See Mwangi's *The Black Bar: Corruption and Political Intrigue within Kenya's Legal Fraternity* (2001) for a fascinating account of the Kenyan judiciary and its historic lack of independence.

Jean and John Comaroff (1993) and Luise White (1995), Macamo sees this as one of the ways in which Africans continue to resist the conditions and terms of their integration into the wider world. He situates this ambivalence in the colonial experience.

> Colonialism was the historical form through which modernity became a real social project on the African continent [yet] colonialism was premised on the denial of the same modernity to Africans [including] human dignity, emancipation and progress. [Thus] African social experience has been structured by the ambivalence of promise and denial that was constitutive of colonialism and, indeed, as we move into what some call a global era, of globalization [Macamo 2005a: 8].

Simon Gikandi shares this view, in his argument that 'colonial modernity dislocated the African subject by propagating its tenets as a universal model, while at the same time denying Africans, on political and social grounds, the possibility of its realization' (cited in Deutsch et al. 2002: 13).

Underpinning this promise-denial encounter is a distinct conceptual history which situates an originary modernity in Europe, based on the belief that 'as a construct of the enlightenment, modernity is a European project' (Zack-Williams 2004: 20). Yet, Deutsch et al. insist,

> While agreeing that the conceptual differentiation between knowledge and experience, story and history, morality and law is the product of a specific historical process which became dominant in Europe sometime between the seventeenth and eighteenth centuries, it is equally clear that this process has received its own shape and its own dynamics in other parts of the world [2002: 3].

For Robinson, this association of Europe with an originary modernity has caused understandings of 'the embrace of novelty as "innovative" in Western contexts but "imitative" in others' including in Africa (2006: 66). She questions Europe's claim to an originary modernity as, for her, 'the very [cultural] promiscuity of Western modernity itself proposes a different, cosmopolitan cartography of modernity, one in which origins are dispersed, outcomes differentiated and multiple and the spatial logics those of circulation and interaction' (2006: 19). Instead, she defines urban modernity as 'the cultural experience of contemporary city life ... and celebration of innovation and novelty' (2006: 4).

In addition to seeing 'modernity' through a hierarchical lens, modernization theories have often emphasized the tension between 'tradition' and 'modernity' within a conceptual framework that sees them as mutually exclusive. This view sustains rigid polarizations between the rural and urban, tradition and modernity, further cementing associations of tradition with notions of the 'primitive', 'backward' and 'irrational'. Comaroff and Comaroff note:

The self-sustaining antinomy between tradition and modernity underpins a long-standing European myth: a narrative that replaces the uneven, protean relations among 'ourselves' and 'others' in world history with a simple, epic story about the passage from savagery to civilization, from the mystical to the mundane [1993: xii].

Yet, as Robinson correctly argues, far from being mutually exclusive, there are in fact strong continuities between these sets of geo-discursive tropes, so that 'traditional' cultural elements are best seen as 'dynamic processes at work within the urban social system rather than vestiges from a tribal past' (2006: 38, citing Epstein 1958: 239).

In their encounter with the promise/denial dimension of colonial modernity, Africans developed resourceful strategies in negotiating this unstable terrain and its accompanying polarizations. In the Kenyan context, Ngugi wa Thiong'o's *The River Between* is an engaging portrait of such creative engagements among the colonial-era Gikuyu. In the novel, where two sections of the community are pitted against each other in a sharp binary between traditional practices and formal education and Christianity, Waiyaki and Muthoni's deaths can be seen to seed the spirit that was later to germinate into Gikuyu independent churches and schools as forms of creative alternatives to the sterile tradition/modernity binary. Similar binary-defying engagements with colonial modernity were widespread across the continent, as suggested by encounters with literacy (Barber 2006), Christianity (Saute 2005), migrant labour (Macamo 2005b) and modern masculinities (Hodgson 1999), through which people forged new and dynamic repertoires of African modernities. Through similar processes, for Francis Nyamnjoh, postcolonial-era Africans are daily 'modernizing the indigenous and indigenizing the modern with novel outcomes' (2005: 4).

It is this resourcefulness that Joyce Nyairo alludes to in her metaphor of the *jua kali* artisan, whom she reads as signalling an ethos of change as the driving force of contemporary African societies through a constant 'flux of revisions [which] signal traditions and identities that are always in the making' (2007: 147). Although it is hard to detach the *jua kali* worker – who works under harsh conditions in the 'hot sun' – from urban poverty, such artisans nonetheless epitomize the resilience, creativity and dynamism that have emerged as responses to the paradoxes of the promise/denial dimension of modernity, which continue to play themselves out in postcolonial African states and, most visibly, African cities.

In view of this, rumour may be seen as an important genre of African modernity, which epitomizes *jua-kali*-style innovative energies while at the same time critiquing the officially proclaimed rationality of postcolonial state institutions and their reproduction of the colonial-era promise/denial tensions related to imported modernities. I suggest that, in creatively drawing on and adding to existing Kenyan social imaginaries, the rumours about the Julie Ward case challenge the assumptions of modernization theories which, as Macamo notes, not only emphasize the tensions between modernity and tradition, but further contend that 'the challenge facing African societies consist[s] in overcoming tradition in order to gain access to the benefits of modernity' (2005a: 2). When the process of law failed to provide convincing answers to questions about Julie Ward's death, the parallel 'courtrooms' of the grapevine reached their own credible verdicts, which were able to fill in the gaps left by the failed legal processes in the state institutions. In a case which displayed uncompromising privileging of monolithic truths, the rumours on Julie Ward's death appeared to interrogate the viability of such a quest under the Kenyan socio-political climate of the time, where state institutions had lost all credibility. The Ward case rumours underline two faces of Peter Ekeh's two publics and their moralities: first, by indexing the political elite's disregard for civil institutions, and second, by illustrating Kenyan publics' navigation of the terrain between compromised modern state institutions and their own rumour-mongering platforms and networks.

In situating Julie Ward's death at the doorstep of criminal political elite, the rumours speak to what Cohen and Odhiambo (2004) term 'the risks of knowledge' in Kenya. In their book of the same title, they refer to contestations around questions of knowing, or in their words, 'the powers and dangers that attach to knowledge in the moving setting of official and public gestures: closures, openings, proofs, convictions, expiations, alibis, narratives and histories' (ibid.: 39). The Julie Ward death and its interpretations – both official and unofficial – illustrate these contestations of truths and knowledge through accessing a wide range of archives, sources, texts, questions, events and information gaps. From this angle, we start to understand the recurrent scripting of Julie Ward as a woman who knew what she should not have known, and her killers as subjects of knowledge that had to be kept secret at all costs, as the rumours and allegations decoded both the ambiguities in her death and the official keenness to validate certain preferred truths.

A striking aspect of the case is the manner in which both Ward's death and its subsequent interpretations collapsed orthodox polarizations between the urban and the rural, the 'modern' and the 'traditional'. Although she died in the wilderness of the Maasai Mara Game Reserve, Julie Ward's death and the search for the truth behind it traversed various topographies, dissolving conventional boundaries between the wild and the modern, the rural and the urban. In addition, although the debate on Julie Ward's death had its epicentre in Nairobi, primarily because the investigations into her death were being carried out in the city (which is also the country's media capital), rumours nonetheless enjoyed wide circulation throughout both Nairobi and the countryside, thus powerfully underscoring their porous boundaries. They also seeped into the formal media, including prominent newspapers such as the *Sunday Nation* and the *East African Standard*, confirming Nyamnjoh's portrait of the African mediascape as a blend of influences, traditions and technologies, where modern communication technologies co-exist in conviviality and interdependence with indigenous media (2005: 4). In recent times, this permeability has been rendered all the more tangible by developments in, and access to, modern communication technologies such as the internet and cell phones, which now give speed and breadth to the waves of pavement radio in processes that further muddy any clear demarcations between tradition and modernity, the rural and the urban, and (by extension) the rational and the irrational.

Modernity and the Grapevine

John Ward and Scotland Yard's dismissal of the anonymous claims and rumours on the basis of lack of proof reflects the conventional disregard of rumours and allegations as lacking validity. This dismissive attitude is premised on conventional understandings of truth and veracity that presume the existence of singular, objective truths, grounded in verifiable evidence. A similar view of truth is often embraced by judicial institutions, which, in the Julie Ward mystery, was the primary – indeed the solitary – site for the search for her killers. However, rumours are often founded on suspicion of such dominant epistemologies, and seek to contest hegemonic truths. Interrogating this monologic view of truth which precludes conspiracy theories and rumours as wanting in veracity, Anita Waters (1997) proposes what she terms 'ethnosociologies', a concept she uses in reference to 'theories that ordinary people use to explain social phenomena' (1997: 114). Taking its cue from Waters and White, this book lays emphasis on the kernels of what Luise White (2000: 34) has termed 'social truths', around which the rumours on the circumstances surrounding Julie Ward's death were scripted.

The allegations implicating key government officials in Julie Ward's death went officially unacknowledged. However, they took root in the popular imagination, and while this may not be an accurate record of how and why Julie Ward died, the knowledge production processes that these rumours entailed are of interest as social mechanisms for the interrogation of official modern state institutions and their preferred truths.

Stephen Ellis' 'pavement radio' in Africa enacts a powerful contestation of truth claims associated with officially-promoted rationalities. Far from being specific to Kenya, this suspicion of formal sites of truth production is a widespread phenomenon in Africa,[15] where the 'truths' circulated in the rumour wavelength enjoy greater popular legitimacy than those produced in the more formal sites. While truth is conventionally legitimized by its provable veracity,

---

[15] See Ellis (1989), Nyamnjoh (2005) and White (2004) on rumour in Togo, Cameroon and DR Congo respectively.

pavement radio derives legitimacy from the suspect nature of official or hegemonic truths produced through modern institutions and processes, which are often assumed to be in some way compromised. As such, it operates on a different index of credibility, which, as Luise White notes, lays greater store on truths seen to be credible to the group in question, than on monolithic understandings of truth and evidence (2000: 34). Yet, at the same time, the written word mobilizes precisely the 'official' kind of legitimacy, which grants written and published rumours further endorsement as 'truth'. Such rumours may gain added 'truth value' when contested by the named suspects and institutions, catalysing yet another cycle of oral/written circulation. For instance, the Kenyan Government's insistence that it had no records of Kodipo's service in the military commanded little credibility for Kenyans as it was obvious to them that the government could easily sanitize its archives of Kodipo. As a cover story in the *Nairobi Law Monthly* rightly observed:

> It is unlikely that even if Kodipo served in the force, those who trained him would venture information to the probe out of mortal fear of being victimised. The government's disclaimer of September 28, 1995 in reaction to the *Mail on Sunday* exposé took great sanctuary in this line of defence. It said Kodipo was never employed in the GSU or any of the police wings, pointing out that his name is nowhere in the service records. Now, that is easy because the government has the records to do with them as it pleases, alteration being one of them [Makali 1996: 22].

As responses to formalized truths, the rumours and allegations about Julie Ward's death represented an important process of reconfiguring conventional regimes of truth and evidence privileged by modern state institutions. Kodipo's claims about Julie Ward stumbling upon death squads hidden in the Mara, for instance, commanded significant credibility in view of the popular belief in Kenya that certain political figures had private armies, some of which took part in the 1991 'ethnic clashes' in the Rift Valley Province, between the Kalenjin and Kikuyu ethnic communities.[16] The notion of 'private armies' features prominently in Kenyan politics; and includes the trained killers alluded to in Big Mohammed's and Kodipo's allegations and a range of vigilante and youth groups hired by politicians to disrupt political rallies or violently 'persuade' an opponent to refrain from running for office.

While the outlined rumours and allegations may seem largely speculative and lacking in concrete evidence, they simultaneously display interesting relationships with the procedures of modern law and science. All rumours are scripted around the core tenets of legal procedures that underpin murder cases: motive and suspects. Each rumour identifies specific suspects, their motives, and in some cases, the logic behind the choices made in the course of the murder.

[16] See Ochola (1992) and Anderson (2002).

The rumours and allegations also drew on certain scientific epistemologies in explaining Julie Ward's murder: a case in point is Big Mo's claim that Ward's remains were incinerated to avoid the possibility of DNA profiling of the killers.

At the same time, the rumours also appeared to question the empirical reach of modern science and law. In highlighting the vulnerability of modern state institutions to manipulation by interested parties, the rumours simultaneously mock the assumed legitimacy of modern state institutions. In this way, they show modernity as a project that, despite its claims to progress predicated on value-neutral rationality, remains open to manipulation. Ward's contested autopsy, for instance, questioned the assumed legitimacy of autopsies as scientific processes believed to be capable of rendering visible the silenced secrets of a death, just as legal truths premised on evidence and witnesses were considered unattainable in circumstances where witnesses either disappeared or were cowered into silence, as illustrated by Big Mo's claim to be afraid of giving formal evidence in court. Gitau wa Njenga writes about Big Mo:

> As to whether he would be willing to take his story to the authorities, he [Big Mo] said: 'I'm more than willing to give evidence in a court of law but the implications and risks outweigh my willingness to do so' ... Big Mo also alleged that witnesses to the crime have since been killed. 'Several of the game warders who worked in Maasai Mara on the fateful night have died mysteriously' he claimed [wa Njenga 2004b].

Big Mo's observations above echo similar mysterious deaths of witnesses in the Robert Ouko murder mystery.[17] Indeed, the one trademark feature of all suspicious deaths in Kenyan history is that, despite the seemingly 'labour-intensive' nature of all these murders, which suggest the involvement of more than one person, nobody ever breaks the code of silence formally, beyond rumours and unconfirmed 'eye-witness' allegations such as those of Kodipo and Big Mo. Under these circumstances, any insistence on 'evidence/proof,' as John Ward and Scotland Yard detective Searle were inclined to, remains futile and unproductive. In some ways, the rumours and allegations were also urgent pleas to Ward and his investigating team to lose their innocence and naïve faith in the modern state institutions, the Kenyan Government, and indeed, the British Government, as he was later to find.

To a large extent, the rumours and allegations' critique of Western modernity's impotence in the Julie Ward case extends to the contradictions embedded in those modern institutions which trace their roots back to colonial rule. As Frantz Fanon (1967) reminds us, the distribution of the promises of colonial modernity along Mamdani's (1996) citizen–subject axis produced a specific kind of native subject who longed for the citizen's privileges: 'The look that the

---

[17] See Cohen and Odhiambo (2004).

native turns on the settler's town is a look of lust, a look of envy; it expresses his dreams of possession – all manner of possession: to sit at the settler's table, to sleep in the settler's bed, with his wife if possible. The colonized man is an envious man' (1967: 30). Colonial Kenya too, observed racial apartheid, unofficially. Gerard Loughran explains:

> Legally, there was no colour bar in Kenya but socially it was inescapable … Racism was institutionalized in government service, with salaries graded by ethnicity: Class A for Europeans, B for Asians, C for Arabs and D for Africans, the latter being mostly drivers, messengers and cleaners … Nairobi was unofficially zoned by race. Africans lived in 'native locations' such as Pumwani, where the young Tom Mboya had a tiny house; Asians gathered in Parklands and Nairobi West; and whites in Muthaiga, Lavington, Karen, Kitisuru and other upmarket areas. Africans were required to carry around their necks the hated *kipande* (an employment card bearing their fingerprints), were not allowed to grow coffee or other cash crops and, however unlikely the prospect seemed at the time, were barred by law from owning company shares [Loughran 2010: 14–16].

At independence, this legacy of partial distribution of the promises of modernity carried on, as Gikandi (2001) and Macamo (2005a) explain. At this level then, the distrust of modern state institutions and their official rationality goes beyond a mere critique of the postcolonial state's failures. It is also a critique of the legacy of colonial modernity, which continues to haunt the postcolonial state. In Gikandi's words, to understand the African crisis in both colonial and postcolonial contexts, 'we must first listen to the stories about the black subject's precarious location inside and outside modernity (Gikandi 2002: 136).

A related critique in these rumours is directed at the judiciary's lack of independence from state power. This was one of the bitter discoveries Ward was to make, as the British press reported: 'He has no faith in the Kenyan justice system. "It's corrupt. The state pathologist who falsified Julie's death certificate is still the state pathologist. The chief of police who refused to instigate a murder inquiry is still the chief of police. These guys walk on water. I have exposed Kenya as a corrupt place but I haven't been able to do anything about the people in power"' (O'Kane 1992: 2). While our discussions underscore Ward's disappointment in the Kenyan state institutions as inept and inefficient, this state of affairs goes beyond a mere 'typical' postcolonial state's compromised institutions. In fact, the question of lack of independence of the judiciary can be traced back to the exercise of colonial control in Kenya, where the judiciary was an important tool in the service of the state, as illustrated by both Mwangi (2001) and Anderson (2005). Again, the Ward case presented an illustration of the paradoxical legacies of colonial modernity that the postcolonial state had found equally handy, and whose contradictions were, in an unfortunate sense, coming home to roost in a case involving a British family's frustrated quest for justice.

While both Atieno Odhiambo (1987) and Scott see rumour as an integral vehicle of alternative discourses, in Kenya rumour is not always the exclusive domain of the discontented publics. Rather, it remains a multivalent medium which sometimes serves the purposes of the political elite very well. Angelique Haugerud (1995) sees such instances of a shared grammar as an indication of the porosity of hegemonic transcripts – and, one may add, counter-hegemonic transcripts. For her, hegemonic transcripts are not marked by distinct boundaries; rather, there are several overlaps and ambiguities in the interactions between the state and the people (1995: 8). The Moi regime often used rumour as an important weapon of control by first circulating and then acting on rumours. A case in point was the 1983 case of the then Minister of Constitutional Affairs Charles Njonjo, where the regime engineered the rumour that Njonjo was planning to overthrow the government. In this instance, a Commission of Inquiry headed by Judge Cecil Miller was set up in response to a complaint by President Moi that 'an unnamed person, with the support of foreigners, was being groomed to overthrow the government' (AfriCOG 2007: 12). This unnamed person was first termed a 'traitor' before finally being named as Charles Njonjo. AfriCOG notes that 'the events leading up to the formation of the Miller Inquiry was [*sic*] a well choreographed political strategy for getting rid of Njonjo, at the time a highly influential member of the government' (ibid.). Njonjo was successfully purged from government.[18] In the course of investigations into Julie Ward's death, the state appears to have supported rumours that Julie Ward was a woman of loose morals, whose promiscuity may have contributed to her murder. Rumour's potential as a vehicle for hegemonic discourses here is an instance of the state's appropriation of oppositional modes of discourse.

In a way, this further cautions against a view of both the oppressed and their hidden transcripts as necessarily progressive or even subversive. These hidden transcripts, while often having their roots in the need to counter hegemonic discourses, sometimes achieve this end precisely by embracing these discourses. Further, these apparently subversive discourses often concomitantly reinforce other oppressive discourses, in the course of subverting one form of oppression. This is illustrated by the rumours, which offered a forum for registering discontent and criticism against the establishment's culture of repression and political intolerance, and to this end provided what James Ogude (2007) has described as an 'imaginative space through which we can debate issues of power and have a second handle onto the public spheres, often posited as being very much out of the reach of marginalized groups'. These rumours however, simultaneously

---

[18] See Mwangi (2001: 69–87) for a detailed discussion of the Njonjo case.

expressed deeply patriarchal gender attitudes, where Julie Ward's sexual relations were lingered upon as justification for her death.

Ogude (2007) cites a similar example in his cautionary note on the tendency
to associate popular cultural productions with progressive and revolutionary
politics. In his discussion of D.O. Misiani's engagement with the repressive political sphere in Kenya, Ogude notes that Misiani uses popular music to critique
the postcolonial state in Kenya as an instrument for the perpetuation of institutionalized plunder and patron-client distributive networks configured along
ethnic lines. However, Misiani's politics are still trapped within the same ethnic
discourse he critiques, evident in his lamentation of the deliberate exclusion of
Luo interests throughout Kenyan political history. For Ogude, Misiani's inability
to transcend the ethnic moral economy can be read as a pointer towards the
paralysing effect of hegemonic discourses, which sometimes institute dangerous
ideological closures. Thus, while taking the point that oppositional discourses
often find themselves defined by, and indeed trapped within the discourses they
seek to subvert, caution must be exercised to avoid imbuing popular discourses
with inordinate amounts of progressive agency.

Given the privileging of legal truths in the Julie Ward case, our discussions
in this chapter suggest that for the Kenyan publics, such prioritization of monolithic truths was a doomed approach, in a context where these truths had to be
produced through the Kenyan state institutions, which commanded little credibility. At the same time, through these rumours, local publics appropriated Julie
Ward's death as a discursive space through which they were able to articulate a
critique of both colonial modernity and its manifestation in postcolonial Kenya.

Returning to the earlier discussion on modernity, then, Dipesh Chakrabarty's
observations on Indian encounters with modernity lend us yet another angle
from which to make sense of genres such as rumour and hearsay. In his critique
of what he terms the transition-narrative to modernity, Chakrabarty reminds
us that colonial subjects in India sometimes operated within the contexts of
'modern' institutions by mobilizing practices that would otherwise be deemed
'antihistorical' and 'antimodern', as a strategy of arrogating themselves 'subject-
hood' (Chakrabarty 2010: 65). This book's critique of modernity is rooted in
the spirit of Chakrabarty's project of provincializing Europe as not so much a
'simplistic, out-of-hand rejection of modernity, liberal values, universals, science, reason [nor] the stance that the reason/science/universals that help define
Europe as modern are simply 'culture-specific' and therefore only belong to the
European cultures. For the point is not that Enlightenment rationalism is always
unreasonable in itself but rather a matter of documenting how – through what
historical process – its "reason," which was not always self-evident to everyone,
has been made to look "obvious" far beyond the ground where it originated'
(Chakrabarty 2010: 67).

Like the *jua kali* artisan, rumour engages the paradoxes of postcolonial manifestations of the promise/denial dynamic of modernity, by weaving together pieces of information from a range of archives, and allowing their multiple verdicts to circulate across the gaps left by the institutions of the postcolonial state. A striking irony in this case remained the ways in which the British colonial legacy of the selective distribution of the benefits of modernity had come home to roost in a postcolonial case involving the quest for truth and justice for a British family. This legacy was equally evident in the narrative tropes mobilized in narrating the Julie Ward case by British and American writers, as the next chapter reveals.

Wildebeest, 'Noble Savages' and Moi's Kenya: Cultural Illiteracies in the Search for Julie Ward's Killers

This chapter reflects on the interactions between British and Kenyan actors in the search for Julie Ward's killers, and how the case is narrated in the three true crime texts. It suggests that Julie Ward's presence in Kenya as a tourist and wildlife photographer was mediated by a certain discursive archive on Africa. Upon her death, British investigations into her murder were tinted by this archive, at the core of which lay assumptions about 'noble savages' on the one hand and the postcolonial African state on the other, both of which were taken to be transparent to instruments of Western modernity in line with what Homi Bhabha has described as colonial discourse's production of the colonized 'as a fixed reality which is at once an "Other" and yet entirely knowable and visible' (Bhabha 1983: 23). Subsequently, the three books on the case – John Ward's *The Animals are Innocent*, Michael Hiltzik's *A Death in Kenya* and Jeremy Gavron's *Darkness in Eden* – also narrated the case through the prism of discourses drawn from this archive of ideas on Kenya and Africa. Yet the Kenyans – both the individual players involved in the case and the state institutions – subscribed to a different set of discursive regimes, some of which were inscrutable to the British. So, I suggest, there was an epistemological disarticulation between the British and Kenyan approaches to the case, as the Kenyans were proficient in both local epistemes and the institutions and values of modern state epistemes, while the British were hampered by their illiteracy in the local textualities which were illegible to orthodox instruments of Western modernity, namely modern law and science. This epistemological disarticulation resulted in what I term 'cultural illiteracy' in reference to some British actors' inability to access the local ideas and practices that were at play in Kenya. This chapter argues that this illiteracy had less to do with an insider/outsider positioning than with the continued reproduction and deployment of assumptions embedded in colonial archives on Africa(ns), which retain epistemes that proved disabling in the quest for Julie Ward's killers. This chapter examines what happens at the intersection between what Neil Lazarus has identified as the three main perspectives from which the question of representation has been approached in postcolonial scholarship: 'first, concerning subalternity and the recovery of popular consciousness; second, concerning the critique of Eurocentrism and colonialist ideology; third (an extension and radicalization of the second), concerning the deconstruction of the "Western" ratio and its discourses and the corresponding production of what the Moroccan writer, Abdelkebir Khatibi, has called "the thought of difference"' (Lazarus 2005: 81). I am interested in the kinds of blind spots, cultural illiteracies and deceit that unfold at the contact zone between subaltern logics, Eurocentric ideologies and Khatibi's thought of difference. I am further interested in the modes of what Mary Louise Pratt terms 'autoethnography', which the Maasai individuals and communities implicated in the case deployed as responses to popular assumptions about the Maasai community in general, and the individual Maasai implicated in the case, in particular.

Europe's construction of the Other as a negation of its normative self has over time become a well-known truism persuasively articulated in, among others, Edward Said's seminal work, *Orientalism* (1978), AbdulRazak JanMohamed's concept of the Manichean allegory (1983) and Fanon's notion of the Negro as a product of a particular European gaze. This history emphasizes the existence of the actual people of colour who remain largely illegible to a Euro-American gaze deeply invested in the stereotypical fantasy people of colour. The imperial project, Said (1978) writes, was conceptualized within a well-developed portrait of the Orient – and by extension, Africa – legitimized by an assumed knowledge that inscribed the West as the 'Seeing Eye'. As Jean-Paul Sartre puts it, 'for three thousand years, the white man has enjoyed the privilege of seeing without being seen (Sartre 2001: 115). This assumed knowledge, based on difference, resulted in highly polarized identities. Africa came to be defined as a negation of the West: it was everything Europe was not. Where Europe was mature, civilized and rational, Africa was seen as child-like, irrational and depraved. This definition by negation suggests a process of self-construction based on the definition of the 'Other' as different, which underscores Europe's assumed superiority as one that is concretized by the denigration of other races. For Hayden White, this self-definition by negation is founded on uncertainty about the identity of the self, which makes it easier to define it by what it is not. As he argues, 'in the past, when men were uncertain as to the precise quality of their sensed humanity, they appealed to the concept of wildness to designate an area of subhumanity that was characterised by everything they hoped they were not' (1978: 152). What remains interesting, though, is the manner in which Europe further appropriated the gaze and the ability to know the Other. Underpinning this was the assumption that the Other – in this case the African – was incapable of returning the gaze. Dipesh Chakrabarty captures this in his observation that 'virtually all branches of European knowledge and science have grown with the confident conviction that the world is knowable only through those categories of knowledge developed in Europe – indeed that the world may exist only in and through those categories of European modernity' (cited in Priyadharshini 1999: 2).

The ostensible mission of the colonial project – civilizing natives – necessitated inducting natives into European cultural and knowledge systems.[1] This lent natives insights into the worlds of the colonizers, while the colonial structures read native cosmologies predominantly through Eurocentric lenses, which mostly dismissed them as inferior and irrational, without quite mastering the logics underpinning their world views. This dimension of the inter-racial relationship has attracted extensive commentary in black writing, both fictional and academic. In the American context, bell hooks remarks that 'black folks have, from slavery on, shared in conversations with one another "special" knowledge of whiteness gleaned from close proximity of white people. [Its] purpose was to help black folks cope and survive in a white supremacist society. For years, black domestic servants working in white homes, acting as informants, brought knowledge back to segregated communities – details, facts, observations, and psychoanalytic readings of the white Other' (hooks 1995: 31). The arrogance of white supremacist regimes is evident when, having nursed the fantasy of exclusive control of the gaze; and having successfully terrorized people of colour into a posture of perpetual reverence and averted gazes, they believed that the 'Other who is subjugated, who is subhuman, lacks the ability to comprehend, to understand, to see the working of the powerful' (hooks 1995: 35). Cameroonian novelist Ferdinand Oyono's 1966 novel *Houseboy* tells of this fantasy of invisibility in French colonial Cameroon, where despite the strict boundaries between the native quarters and the European quarters, domestic service in the French quarters afforded natives intimate access to and knowledge of colonial French lives, while the French remained blind to the natives' real lives, beneath the mask of servitude: 'in Dangan, the European quarter and the African quarter are quite separate. But what goes on underneath those corrugated iron roofs is known down to the smallest detail inside the mud-walled huts. The eyes that live in the native location strip the whites naked. The whites on the other hand go about blind' (Oyono 1966: 71). This set-up was to a certain degree replicated in the Julie Ward case.

In an essay reflecting on the historical reasons behind the persistence of what

---

[1] Ostensible, because the actual mission of the colonial project was far less invested in natives' souls or quality of life. Will Jackson offers an excellent example of the calculated deployment of the rhetoric of benevolent paternalism to exclude Indians in Kenya from owning land in the fertile so-called white highland by British settlers who considered themselves uniquely cut out for the task of civilizing Africans and argued that increased Indian presence would be harmful to Africans: 'not only would Indians monopolise those subordinate skilled and semi-skilled positions to which Africans might aspire but they would also be utterly unable to exercise that civilising influence to which only Europeans were equipped. "It is our firm conviction," the report set out, "that the justification of our occupation of this country lies in our ability to adapt the native to our own civilisation. If we complicate the task by continuing to expose the African to the antagonistic influence of Asiatic, as distinct from European, philosophy, we shall be guilty of a breach of trust"' (Jackson 2011b: 348, citing East Africa Protectorate Economic Commission 1919).

he terms 'Kenya Colony's romantic mythology', Will Jackson sees this image as a product of the manufacture of Kenya 'as a tourist commodity'; a process which in turn 'depended on making manifest prospective tourists' prior ideas' (Jackson 2011b: 345, 346). He historicizes the colonial production of Kenya, the tourist commodity, as a strategic political response to counter negative publicity generated by the Mau Mau state of emergency, and an economic strategy that tapped into a post-war British expatriate market by offering a leisurely outdoor encounter with a landscape that had been imagined as both savage and beautiful (ibid.: 353).

It is impossible to discuss Julie Ward's murder without discussing Kenya, the tourist commodity, as the landscape – both geographical and discursive – in which this tragedy took place. In the 1980s, and to some degree, to date, the pleasures promised by the Kenyan game reserve were primarily targeted at a white clientele. South African writer and scholar Njabulo Ndebele makes similar observations about wildlife tourism in South Africa in his autobiographical essay 'Game Lodges and Leisure Colonialists' (2007) where he explores black experiences of the game lodge as a space colonially framed for white pleasure. For Rob Nixon, Ndebele's essay revisits his earlier concern with spectacle in black South African writing under apartheid, this time by asking 'what would it take for a black South African to enter the game lodge as an unspectacular, unwatched, *ordinary* tourist, thereby transforming ecologies of looking?' (Nixon 2011: 183; original emphasis). These ecologies of looking are anchored on the notion of the picturesque as what J.M. Coetzee terms 'physical landscape conceived pictorially' (1988: 40).

Nixon and Jackson's readings of the game reserve and the fictions that shape their brand rhyme in striking ways. Nixon's game reserve as 'a sanctuary from labor and from history's brutality; [where] history's corrugations have been Botoxed from nature's visage' (2011: 184) might as well be echoing Jackson's colonial picturesque as 'the visual grammar by which what was politically contingent was made beautiful and thus benign' (Jackson 2011b: 355). Jackson further sees a certain genre of writing on Kenya as participating in this production of tourist Kenya, while 'Botoxing out' the brutalities to which we owe its haunting beauty: 'to write lyrically of Africa and so render both colonised space (and the author's presence therein) as beautiful was to make what was in fact structured fundamentally by relations of political and economic power appear to be something naturally or divinely ordained, remote from the banality of politics and free from the taint of human responsibility' (ibid.). That Jackson and Nixon's perspectives are in tune with each other, despite their focus on Kenya and South Africa respectively, in itself underlines a distinct packaging of wildlife tourism in Africa that is hardly unique to Kenya. As Nixon further notes, given the linkages between violent labour histories, forced removals and the formation of game reserves in settler colonies, game reserves embody a 'labor-intensive production of labor's illusory absence, an absence critical to the eco-archaic's role in producing a sweat-free, soft-focus, natural tranquillity that appears at once effortless and untouched by human history' (Nixon 2011: 184).

In the Footsteps of Mr Kurtz and Baroness Blixen

Apart from the writing of Karen Blixen, Robert Ruark, Winston Churchill, Elspeth Huxley and other such writers who popularized Kenya in Euro-American imaginaries, contemporary white writing on Kenya has remained largely under-examined in Kenyan literary scholarship. This marks a focal point of this book, in so far as it engages with strands of contemporary Anglo-American imaginaries on Kenya. In reading the three books on the case and the ideological underpinnings that shape their narration of Julie Ward's death, an understanding of the settler literary tradition in Africa and specifically, Kenya, is important.

Settler writing played an important role in the production of Kenya as what came to be known as 'white man's country'. This fiction, coupled with an extensive library of life writing, provided an effective vehicle for the propagation of colonial ideology, myths and stereotypes about Kenyans as part of the justification for continued British occupation of the country (Maughan-Brown 1985). In most of this writing, David Maughan-Brown notes, there is little engagement with the concrete socio-economic forces of colonialism and their influence on the black population; rather, what emerge are powerful portraits of Will Jackson's afore-mentioned colonial picturesque.

In contemporary British imaginaries, Apollo Amoko notes in his essay on representations of the Moi regime Kenya in the British media, there is the continued (re)production of Kenyans as a savage, backward people, victims at the hands of 'the stock savage, Moi,' for whom the white man – whether the white Kenyan politician or Euro-America as a whole – is a messianic saviour, out to rescue them from retrogressive politics and oppression (Amoko 1999: 229). His observation that the colonial discourses and stereotypes of Kenya are still at play in contemporary British imaginings of the Kenyan political sphere is instructive. This is the other face of Kenya in the Euro-American imagination, the antithesis of the tourist's haven, where we have the socio-political jungle. This face of Kenya figures in the media, fiction, feature films and documentaries whose iconography includes emaciated women and children, and stories of poverty, disease and senseless violence.[2] These various representations of

---

[2] Photojournalist Kevin Carter's much-publicized picture of an emaciated Sudanese girl stalked by a vulture as she walks to a feeding centre is an illustration of this face of Africa, as the picture became the icon of Africa's crises. According to media reports, this picture drew tears all over the world and there was a momentary respite in compassion fatigue as aid poured into Southern Sudan. But the fate of the girl remains unknown as Carter is said to have broken down in tears after taking the picture and chasing off the vulture, as the girl journeyed on.

Africa are useful in understanding why constructions of Kenya and Africa at large, which though proven to be misconceptions time and again, nevertheless continue to hold sway in Anglo-American imaginaries, in a way illustrating the cognitive power of myth and stereotype and their embeddedness in the Euro-American psyche. It is important to set this context of popular perceptions of Kenya as a background against which one must read Julie Ward's murder in the Maasai Mara, the centrepiece of tourist Kenya. These perceptions preceded Julie Ward's visit to Kenya.

To a large extent, Anglo-American narratives of the Julie Ward murder were distilled through a literary tradition that represents black Kenyans as a people given to impulsive violence and callousness. Such ideas had been constructed in Anglo-American writing on Kenya during the colonial decades, and especially in the portrayal of the Mau Mau freedom fighters as brute terrorists, the 'wild savage' opposite of 'noble savages'. Robert Ruark's *Uhuru* (1962) offers an excellent narration of this fantasy, in the shape of Kidogo, a Ndorobo man whose Swahili nickname translates to 'little/small'. Despite working closely with the white hunter protagonist Andrew Dermott, Kidogo remains rooted in his Ndorobo worldviews and therefore, unthreatening to British interests, as a perfect 'noble savage', while on the other extreme lie the 'wild savages', the brutal Mau Mau who casually behead an American tourist in a horrendous bloodbath. While the Julie Ward murder happened in a Kenya marked by different socio-political realities, there are audible echoes of Anglo-American settler iconography of Kenya(ns) in these books.

The three books on the Julie Ward case provide interesting insights into the meaning-making practices that the authors engage in as they narrate the Julie Ward case. Although they belong to the true crime genre – which carries with it claims to certain notions of 'truth' – the books are nonetheless engaged in a process of decoding and encoding available information on the death, and weaving this into a narrative. This process exemplifies Stuart Hall's observation, noted earlier, that a 'raw historical event' cannot be transmitted in that form; it must 'become a story before it can become a communicative event' (2002: 302). For him though, this process is far from technical, as it involves a whole range of cultural and ideological positions that provide lenses through which historical reality is read and represented. These lenses are central to the connotational level of meaning-making, where texts 'contract relations with the universe of

---

The ethical and professional issues surrounding journalistic practice are beyond our scope, but for our purposes, this illustrates the symbiotic relationship between representations of an Africa ravaged by conflict, famine and disease and the humanitarian causes, whose interests sometimes go beyond service to humanity. See Susan Moeller's *Compassion Fatigue: How the Media Sell Disease, Famine, War and Death* (1999) for a detailed discussion.

ideologies in a culture, [and] domains of social life, the segmentations of culture, power and ideology are made to signify' (Hall 2002: 306).

While Julie Ward's death took place in a Kenya marked by different socio-political realities – close to three decades after the official demise of colonial rule – there are frequent echoes of settler iconography of Kenya(ns) in these three texts: they make numerous allusions to an older library of settler fiction on Kenya and Africa in ways that betray their situatedness in British colonial representational archives. It is in these echoes – and the outright muting of other archives on Kenya/Africa – that one begins to see how, in Hall's words, the universe of ideologies and culture are made to signify (2002: 302) and shape the interpretative lenses through which Julie Ward's death in Kenya is read and written by these authors. As Vron Ware rightly points out, Hiltzik's 'evocation of Karen Blixen's *Out of Africa* in his own description of the landscape confirms that colonialism provides the lens through which the mystery of Julie Ward's murder is being viewed, almost thirty years after independence' (1992: 130). Perhaps in recognition of Julie Ward's trip as unfolding in the footprints of earlier European visitors to Africa, the three books on the case signpost her journey across Africa with revering reference to the memory of figures such as Mungo Park, David Livingstone, Henry Stanley, Karen Blixen and Lord Delamere among others.

This evocation of colonial history is evident in Gavron's *Darkness in Eden*, as he locates Julie Ward's trip to Kenya in the footsteps of a string of colonial figures:

> Julie Ward was by no means the first traveller to find 'Shangri-la' in the grandeur and freedom of Kenya. Early descriptions by the explorers and pioneers of East Africa are peppered with references to paradise and God's own land … 'A veritable land of Goshen', recorded Joseph Thompson in *Through Maasailand*, published in 1885. 'Everything', Karen Blixen said, 'was made for greatness and freedom, and unequalled nobility'. And Elspeth Huxley, who arrived in Kenya in 1913, had this to say of Lord Delamere's first view, in 1897, of what became known as the White Highlands: 'Here indeed, he must have thought, was a promised land, the realization of a Rider Haggard dream' [Gavron 1991: 56].

This summoning of imperial memories not only confirms the continued availability and deployment of these narrative archives in interpreting contemporary experiences, but further, it betrays a frozen backward gaze at these colonial archives while imagining a readership invested and steeped in these memories. Will Jackson comments on this phenomenon, noting that

> while Kenya's colonial mythology has been picked over extensively by literary critics … what remains strikingly absent is an historical explanation for why Kenya Colony continues to be associated with a particular combination of romance and

adventure almost fifty years after political independence; [why is it that] as practitioners of the 'new imperial history' continue to pull apart triumphalist colonialist narratives elsewhere, in the case of Kenya the dominant *colonial* version of events [has] remained more or less intact? [Jackson 2011: 345; original emphasis].

In the Ward case at least, one way of understanding this retrieval of these colonial histories is as a summoning of the familiar in making sense of a tragedy whose twists and turns marked a shocking rupture of accepted common senses about the British–Kenyan and, by extension, the tourist–host relationship. These colonial archives may however, have negatively impacted on the quest for truth and justice in the case, as Chapter 7 illustrates.

In his book, *A Death in Kenya*, Michael Hiltzik attempts to piece together Julie Ward's journey on the overland drive across the continent. In reconstructing the group's journey, Hiltzik superimposes his vision of what they may have seen as they drove across the continent, a vision which unproblematically embraces the twin tropes of the savage, exotic jungle and its reverse, the socio-political jungle, as the prisms through which he narrates Julie Ward's trip to Kenya and her subsequent death. A blurb on the book's jacket signals these lenses: 'This is the heart wrenching, compelling story of the dark secrets hiding under Kenya's haunting beauty ... a remarkable journey into the dark side of the Dark Continent.' In similar fashion, Gavron's blurb – 'a book that shows that in Kenya savagery and beauty can walk side by side' – summarizes this recurrent motif of beauty and brutality in ways that powerfully evoke Derek Gregory's reminder that it is 'imperative to understand the ways in which anxiety, desire and fantasy enter into the production of imaginative geographies' (Gregory 2000: 313).

Both Hiltzik and Gavron deploy a certain 'vacuating' gaze as they sweep across the continent tracing Julie Ward's journey to Maasai Mara. Throughout this trip, they empty the landscapes of both local people and local histories, only selectively seeing the occasional faceless masses and the power-mad politicians. The landscapes are described through the dual lens of their exotic, natural beauty and the accompanying white histories of the spaces on the one hand, and their postcolonial political histories on the other. This vacuation of the land evokes an earlier emptying of the continent, to legitimize its appropriation. In Hiltzik's and Gavron's books, these spaces are not just emptied of local people and their histories; they are re-mapped with a distinct white colonial history. When the travellers cross into Mali, Gavron picks out the two landmarks, Niger River and Timbuktu, about which he writes:

The truck crossed into Mali and eventually arrived in Timbuctu. *The legendary city of gold and ivory is now a dull, brown, dusty town, with little to recommend it apart from its name.* Several hundred years ago the Niger River changed its course and stranded the city a dozen miles from its banks. Mungo Park, the great explorer, paddled up the

Niger in 1807 and passed Timbuctu without realizing the city lay just beyond a field of sand dunes. Park met his death upstream a few weeks later, in a hail of poisoned arrows. Timbuctu was not a particularly happy city for the HoBo group either and one of the girls had a bad case of sunstroke and had to be tended by Julie for a few days before the truck could carry on [Gavron 1991: 49, emphasis added].

Despite the abbreviated nod to its 'legendary status', Timbuktu's claim to fame for Gavron, appears to be that Mungo Park narrowly missed it, and went on to fall into the white man's grave under the locals' poisoned arrows. Over a century later, the tour group battles sunstroke, yet another 'African' peril. It is however the silence on Timbuktu's other histories that is striking here, especially given Timbuktu's architecture and most importantly, its contributions to scholarship for which it lies at the centre of an important intellectual tradition in Africa.

Hiltzik's book too lingers on the Niger River, reconstructing an incident when the group's truck got stuck halfway across the Niger River.

The travellers eyed the water around them with deep apprehension, terrified to stay in the listing vehicle, but panicky at the thought of Bilharzia, the parasitic scourge of stagnant African waters. *Bilharzia afflicts people who bathe or drink the water of rivers and lakes throughout sub-Saharan Africa ... in fact hardly a watercourse in Africa is free of the parasite ...* In the first hours some of the trekkers swore they would live on the truck until it was freed [ibid.: 28, emphasis added].

By spreading Bilharzia to all the continent's waters in a haughty health panic, Hiltzik writes this incident through the trope of Africa as the white man's grave and the stereotypical African jungle of disease. John Ward too nursed similar fears over his daughter's journey across what he seemed to consider a den of disease, a concern he raises in *The Animals are Innocent*.

Now that Muff had safely reached Nairobi we didn't look for the postman quite so anxiously as before. During her journey through Africa, I think we all had some private fears for her. Mine was illness: typhoid, yellow fever, polio, malaria, hepatitis, cholera. You name it. Africa has it on the illness menu. So, when Muff reached Nairobi unscathed by these awful diseases which can ruin your health for life, I was relieved [Ward 1991: 37].

So apprehensive was John Ward about Africa's 'illness menu' that when he eventually went to Nairobi for the first time, he remained baffled at the white community's choice to live there:

I find the life-style of the white population in Nairobi hard to appreciate. In fact, I cannot understand why they choose to live there at all. There are few cultural activities. And there is the constant risk of illness; everyone seems to have had malaria at some time or another and much worse ailments are ever-present [ibid.: 155].

Hiltzik, Gavron and Ward's health panics about 1980s Africa owe their roots to a much older colonial library. In the three writers' selective re-scripting of the landscape, only the dictators warrant individual mention, thanks to their place in the foreign correspondent's phrasebook as familiar short-hand for the failures of the postcolonial African state. As the group drives into central Africa, Hiltzik dons his political commentator's cap and maps out a selective political geography of the various countries. In the Central African Republic, he gives a shrill sermon on President Bokassa's misdeeds, which he describes as 'impossibly hideous brutalities in the imperial palace, a caricature of African monstrousness' (1991: 34). He dedicates an entire chapter to a sketch of the political topography of Africa, giving a roll-call of countries by their presidents' misdeeds, crowning it with Zaire's Mobutu. Here he juxtaposes the impenetrably dense rain forest with the equally impenetrable political system and chaos of the country in a register that recalls Richard Grove's description of colonial incursion: 'European colonial invaders of the tropics were frequently faced with a highly unfamiliar set of circumstances in which risks in the physical environment (in terms of disease, soils, water supply and fuel provision) were paralleled only by the dangers apprehended as being posed by an often equally poorly understood indigenous population ... In other words, an unfamiliar environment and populace might both present untold risks in knowing and controlling' (Grove 2010: 213). Hiltzik's text selectively maintains a studied silence on colonial violence and postcolonial manipulations by former colonizers, and their complicity in the creation of these latter-day 'monstrosities'. These complicities are safely obscured by lush rainforests, rare gorillas, and the excesses of the Mobutus and Bokassas. While it is hard to deny long histories of inefficient and often brutal political cultures, it is nonetheless important to heed Branwen Gruffydd Jones' caution that 'the conceptual language of state failure meshes easily with a broader and long-entrenched Western imagination of chaos and anarchy in Africa: a general lack of capacity to develop, to rule or to be peaceful' (Jones 2013: 49).

But the most articulate, yet subtle allusion to colonial epistemology with regard to Africa is the picture of Julie Ward hugging a young chimpanzee, which is reproduced on the covers of both Ward's and Hiltzik's books and which often graces media reports on the case (see also p. ix and jacket of present book). The picture was wrongly reported to have been taken when the tour group visited an animal orphanage in Cameroon. Commenting on this aspect of the trip, Hiltzik informs his readers: 'In the foothills of Cameroon, *chimps are hunted for their meat in the usual heedless fashion of Africans: the hunters took away the mothers and left their infants to die unnurtured in the bush*' (1991: 34; emphasis added). Julie Ward hugs one such orphan in the picture, as both Gavron and Hiltzik give detailed descriptions of her silent anger at the hunters. By selecting this as the emblematic photo of Julie Ward after her death, we have a construction of her murderers as stereotypically callous Africans. This line of thought is captured in

John Ward's book's title, *The Animals are Innocent* which also bears this photograph on the cover. At play here are specific cultural epistemologies, especially in the subtle allusions to cannibalism. This allusion glances back to the classification of species in biology, coupled with Darwinian thinking on evolution, both of which argue that human beings evolved from primates, and indeed the chimpanzee is a distant cousin. That this is the picture chosen to represent Julie Ward after her death is instructive. Implicit in this picture is the suggestion that, like the chimpanzee's mother, she too fell victim to the predatory violence of Africans.

In all three books, allusions to colonial archives of ideas, books, people and experiences function as what Jack Moore (1984: 65) terms 'signposts in the wilderness' for the target readership. In drawing on exclusively white, mainly Euro-American archives, the texts would seem to be using such familiar histories as what Simon Gikandi (2000b) would term a legible referent, in the face of the discursive rupture that Julie Ward's murder represents. In this way, the authors overwrite present instability – where modern law and science have failed to unravel the murder mystery – by summoning preferred histories which impart an illusion of mastery of the continent and her people.

The three books' dependence on a distinct Euro-American archive on Africa and Africans which betrays echoes of colonial mentalities can further be interpreted as yet another co-ordinate in the return of the repressed in British imaginaries. Indeed it is possible to understand the continued deployment of ideas drawn from such outdated archives as an indicator that they remain embedded in the Euro-American cultural psyche, available for retrieval whenever the fantasy of knowing and control demands it. Hayden White advises that

> concepts which in an earlier time functioned as components of sustaining cultural myths and as parts of the game of civilization … have one by one passed into the category of the fictitious; they are identified as manifestations of cultural neurosis and often relegated to the status of mere prejudices. [Yet] the unmasking of such myths as the Wild Man has not always been followed by the banishment of their component concepts, but rather by their interiorisation. For, the dissolution by scientific knowledge of the ignorance which led earlier men to locate their imagined wild men in specific times and places does not necessarily touch the levels of psychic anxiety where such images have their origins [1978: 153].

In a Freudian sense then, the discursive rupture of Julie Ward's death, which seemed to collapse all existing assumptions about the sanctity of the tourist, and which remained elusive to the privileged modern institutions of science and law, activated these deep psychic anxieties, necessitating a summoning of the familiar, thus resurfacing a white supremacist, Euro-American cultural unconscious and its attendant memories, if not of full authority, then at least some degree of colonial control.

Beyond the clichéd stereotyping in these narratives, though, an important concern is how these discursive templates tinted the search for the truth behind the mystery of Julie Ward's death. What approaches were embraced in the quest for her killers and in what ways did these reflect the ideological and cultural configurations discussed in this chapter? And with what results?

Tourism and the Maasai Question in the Julie Ward Case

The figure of the 'noble savage' mediates the contours between what Hayden White describes as civilization and wildness, and the associated couplet of humanity and animality (1978: 151). Initially, the 'wild man' was associated with backwardness, wildness and failure to comply with the evolutionary march of civilization, modernity and progress. With greater reckoning of the drawbacks of Western modernity, the 'wild man', now designated 'noble savage', came to be the receptacle of nostalgic longings for an idealized past. He was transformed into 'the ideal model of a free humanity, his presumed attributes made the essence of a lost humanity, and his idealized image used as justification for rebellion against civilization itself' (ibid.: 168). Commenting on this fetishization of the 'noble savage' in the New World, Hayden White considers it noteworthy that the 'idolization of the natives of the New World [as 'noble savages'] occurs only after the conflict between the Europeans and the natives had already been decided and when, therefore, it could no longer hamper the exploitation of the latter by the former' (ibid.: 186). Rob Nixon's work on the game lodge as a product of aggressive modernization is in tune with this argument: the game reserve and the native reserve were both located in a different temporal scape from South/ Africa's white, mining-driven modernity, despite coming about due to that modernization; 'the game reserve as a hyper-visible space of "ancient" wildness administered for touristic consumption, the native reserve as an anachronistic space structured around invisibility, where crowded human suffering and attendant ecological calamity were concentrated in "out of the way" places' (Nixon 2011: 190). A similar impulse played out in Kenya in the case of the Maasai.

With little say in the matter, the Maasai have had a long-standing monopoly role as East Africa's 'noble savages' which has with time earned them a spot at the centre of the Kenyan tourist industry. The construction of the Maasai as tourist attractions in the region's cultural tourism can be traced back to early colonial settlement in Kenya, when they were displaced from around the present-day Nairobi area and later the Mara plains were declared state reserves for animal conservation in a move that illustrates Nixon's 'Botoxing out' of historical brutalities. The Maasai were pushed out of their ancestral lands and confined to Maasai reserves.[3] But the British were also struck by the Maasai

---

[3] See Parselelo Kantai's 'In the Grip of the Vampire State: Maasai Land Struggles in Kenyan Politics' (2007) and Fr John Anthony Kaiser's *If I Die* (2003) for detailed discussions of the displacement of the Maasai from present day Laikipia region.

culture and elegant bodily build, leading to a gradual attempt to conserve them as a tourist attraction too. Here, we recall Bayart's observation that 'the process of 'civilizing' the natives of Africa quite often consisted in traditionalizing them, by assigning to them ethnic identities or codes of customary law which were largely invented' (2000: 251). This process has been continued in post-independence Kenya, and indeed, the Maasai *moran* donning a red-checked *shuka* (sash, long decorative piece of cloth), colourful beads and a long spear are part of the branding of Kenya as a tourist destination, alongside the wildlife and white sands at the coast. The emblematic 'noble savages' believed to have successfully resisted Western modernity have now become an iconic marker of Kenya, the tourist paradise.

These are the kinds of 'noble savages' the British had in mind in the course of their investigations into Ward's death. As John Ward describes them on his first trip to the Mara in search of his daughter, before he learnt she was dead:

> In this part of Kenya [Narok region] the Maasai tribesmen are nomadic. They graze their few cattle on the dry grass of the plain, building themselves a temporary hut surrounded by a corral into which the cattle are herded at the end of each day … When an area is grazed out, the Maasai move on a few miles further, to where the grass is longer. The Maasai have been living this life since time began. *I found it unreal that only that morning I had stepped off one of the latest and most advanced jet aircraft in the world and here I was, that same afternoon, looking at a race of people for whom time had stood still* [1991: 62, emphasis added].

Ward's observations here reproduce the 'noble savage' understanding of the Maasai while simultaneously partaking in a process started decades earlier by the British colonialists: the fossilization of the Maasai as a people 'for whom time had stood still', people who had resisted modernity. Similar assumptions filter through in Gavron's and Hiltzik's narratives, where one notices a constant attempt to represent the Maasai as harmless 'noble savages', while blame is laid at the doorstep of state officials including the various police officers and the park employees. On this same trip, as they search for his daughter Ward writes:

> Whenever we saw a *manyatta* (corral) within sight of the road, we went to take a look. 'It's not really worth looking', said Glen. 'If the Maasai had found her she would be safe. They are a gentle people and would respect a woman and made sure she came to no harm.' Just the same I made sure we looked [1991: 62].

The portrayals of the Maasai in the three books is noteworthy, more so as all three men who were charged with the murder and acquitted, were Maasai employees at Maasai Mara: two junior game wardens, Peter Kipeen and John Magiroi, in 1992, and the chief warden, Simon Makallah, seven years later. However, all the texts on the case mute these men's conventional Maasai identity as per the colonial archives as 'noble savages', and choose to see them as civil servants, rather than *Maasai* civil servants. This is chiefly because the image of the postcolonial African state as inefficient, apathy-ridden and corrupt is the polar opposite of the image of the 'noble savages' who have successfully resisted the march of modernity. In some ways, this selective scripting betrays attempts to preserve the romantic image of the Maasai-as-noble-savages, by displacing any suspected misdeeds of individual Maasai on their other identities as players in a postcolonial state, implicitly underlining the corrupting impacts of 'incomplete' modernity.

Gavron, Ward and Hiltzik were not alone in this fossilizing script of the Maasai. Surprisingly, Judge Abdullah Fidahussein makes similar observations, by way of comment on the conduct of the Scotland Yard detectives – Searle and Shipperlee – who investigated the case and arrived at the decision that two Maasai game wardens, Jonah Tajeu Magiroi and Peter Metui Kipeen had a case to answer:

> it may be proper to consider at this stage further *repeated interrogations of these two clumsy rustics of the wilderness by the sophisticated sleuths of the Scotland Yard.* These two were subjected to rigorous and searching interrogations which sometimes bordered on to offensive and to which the two rangers did not take kindly … *One would expect these experienced detectives to be more considerate in gaining the confidence of these Masai men entering modern times so recently,* instead of brow beating and intimidating them [Fidahussein 1992: 80, emphasis added].

Judge Fidahussein repeatedly underlines the two men's 'Maasainess' and their ostensible lack of exposure to modern logics. In the same judgement, he points out that in their enthusiasm to find culprits behind the murder, the three Scotland Yard detectives

> forgot that they were dealing with youthful Masai Morans from the wilderness, whose intellectual capacity to perceive things, state of things or relation of things may not be equated in the same breath with perception of a sophisticated city dweller … I regard estimate of distances coming from a Masai Moran of the wilderness as unreliable, not a lie [Fidahussein 1992: 81].

This decision on the Judge's part was important in countering the Scotland Yard detectives' claims about the two game wardens as having lied in response to questions about distance, and therefore actively subverting the quest for truth in the case. In this instance, Judge Fidahussein underscores one of the core challenges to the quest for truth in the case: the fact that the law and the investigations were anchored on modern logics relating to modern ways of measuring distances – an important factor in the case – while the key respondents, the game wardens, were either not fully compatible with these logics of distance, or feigned unfamiliarity with these logics by playing on precisely these perceptions of Maasai illiteracy to modern logics, as a defence strategy. To some extent, the earlier-cited case of the British Army's alleged three-decade reign of rape in Kenya underscores this difficulty at the basic level of literacy and the alleged victims' inability to determine dates and times using the modern calendar. But this ostensible portrait of the Maasai as an ethnocultural community outside the dictates – and violences – of modernity would also be a useful defence. During his interrogation in court, Peter Kipeen pointed out that it was 'a great sin for Masai man [*sic*] to kill a woman' (Fidahussein 1992: 78), a defence that tapped into his Maasai ethnocultural identity as proof that he was not the culprit, while reminding the court to treat him as a *Maasai* respondent, and therefore, acknowledge his Maasai cultural citizenship.

This assumption of the Maasai as a fossilized community, illiterate in the protocols of modern law, represented one of the instances of cultural illiteracies of the British investigating team. As the investigations unfolded, the predominantly Maasai staff of the park observed what Vron Ware (1992: 133) terms a mafia-like code of silence, obstinately refusing to volunteer any information or to be witnesses. Ward and the Scotland Yard detectives seemed to be unschooled in the nuances of social capital and patronage relationships in Kenya as played out among the Maasai linked to the game reserve and the state at large. Ward inadvertently reveals this, in his book, while commenting on the investigating police officer, Muchiri Wanjau, whom he considered inept:

> The Maasai Mara is a difficult place in which to operate. Much later it was described to me as a 'private kingdom,' and in many ways it is. The Maasai tribe, who almost exclusively make up the rangers of the Maasai Mara, are a close-knit community … The Maasai family network is very strong. A family member, no matter how remote, is always known and supported. Indeed, there is a tribal obligation to do so. Wanjau is not a Maasai and is therefore treated with nearly as much suspicion as I am in the kingdom of the Mara [Ward 1991: 94].

Although Ward picked up the fact that over 90 per cent of the staff at the Maasai Mara were Maasai, his interpretation of this simplistically reads it as a display of 'tribal' bonds, in keeping with the dictates of Maasai culture. While this may indeed have been the case, it went beyond tribal bonds: in this instance, it was a complex mixture of patronage politics and the accompanying social networks which appear to have determined allegiances, coupled with a basic instinct for self-preservation, in light of the brutality of the murder. Ward failed to realize that under these circumstances, the modern legal processes that were privileged in the case were at odds with these patronage networks and its grip on the Maasai employees of the reserve, and the Maasai villagers, in terms of senses of loyalty and aligned interests and what this implied for the case. At play here was the same cynicism towards modern state institutions, as the cynicism displayed by the rumours about the involvement of highly placed political figures in Ward's death. In this environment, where the promises of modernity flowed along patronage networks, an instinct of self-preservation – in the face of a brutal murderer and a patronage-based statecraft – coupled with the lack of credibility of the state institutions meant that the Maasai employees of the park had to choose between Ward and the police on one hand and their immediate workmates and colleagues on the other. The choices made here were in line with Ekeh's two publics and the moral imperatives that govern membership in these two spheres.

For Vron Ware, part of the problem here arose from the fact that the Maasai live outside of modernity and its rationale-based civilization. Ware is right about the difficulty of engaging with some Maasai along the dictates of a rationale-based modernity, through the formal legal processes. However, she too buys into the Maasai mask of 'relics of primordial history, who have successfully resisted modernity', which in many senses is just that: a convenient mask that occasionally comes in handy. In reality, quite apart from seemingly not sub-scribing to the kinds of legal rationalities that govern criminal law in Kenya, these particular Maasai were faced with a choice between co-operating with 'the law' in favour of 'the British', and protecting members of their community, who were part of their immediate social network and likely to do them a good turn when they needed it. If we also consider that the second-hand clothes seller who told Ward about allegations of a high-profile politician's involvement in the murder claimed to have heard these allegations all over the game reserve and surrounding villages (Ward 2012: 34), then Ware's Mafia-like code of silence would seem to have been a result of a fair assessment of the situation, and the potential injustice of it, in their belief that Makallah, Kipeen and Magiroi, if at all involved in the murder or disposal of the body, were certainly the small fish, who could easily become the sacrificial lambs, while the person who ordered the murder, and had a motive for the murder, went scot-free, protected by the shroud of impunity that attaches to proximity to power. Recalling Nahashon Isaac Njenga's fate in the Tom Mboya murder, where the big man allegedly behind the murder remained free, this would be a realistic assessment of the situation, whatever its moral weight. Two decades later, asked whether Makallah was the murderer, Supt Muchiri – the first detective to investigate the murder a few days after the remains were found, and who subsequently confessed to Ward that he was ordered to lie about his findings – would respond, 'it wasn't him. He was told to get rid of the body, but he didn't kill her. I think it was *Mr B.*'s bodyguards' (Ward 2012: 43).[4]

While Maasai literacy levels remain among the lowest in Kenya, and while it is indeed true that they are among the communities that have retained a

---

[4] Ward writes that Supt Wanjau approached him on his own volition in March 2009. They met at 10 a.m. on 31 March at Serena Hotel, Nairobi, and talked for two and a half hours (Ward 2012: 42).

powerful bond with their ethnocultural values and practices – thus appearing to have resisted modernity (or been deliberately fossilized as having resisted modernity), they were not entirely ignorant of what was at stake in the case. To assume so, as Ward does, is (inadvertently or otherwise) to embrace patronizing colonial assumptions about Africans' intellectual capacities. In fact, despite their illiteracy, the Maasai have been awake to the various patterns of their commodi-fication as 'noble savages', and the goldmine that cultural tourism has become in Kenya, and they have cashed in on this in many ways, ranging from travelling to Europe (and lately South Africa) as cultural ambassadors, charging tourists for taking their photographs and concocting non-existent customs to gratify tour-ists' desire for the exotic, all the way to variations of sex tourism at the Kenyan coastline, sometimes resulting in marriages with the more adventurous tourists (mainly white women) and performing rituals to install equally adventurous white men as 'elders' in the Maasai nation. So lucrative is the exoticized Maasai identity as cultural commodity that it increasingly features fake Maasais spin-ning fantastic mélanges of Maasai cultural practices for tourist consumption, in true Kenyan entrepreneurial spirit. One Maasai 'traditional dancer' Johnson Pesi shares an inside view of this Maasai shrewdness:

> There is not much exchange between us [and tourists]. We don't tell the tourists about our culture, and they don't tell us about theirs. We don't sell them what we own: we make them something similar to what we own, especially to be sold. The songs we sing are not the real songs that we sing during our own ceremonies, so they don't affect our culture. It's just a fake thing for tourists. I am dressed as a mo-ran (Maasai warrior). But I'm not yet a moran; I'm preparing to become one [Sayer 1998: 63].

Pesi's creation of new artefacts, songs and dances for tourist consumption speaks to Mary Louise Pratt's idea of autoethnography. Pratt uses this term to refer to 'instances in which colonized subjects undertake to represent themselves in ways that engage with the colonizer's own terms' (1992: 7). As she writes, 'if ethnographic texts are a means by which Europeans represent to themselves their (usually subjugated) others, autoethnographic texts are those the others construct in response to or in dialogue with those metropolitan representations' (ibid.). Pesi, then, gives us a glimpse of this autoethnographic response to tour-ists' fantasies about Maasai exoticism. To borrow Will Jackson's phrase, they make manifest these fantasies in a strategic self-exoticization that is a form of benign deception that enables them to make some money without compromis-ing their cultural practices and artefacts, by selling these to tourists who do not share or appreciate the epistemic and cultural values they represent.

In keeping with this trend, the Maasai Mara's employees were later to enact a variety of subtle, yet distinctive forms of passive resistance in their total refusal to in any way co-operate with or support investigations into the murder. Where earlier he would be accorded tourist-status with the requisite gratification of his every whim (Ward 1991: 125), John Ward was now treated as an unwanted enemy by the staff at Maasai Mara, and soon found himself facing forms of petty resistance, which included refusals to make transport and drivers available, and even to guide him to the spot where his daughter's remains had been found, as he went about his investigations. The investigating police officer in charge of the case, Muchiri Wanjau, found himself in a similar position: 'It's almost impossible for me to work in the Masai Mara now … The rangers will not help us and I have to take police vehicles from Nairobi because they will not let us use theirs' he reported to Ward (1991: 189).

It must be noted though, that these stereotypical understandings of the Maasai were hardly the full story. There was yet another pattern of values and practices which were evoked at various stages in the Ward case that underlined various parties' double belonging in both the modern universes of law, science, search helicopters and top-of-the-range German cars driven to the murder scene, and a second universe governed by spiritual protocols or what I term ethnoculture. These emerge at four interesting points across the case, revolving around the figure of Valentine Uhuru Kodipo as a self-confessed witness of the murder and the Ward family.

In his detailed description of the murder, Kodipo claims that after torturing her and whipping her with hippo-hide whips, she was struck with a 'Masai wooden club' which bore a heavy wheel nut at its tip:

> The man in charge told another man – a much feared political murderer – to end it. This man went to a vehicle and pulled back the front seat. Behind it was a carved Masai wooden club – with the wheel nut of a tractor on the top. He took it and hit her once on the back of the neck at the base of the skull. She fell down immediately and her body twitched for some minutes before she was quiet [*Nairobi Law Monthly* 62, March 1996: 24].

For John Ward, Kodipo's claims seemed to be legitimized by medical science, as UK-based pathologists confirmed that Kodipo's description of how his daughter's body twitched before she died was medically accurate. Prof. Gresham further described the head as showing 'the classical signs of decapitation' (Ward 1991: 50). This description represents one of the disconcerting moments in the case, when modern science – here represented by pathology – comes face to face with the dictates of ethnoculture, if Kodipo's evidence is to be believed. Kodipo claims that the killers decided to butcher Julie Ward's body into small pieces, but the politician further ordered them to decapitate her head:

> The president's close confidant picked up the severed head by the ear and ordered me to drive behind him to Makari [outpost in the Maasai Mara Reserve]. It was only about one kilometre, but it took us almost an hour because he was walking

slowly with the head dangling by his side, dripping blood, while my car headlights lit up the road for them ... He did not want to drive because he did not want blood in the vehicle, and also it is a Kalenjin ritual to walk with the head of your victim [*Nairobi Law Monthly* 62, March 1996, 24].

While this book is not interested in determining the truth or otherwise of the various claims and allegations, it is nonetheless noteworthy that Kodipo's claim about walking with the head about a kilometre away appears to cohere with the discovery of Julie Ward's skull about 1.7 km from the seat of fire. Yet another tragic angle to the case emerges here, when two policemen casually deliver the head to John Ward's hotel room at Serena Hotel one night, as described in the introduction. Apart from its sheer absurdity and callousness, this would be considered an unusual, even abominable treatment of the dead in the eyes of many Kenyan nations' cultural common senses. One possible reading of this incident is that the two policemen at that moment understood themselves as policemen, and not citizens of their ethnocultural worlds, with its attendant protocols of decent treatment of the dead.

Kodipo's descriptions of the cultural protocols that govern murder – presumably drawn from an older ethnocultural morality that once governed sanctioned military action –further complicate our reading of this case. The idea of raping, torturing and gruesomely murdering a woman assumed to be a threat to modern political power (as per Kodipo's version), driving around a game reserve in a Mercedes Benz, then proceeding to observe ethnocultural military protocol is perplexing in its collage of moral referents that signal active belonging to multiple, seemingly entangled epistemic moral worlds which were crisscrossed with little contradiction. This collage of referents is further mirrored in the afore-mentioned 'Masai wooden club' with a tractor's wheel nut, which similarly blends together a seemingly contradictory set of cultural and technological tropes: Maasai-ness as an identity that has come to accumulate particular ethnocultural baggage in tourist Kenyan imaginaries, the wheel nut of a tractor as associated with modern, mechanized, farming, and private militias training in the Mara. Considering rumoured speculations that Julie Ward may have stumbled upon private militias training in the game reserve, and given that two years later, trained militias were to masquerade as 'tribal warriors' in the so-called ethnic violence that haunted Kenya's first multi-party elections in 1991, Kodipo's claims underscore not only this multiple mobilization of different moral epistemes, but further signals politically manipulated appropriation of ethnoculture. As Peter Kagwanja has argued, concerning the so-called ethnic violence, and the Mungiki movement, this entailed a cynical masking of modern militias as a resurgence of ethnocultural military practices and histories (Kagwanja 2003). Two decades on, a similar set of questions would emerge in the International Criminal Court's case against Kenyan

President Uhuru Kenyatta and his deputy William Samoei arap Ruto, regarding whether the so-called Kalenjin youths and the Mungiki groups at the centre of the bloodshed were mobilized or acted spontaneously in the outburst of post-election violence in 2007–8. The assumption here appears to be assumed distinctions between organized military action under orders of a modern politician and spontaneous defensive military response by 'ethnocultural' young men as per ethnocultural military protocols.

A third feature of ethnoculture took the form of a clairvoyant: John Ward writes about watching TV one day and seeing an episode of a programme featuring a clairvoyant who had special powers. Desperate, and figuring they had nothing to lose in consulting her, even though he did not believe in such powers, he contacted her and visited her in Kent in south-east England. Ward approvingly notes that there was no hocus-pocus, dimmed lights, drawn curtains or crystal ball, but she requested they bring something that belonged to their daughter for her to hold (Ward 1991: 369). Ward and his wife, Jan, took along Julie Ward's money belt which she had worn on the journey to Nairobi, along with several pictures of key figures in the case, some unpublished, and therefore, not previously known to Nella Jones, the clairvoyant. When she talked,

> phrases came out at random. Many fitted the scene in a general way and some much more precisely. She asked questions. 'Who is the man with a scar on his arm? Something like a burn. The skin is shiny. He is quite old and has bad teeth. He's the weak link. Try to find him. He drives. Delivers food.' I got out my gallery of photographs and laid them on the floor in front of her armchair. All together there were twenty-eight different African men in the pictures. 'Oh,' Nella said immediately, 'that's him. That's the one.' Leaning forward, she picked up the photograph of Peter Kipeen. It had never been published and there was no way that Nella had seen the picture before … After instantly selecting Kipeen, the next one was Karori. She could not have known his photograph either. 'He took something of Julie's. He's driven the car. I think he got it stuck.' [Ward 1991: 369–70].

When shown aerial photographs of the Sand River, Jones pointed at the exact spot where the jeep was found. On looking at pictures of different buildings in the Mara Game Reserve, Nella Jones held one of a corrugated latrine shed in Makari Outpost, in the Mara: 'Her face, screwed up in disgust and horror, was turned away. She was holding the photograph of the latrine as far away as possible, and her hand was shaking. I took it from her. "It's alright" she said after a few seconds. "But that one was horrible. Why was she shut in there?" She spoke as if she thought I knew' (Ward 1991: 370). On his next trip to Kenya, Ward hired someone to search the latrine thoroughly, with a strong magnet, in the hope of finding bits of evidence, possibly his daughter's missing camera. No useful evidence was found.

I read the clairvoyant as an example of ethnocultural interventions in the case, whose involvement highlights the levels of desperation by the Ward family in their quest for information on what had happened to their daughter and why. Read alongside each other, these various segments of ethnocultural practices in the Ward murder and quest for justice map yet another set of world views that would come to bear on the case, while reiterating another facet of the intricate moral considerations that were at play in the case, even at the very moment of her murder, if we were to believe Kodipo's version of the truth.

In keeping with the entanglements of values, practices and beliefs that collided, knotted and interwove through the Ward tragedy, I read these figurings of ethnoculture across the Kenyan–British bridge as one corner of a triangular epistemic triangle that framed the Kenya–Britain relationship in the case, with the other two corners featuring stereotypical perceptions of the Maasai and actual Maasai's contingent embrace and rejection of these perceptions. In view of the outlined instances of Maasai shrewdness it is evident that in some senses, the 'noble savages' may not have been as ignorant as popular assumptions led Ward and his team to believe. Indeed, it is possible that their identity as 'noble savages' provided a convenient mask behind which to enact their passive resistance and stem the imminent possibility of one of their own being punished for a murder they never ordered. So, the scripting of the Maasai as a majestic tourist attraction of 'noble savages' who have successfully resisted the destructive effects of 'incomplete' modernity falls apart in the case of these particular Maasai who were masters of inscrutability and were clearly very rational actors in this game, despite their assumed illiteracy in the conventions of modern legal practice. In all this, John Ward and his team's unfamiliarity with these subtle nuances of informal local textures, values and socio-political imperatives created a hurdle that proved difficult to navigate in the quest for the killer(s).

Double Realities and *Trompes l'Œil*[5]: Playing Hide and Seek with the Master's Truths

For long, Europe presented itself as the womb of originary modernity, a view sustained by the assumption that 'as a construct of the enlightenment, modernity is a European project' (Zack-Williams 2004: 20). This modernity is often taken to signal progress that is assumed to be worth aspiring to, for all societies. The investigations into Julie Ward's death in Kenya, framed around the

---

[5] I am using this phrase in its original sense, to mean acts of window-dressing. See also Jean-François Bayart's 'Africa in the World: A History of Extraversion' (2000). Bayart identifies this as an important feature in the political lexicon of the African state, which has historically been used to 'perform compliance' with Western dictates, and thus preserve relations with the West. Although Bayart uses it in relation to donor-Africa relations, I find the phrase equally apt in understanding acts of 'window-dressing' that were performed by Kenyan institutions in the search for Julie Ward's killers.

instruments and values of Western modernity and filtered through circulating discourses about the typical postcolonial African state, were however faced with instances of inscrutability, coupled with subversive performances of these circulating discourses.

In conducting his investigations, John Ward was operating with idealistic assumptions about state institutions and their responsibilities to the citizenry, suppositions which were thwarted time and again. Unfamiliar with some elements of Kenyan statecraft, he was proceeding from assumptions which, though applicable on paper, were inapplicable in the practice of governance in most Kenyan state institutions. One such example was the post-mortem process, which is a fairly reliable scientific tool for determining time and manner of death. Although the first autopsy conducted by the police pathologist Dr Adel Shaker revealed that the remains had been severed with a sharp instrument, the report was allegedly altered by the Chief Government Pathologist Dr Jason Kaviti.

For John Ward, this was a deplorable act, as it was unheard of for a doctor to alter a colleague's report (Ward 1991: 119). In response, Ward, accompanied by an official from the British High Commission in Kenya, sought out the pathologist, expecting that Dr Shaker would obviously stand by his earlier report. Again they lacked an understanding of the workings of state power in Kenya and the lengths to which certain individuals were willing to go to ensure that the preferred truths about his daughter's death were legitimized. Soon after, he found that Dr Shaker was totally cowered and afraid to be seen talking to them. What Ward may have overlooked at the time is that as an Egyptian Copt who had sought asylum in Kenya from religious persecution in Egypt, Dr Shaker's refugee status gave the government significant leverage in 'persuading' him to reconsider his earlier post-mortem report and his co-operation with John Ward. For good measure, this was coupled with an accusation of corruption which the police department used as a trump card and a latent threat of criminal prosecution which could be activated at will (Ward 1991).

In the course of his investigations, John Ward constantly came up against walls of resistance from state institutions. After the remains were found, the Police Commissioner, Phillip Kilonzo was reluctant to open a murder case and insisted that they were not looking at a murder (Ward 1991: 111). Later on, with the altered autopsy report, there was an inquest to establish the cause of death, despite the fact that the first post-mortem report had returned with a verdict that suggested murder, a view that was reiterated by a second pathologist, Prof Austin Gresham. The Police Commissioner's refusal to admit that this was a murder case, instead pushing for an inquest, was a strategic delaying tactic. It further served to lengthen the process of searching for the truths behind Julie Ward's death.

As investigations unfolded, John Ward found himself succumbing to local ways of doing things, although, as luck would have it, he trapped himself in them. At one point, he needed to follow a possible lead across the border into neighbouring Tanzania. The person in question was on a four-day tour of Mt. Kilimanjaro and Ward wanted to meet him before he left. However, there was a slight complication with the international flight permit which his chartered pilot had to apply for from the Department of Aviation, a process that required seven days' notice, but could be 'hastened' for a fee, he was informed. Ward successfully bribed the airport official to 'facilitate' speedy processing of his flight clearance, imagining himself to have mastered how things worked in Kenya. A few weeks earlier, Ward had also bribed a different customs official at the airport, to allow him to take soil samples collected from the seat of fire in the Mara, where his daughter's body had been incinerated, to the UK for forensic testing. When the official demanded Ward's export permit from the government, permitting him to ship out the soil samples – a process that would have delayed his travel plans, if not flatly prevented him from taking the samples – he gave the man Ksh 200, and was allowed out without further complications. Ward however, made the mistake of including these encounters in his book, *The Animals are Innocent* (1991: 183–7), using them to illustrate his conviction about the rampant corruption, inefficiency and weak public service in Kenya, forgetting that, by the dictates of the formal legal systems – to which he subscribed – this was a written admission of corruption. These incidents were later to be used by Simon Makallah's defence lawyers in court during the murder trial against Makallah in 1999, to question Ward's credibility as a witness, suggesting that his evidence was questionable, given this dishonesty.[6] Incidentally, earlier, a baggage handler at Wilson Airport had claimed that at a fee of Ksh 2000, he would steal an aircraft manifest and make a copy available to Ward, which showed proof that *Mr B.* and his daughter had flown from the Mara to Nairobi on a private aircraft a couple of days before her murder to collect a vehicle part (a possible reference to the faulty fuel pump). Ward objected to paying the bribe upfront, out of concern that it could be a 'set up' to accuse him of bankrolling a robbery. He instead offered to pay Ksh 5000 once he received the information, provided it was genuine. The baggage handler rejected this offer as he was unwilling to take the risk without a 'deposit' and Ward never determined the veracity of his claims (Ward 2012: 37).

Both Ward and the British investigators oscillated between expectations about how state bureaucracy should run and assumptions of inept African state institutions, manifested as inefficiency and petty corruption. However, their main weakness was in failing to manage this ambivalence creatively in the interests of the case. In the end they unwittingly strengthened the Kenyan case in the legal arenas, as various parties were able to latch on to circulating discourses about Kenya and use these to free themselves from stickier charges.

---

[6] Mulaa 'I bribed government official, admits father', *Daily Nation*, 10 April 1999.

These circulating assumptions about Kenya and Africa provided convenient props which would seem to have worked to further mask certain truths, even though the British stakeholders mistakenly took these assumptions to be useful insights in making sense of various people's behaviour.

The first instance of this relates to the motive behind the state cover-up. Conventional wisdom about the centrality of the tourist industry to the Kenyan economy was a readily available rhetoric which provided a useful way of explaining the seemingly concerted efforts by Kenyan state institutions to cover up the facts of the case, or to favour the view that it was an accidental death rather than a murder. In working with these assumptions, both the British media and John Ward made sense of these cover-ups in ways they deemed credible within their scheme of thought. For many Kenyans, and for anybody familiar with the state's track record of ingenious imagination in such matters, however, the theory of protecting the tourism industry had less purchase than the need to protect certain politically connected individuals who may have been implicated in the murder. If anything, the cover-up drew greater negative attention to the industry.

The second instance played on ideas of the corrupt African state. The centrality of corruption as a cliché feature of African state institutions in Western imaginaries and the practices of stakeholders in these institutions were strategically used to shield the various witnesses against more serious accusations. Two examples illustrate this: Ward's legal team had created a profile of the chief suspect, as someone who was both totally familiar with the park and who had enough authority over its staff to allow him 24-hour access to all of its corners without too many questions being asked (Ward 1991: 271). Somebody who could dispose of the body at an obscure spot off the main tracks of the park. This profile fitted the Mara Chief Warden at the time, Simon Makallah. During the inquest into the death, Makallah had made a possibly incriminating observation that if Julie Ward's jeep had had four-wheel drive function, it would not have got stuck in the gully where it was later found. This proved to be dangerous information, for, being a jeep of a make which ordinarily came with a four-wheel drive function, the prosecution argued, Makallah had to be more familiar with this particular jeep than he was letting on, to know that this particular jeep's four-wheel drive was not functioning, which suggested that he must have driven the vehicle at some point. In response to this charge, Makallah swore that he was unable to drive and he did not have a driver's licence. In a statement dated 16 August 1989, Makallah wrote: 'I wish to confirm that I do not know how to drive a motor vehicle. *I have never driven any motor vehicle since I was born.* I have never done any driving test therefore I do not hold any driving licence' (cited in Aganyanya 1999: 32; emphasis added) reiterating a claim he had made in three previous statements. When several witnesses, including Mara staff, testified about his ability to drive – in fact he had driven John Ward on more than one occasion, to the site of the remains, as Ward conducted his investigations in the Mara – Makallah eventually confessed that he had lied because the Narok County Council was strictly against park officials driving park vehicles without drivers' licences, and he did not have one at the time, even though he knew how to drive albeit not competently, so he was lying to protect himself against any disciplinary action from the Council and not necessarily because he had driven Julie Ward's jeep at some point (ibid.: 32–4). Makallah further underlined that Narok County – under whose jurisdiction the Mara Reserve fell – was under the management of a new council after the 1988 elections and he was not in their good books, especially having recently received instructions that only licenced drivers should drive county council vehicles (ibid.). This argument did not exactly explain how he knew that this particular jeep's four-wheel drive was not functioning, but it certainly lightened the suspicion against him. For the presiding Judge at Makallah's murder trial, Daniel Aganyanya, inferring from Makallah's dishonesty about his ability to drive that he drove Julie Ward's jeep, and therefore was complicit in her murder, was a legally unsustainable argument, especially in the absence of additional evidence linking him to the deceased's jeep.

The second instance involved David Nchoko, the clerk on gate duty at the Mara's Sand River Gate on the day Julie Ward was last seen. Nchoko claimed that Julie Ward had left the game reserve on 6 September at 2:27 p.m. He could remember this because she had signed the exit book, as was expected of all tourists, after paying Ksh 200, for the tents which had been on the campsite for an extra two days, when Ward's car broke down on the other side of the Reserve, and she was forced to spend the two nights at Keekorok Lodge. However, close scrutiny revealed that Julie Ward's signature was forged. Additionally, the receipt for the Ksh 200 appeared to have been written out several days later. Initially, Nchoko remained adamant that Julie Ward had signed herself out and left the Mara, alone, which also happened to be the official story. After handwriting experts confirmed that the signature in question was not in Julie Ward's handwriting, Nchoko admitted that actually, he had made the entry and signed against Julie Ward's name afterwards, not because he wanted to create the impression that she had left the Mara when he knew she had not (Ward 1991: 178, 204) but because he had forgotten to give her the register to sign when she was leaving and since she had already left, he was forced to sign on her behalf to save himself from possible disciplinary action for lacking vigilance in his work (Ward 1991: 249–51). The receipt was explained as another genuine oversight: he claimed to have accidentally skipped several pages in the receipt book when writing out Julie Ward's receipt, which explained why subsequent payments appeared earlier in the receipt book. This seemed to be yet another fabrication, which, though revealing Nchoko to be at worst, possibly a dishonest gate-keeper who pocketed some of the park's revenues from camping fees, deflected suspicion from the more serious speculation that he may have faked Julie Ward's exit to give the impression that she had left the Mara, because he knew what had happened to her before it became public knowledge. So, both Makallah and Nchoko were able to seize existing ideas about the inefficiency, corruption and dishonesty of civil servants, and African state institutions broadly, and use these to shield themselves from the far worse accusations of complicity in murder. Most importantly, these defences seemed persuasive in the courtroom, based on this already circulating knowledge of what Bayart (2000) calls Africans' 'strategies of extraversion'.

Through the court case, as it unfolded, certain strands of local realities, behaviours and what had come to be accepted as common informal cultural practices in contemporary Kenya were cited and became admissible as legitimate arguments validated by codes of behaviour that have over time been accepted as cultural common senses of the typical postcolonial African state. It is against this background that Nchoko could credibly explain away his overlooking several receipts in the Maasai Mara receipt book as a mere case of forgetting, or at worst petty fraud, a crime which pales into insignificance beside accusations of murder or being an accomplice to murder.

Remarkably, the case further qualified the workings of corruption in two important ways. In a detailed statement explaining his alterations on the postmortem report, Dr Kaviti explained Dr Shaker's sudden departure from the country as related to his allegedly corrupt activities. Dr Kaviti claimed to have received several verbal complaints that the pathologist was illegally charging families of deceased persons additional money to perform autopsies. In response to this situation, he apparently had Dr Shaker transferred to the Police Surgery at the Nairobi Police Headquarters, but soon learnt that he had demanded a bribe from a drunken driver, in exchange for a favourable P3 Medical Examination Report. Once this accusation was allegedly confirmed to be true, Dr Kaviti reportedly intervened by consulting the Director of Criminal Investigations (CID) and getting him to request the court that the case be withdrawn on condition that Dr Shaker left Kenya immediately after and did not seek employment anywhere else in the country. According to Dr Kaviti, this was considerate intervention on his part, as he knew that if convicted, the younger doctor would be imprisoned with no option of a fine. This incident is intriguing, considering the layers of state interventions in the Ward matter. As it turns out, the rhetoric of corruption can be deployed in different permutations to validate different perspectives, including by the state itself. Given Supt Wanjau's subsequent claims that his boss, the Director of the CID ordered him to 'look elsewhere' when his initial investigations pointed towards *Mr B.* as his main suspect (Ward 2012: 42), it is surprising to have this same Director of the CID so concerned about a possible prison sentence for an allegedly corrupt Dr Shaker. Wanjau himself claimed to have been transferred from CID headquarters to a remote office, before being fired with four days' notice, soon after his investigations of the murder, and despite allegedly complying with his boss' orders to make his report point towards suicide. Ward reports that Wanjau refused to sign the Official Secrets Form for confidentiality after being fired, unless the state paid him all his dues. When he applied for a licence to practice as a private detective, Wanjau's application was declined but, as he told Ward, he 'found a way round the problem' (Ward 2012: 43).

It is important to note that corruption was far from an exclusively Kenyan affliction in the case, as Ward was to learn years later, in relation to British complicity in the cover-up, and as we discuss later in the book. But long before this realization, there was an earlier encounter with a corrupt British dentist, whose corruption got unmasked in a most absurd manner: when his daughter's remains were recovered, including her lower jaw, Dr Shaker requested her dental records to determine her identity. Ward went to see his daughter's dentist back in England to request the records. Noting the dentist's nervousness, Ward got suspicious, declined a copy and insisted on the original records. Back in Nairobi, Dr Shaker was able to confirm the worst: that the remains were Julie Ward's. But he had also picked up something else: the tooth fillings on the dental charts did not match the actual fillings on the jaw. The chart showed two additional fillings which were not on the actual teeth, as the teeth in question were clearly healthy. Dr Shaker shrugged this off as possibly an error on the dentist's part, but remembering the dentist's nervous hesitation to hand over the records, Ward wondered whether it was a genuine error: 'Had I inadvertently stumbled on a dental practitioner who was charging the National Health Service for fillings he hadn't performed? If that was the truth, what an incredible way to be caught out!' Ward remarks, in one of a handful of moments of dry humour in his book (Ward 2012: 108).

In sum then, Julie Ward's presence in Kenya and the subsequent quest for her killers was framed within a circulating archive of ideas on Kenya and Africa mapped on a continuum. Primary among these ideas were notions of the pure wilderness, noble savages and, at the other extreme of this continuum, the corrupt African state and its inefficient bureaucracies. The persistence of these ideas in Gavron, Ward and Hiltzik's imaginations, as the lenses through which Africa is interpreted indicates a certain return of the repressed in Euro-American social imaginaries. Despite major transformations in African societies, they continue to be interpreted through these lenses. In this murder case, these ideas lacked relevance in accessing local textualities and the dual universe of what Bayart (2000) calls 'the visible and the invisible' that was at play in Kenya. Where mainstream understandings of African tourism and indeed the colonial archive cast Africans as the spectacle, the object of the gaze, ultimately transparent to the instruments of Western modernity, in reality, they are complex subjects, who have mastered both the gaze that constructs them and the accompanying premises of these constructions, and have been able to navigate their way around Western modernity, as master tricksters, playing hide and seek in the terrain of epistemological disarticulation created at the contact zone between Africa and colonial modernity. But if, as much postcolonial scholarship reiterates, stereotypical perceptions of Africa revealed more about the Euro-American gaze than about Africa, it may be insightful to revisit wildlife tourism, as an important co-ordinate of colonial and postcolonial whiteness in Africa, and to reflect on the ways in which whiteness functioned in the Ward tragedy.

Farms in Africa: 6
Wildlife Tourism, Conservation and Whiteness in Postcolonial Africa

Within the colonial context, the myth of white supremacy legitimized imperial conquest, control and the accompanying privileges. This myth was materially and ideologically sustained by colonial state apparatuses – both repressive and ideological – including the law, the church, schools and colonial administration, all of which policed the boundaries of Mamdani's (1996) citizen–subject axis. Through these apparatuses, the dividends of whiteness were assured, culminating in the accumulation of social, cultural and economic capital, and the entrenchment of white privilege. With the demise of colonial rule, these institutional and ideological infrastructures were largely dismantled. Yet, despite this, as Alfred López (2005: 20) notes, whiteness still presents itself as an aspirational ideal in the postcolonial world, while retaining much of the privilege and prestige it held at the height of colonialism, begging the question: how is whiteness constructed and performed in postcolonial Africa?

In her study *White Women, Race Matters: The Social Construction of Whiteness*, Ruth Frankenberg makes an important observation about the workings of whiteness: 'the material and discursive dimensions of whiteness are always, in practice, interconnected. Discursive repertoires may reinforce, contradict, conceal, explain or 'explain away' the materiality or the history of a given situation' (1993: 2). It is this interaction between the discursive and the material dimensions of whiteness that this chapter seeks to explore, with particular focus on wildlife tourism and conservation. Using the case of two Kenyans who were shot dead by pioneer settler Lord Delamere's great-grandson, Thomas (Tom) Cholmondeley, a 1989 feature film on poaching set in Kenya, *Ivory Hunters*, and the narration of the Julie Ward case in the three books on the case, the chapter examines wildlife, tourism and wildlife conservation as important registers in the performance of certain strands of whiteness in postcolonial Kenya. Our key interest here lies in tracing these discursive tropes of postcolonial whiteness. In what ways do they mirror the tropes of colonial whiteness? To what extent was Julie Ward's presence in Kenya, her death and quest for her killers mapped onto these grids of contemporary constructions of postcolonial whiteness? What tensions and contradictions emerge from the continued deployment of wildlife tourism and conservation in the construction and performance of whiteness in postcolonial Africa?

On 19 April 2005 Tom Cholmondeley shot dead Kenya Wildlife Society (KWS) ranger, Samson ole Sisina on his Soysambu Ranch, which is part of the Delamere Estates in Kenya's Laikipia District. Faced with murder charges, Cholmondeley claimed that he thought ole Sisina was an armed robber. According to a report by the Law Society of Kenya (2007), ole Sisina had gone to the ranch to investigate allegations of illegal trade in game meat on the ranch following a tip off. Ole Sisina was accompanied by fellow KWS rangers Lillian Ochieng Ajuoga and Kushnow Mamo, and they had procedurally logged their mission in the KWS offices. Posing as meat buyers from Nairobi, they were allowed into the ranch.

> At the (Soysambu Ranch) slaughterhouse, Mamo talked to the manager Benson, who informed him that there was no game meat at Soysambu since wildlife cropping had been outlawed ... The KWS crew left the farm. A few metres from the gate, they met a Land-Rover pick-up with about ten occupants. They also saw a buffalo carried in a suspicious manner. Then one man carrying 'matumbo' [tripe] alighted, who identified himself as a guard. He revealed that a white man had killed the buffalo. The KWS crew expressed an interest in the game meat. They were directed to follow the Land Rover that had sped off. ... At the slaughterhouse, they found the buffalo being skinned and it is then that they identified themselves ... and informed the group that they were under arrest. They rounded up the group and handcuffed those who were restless and who in their judgement, might have caused trouble. The manager wanted to inform his boss, Tom (Cholmondeley) about the incident but the KWS crew declined ... Mamo and Lillian stayed in the slaughterhouse with the suspects while ole Sisina kept watch outside. Meantime Lillian and the deceased were communicating despite being separated by a crush ... Lillian saw Tom who was holding a revolver rush towards the slaughterhouse. Tom saw Lillian. Tom is an honorary warden and knows Lillian personally because they had met on many work-related occasions. Lillian informed ole Sisina that Tom was coming and that he was armed. She then heard Tom say words to the effect that 'What is KWS'? Immediately, Tom fired 4 rounds, in rapid succession at the crush where the deceased was. Lillian and Mamo waited in vain for the deceased to enter the slaughterhouse ... Lillian, who was the head of this KWS mission, had not given an order to fire to any of the crew members. Meantime, Mamo and Lillian, who were both lying flat on the floor, repeatedly shouted at the top of their voices the words 'KWS! KWS!' ... Tom then told Lillian and Mamo that he had shot dead one of them ... Immediately, Lillian called her superiors from her mobile to report. Tom ordered that Lillian's phone be taken away. Tom began making calls on his phone saying that he had killed an 'armed robber.' He called three of his security guards who brutally beat up Lillian and Mamo [Law Society of Kenya 2007: 17–19].

I have quoted the report at length because the circumstances surrounding this particular murder are important to our discussion in this chapter. Further, although the case attracted a lot of media attention, the details of the circum-stances were not public knowledge. Charged with murder, Cholmondeley's case was soon struck off as 'the Attorney General entered *nolle prosequi* in the murder charge against Cholmondeley on the basis that there was insufficient evidence to support a murder charge' (ibid. 73). This is the case that reportedly got Director of Public Prosecutions, Phillip Murgor, relieved of his duties (as mentioned in Chapter 1) before he could institute a new task force to investigate the Ward murder.

On 10 May 2006 – little more than a year later – Cholmondeley shot and killed a second man, Robert Njoya Mbugua. According to the 2006/2007 Kenya Human Rights Commission Bi-Annual Report (ibid. 72–74), Cholmondeley was taking an evening stroll in Soysambu Ranch with his friend Carl Tundo when they bumped into Njoya and two other men from a neighbouring village. The three men were carrying a dead impala, which they had caught on one of the snares they had laid on the ranch. Allegedly familiar with Cholmondeley's legendary rage, the three men dropped their catch and fled. While his two colleagues escaped unscathed, Njoya and two dogs were struck and killed by bullets from Cholmondeley's game hunting rifle. Facing his second murder charge, Cholmondeley claimed the men had set their dogs on him and he had shot at the dogs, but accidentally hit Njoya. Cholmondeley got an eight-month jail sentence.

The Cholmondeley killings speak to the Julie Ward murder in ways that il-luminate questions of control and ownership of land and wildlife as important co-ordinates of whiteness in colonial and postcolonial Kenya. Read alongside the Julie Ward case, the three murders raise pertinent issues on postcolonial constructions of whiteness in contemporary Kenya. This chapter argues that this register of whiteness reveals the accentuation of the fascination with wildlife and nature, which, though having its genesis in colonial Kenya, has calcified into a distinct economy of ideas on white identity in postcolonial Kenya. Rob Nixon captures this eloquently when he writes that, alongside other cultural practices that have historically served the purposes of black exclusion, we must add 'the cultures of nature as well, including the culture of wildlife tourism whereby a provincial whiteness is fortified by white pilgrims from abroad' (Nixon 2011: 187).

Land, Wildlife and Whiteness in Post/colonial Kenya

Ruth Frankenberg's (1993: 6) definition of whiteness as 'a set of locations that are historically, socially, politically and culturally produced and ... intrinsically linked to unfolding relations of domination' captures this chapter's interest in whiteness within the postcolonial context in Africa. Tracing its roots back to centuries of sustained construction of white supremacy, whiteness is primarily defined by its invisibility. For Richard Dyer (1997: 1), white claims to a normative position against which all non-whites are measured and found wanting is founded precisely on their assumed 'unraced' status where, as Frankenberg notes, white people often view themselves as non-racial or racially neutral (1993: 1). This claim to normativity in turn masks the social relations that ensue from it and the privileges that accrue to it. For this reason, George Lipsitz emphasizes that although whiteness is a scientific and cultural fiction it is also 'a social fact, an identity created and continued with all-too-real consequences for the distribution of wealth, prestige and opportunity' (2006: vii). This view mirrors Frankenberg's understanding of whiteness as a set of linked dimensions: 'First, whiteness is a location of structural advantage, of race privilege. Second, it is a 'standpoint', a place from which white people look at ourselves, at others and at society. Third, whiteness refers to a set of cultural practices that are usually unmarked and unnamed' (1993: 1). Frankenberg here captures three definitive pillars of whiteness, namely racial privilege, the assumed control of the gaze over others, which simultaneously makes it invisible, and its sustenance through certain cultural practices.

One of the accepted truisms in whiteness studies is that whiteness manifests itself differently in different social, economic, political and cultural contexts. A second truism is that definitions of who is white have historically been unstable, constantly changing, as illustrated by the Irish, Jewish and Afrikaner experiences in Britain, Germany and South Africa respectively. Despite this though, the myth of white supremacy over other races – largely hinged on an axis of proximity to blackness – has been a historical constant, confirming Frankenberg's reminder that whiteness is 'intrinsically linked to relations of domination' (1993: 6). Alongside the relations of inter-racial domination, David Roediger (2000) reminds us of the ingenuity of whiteness in masking intra-racial exploitation. Roediger builds W.E.B. Du Bois' notion of the public and psychological wage of whiteness to remind us of the ways in which among poor white communities in the US, the 'pleasures of whiteness could function as a "wage" for white workers' and be considered to compensate for 'exploitative class relationships' (Roediger 2000: 13). For Du Bois and Roediger, these wages of whiteness blinded white workers to their shared interests with the black poor, and made them accept 'stunted lives for themselves and those more oppressed than themselves' (ibid.), in their continued subscription to the logics of white supremacy.

In her essay, 'Letting the Side Down: Personal Reflections on Colonial and Independent Kenya' (2001), Celia Nyamweru underlines the difference between settler colonies and colonies of administration: 'colonies of administration, of which Ghana and Nigeria are the most significant examples in Africa, were those in which White people never acquired rights to land beyond residential plots … Kenya, on the other hand, was a colony of settlement. From the late 1800s onwards, it was the avowed policy of the British Government to facilitate

White settlement in the cool highland areas' (2001: 171). At the core of Nyamweru's distinction between the two colonial systems lie relationships with land. In settler colonies, control and ownership of prime land was an important coordinate in the construction of white supremacy. This land was alienated from its owners, a process that was discursively mediated by the vacuation of the land as large expanses of empty space without owners, in inadvertent or feigned ignorance of local land use and ownership cultures, which gave the impression of 'unoccupied' land.

Owing to the largely brutal circumstances that historically marked black contact with whiteness, in African imaginaries, whiteness largely remains intimately linked to slavery and colonial domination. Across the continent – South Africa included – what Michael Chege (1998) terms 'white Africans' remains an aspirational identity, which is largely contested; citizenship – e.g. being a Kenyan, Nigerian or South African citizen – and 'Africanness' are yet to be fully considered synonymous.[1] J.M. Coetzee's description of a community which is 'no longer European, not yet African' (1988: 11) remains relevant decades after he made this observation. In Kenya, J.M. Coetzee's description largely resonates for two reasons. First, the white community in Kenya continues to form what Kennedy (1987) terms 'islands of white' in his book of the same title. The white community in Kenya is known for occupying a deceptively isolated position both geographically and politically, primarily visible as tourists, diplomats, expatriates, largely isolate white Kenyans, and as part of the vast humanitarian industry in the region. With the possible exceptions of figures such as Basil Criticos and Richard Leakey, the white community continues to live in its largely-exclusive white enclaves, and is fairly disinterested in venturing into black Kenyan society. Indeed, one may argue that the illusion of multiracial presence in spaces such as the previously white leafy suburbs, elite schools and country clubs dotting all Kenyan towns, while showing the semblance of multiculturalism, in reality embody what bell hooks, in a different context, refers to as 'integration' (1994) of a select few elite black Kenyans into the existing master narrative of whiteness rather than a meaningful transformation. These spaces continue to uphold white cultural normativity. Second, there has been little negotiation of land ownership patterns, and a good percentage of white society in Kenya continues to own huge tracts of land dubiously acquired at the height of British colonial settlement.

It is almost impossible to discuss whiteness in Kenya – both colonial and

---

[1] The notion of 'Africanness' is one that is largely vague and steeped in mythology, which often steers dangerously towards essentialism. At the same time, skin-deep racial differences and African 'reverse racism' aside, white citizenship in Africa is often mediated by selective and strategic embrace of African identity intertwined with tenacious grip on various strands of 'Europeanness', often in form of dual citizenship, both cultural and political.

postcolonial – without making mention of the Delamere family. In itself, this is an indicator of the continuities between colonial and postcolonial whiteness in Kenya, and not entirely on the basis of the family's cross-generational longevity. In fact, the Delamere presence in Kenya in some ways illustrates the continued production of settler colonial whiteness in postcolonial Kenya. As Elspeth Huxley's biographical portrait of the pioneer settler Lord Delamere aptly titled *White Man's Country* presents him, Delamere was one of the architects of Kenya as white man's country.

Land annexation was an important vector of British settlement in Kenya, which was supported by colonial administrative apparatuses. Huge tracts of rich agricultural land were appropriated for settlement by white farmers and the area renamed White Highlands, while the game-rich land in Southern Kenya was converted into game parks and game reserves, turning the original owners – the Maasai community– into what Rob Nixon calls conservation refugees, a people with 'an ancestral history of being territorially dislodged by game lodges and other conservation projects that … created, under the banner of wildlife conservation, dispossessed conservation refugees' (Nixon 2011: 182). Much of this land was turned into white-owned farms, and present-day Tsavo, Amboseli and Maasai Mara Game Reserves, alongside a number of largely white-owned game ranches, including the Delamere Estates.[2] Joshua Hammer writes in his 2006 article on the Cholmondeley killings, aptly titled 'The Kenyan Cowboy':

> The Delameres are the most prominent members of an elite group of landowning families that profited from treaties forced on indigenous tribes by the British colonial government at the turn of the 20th century. Although many whites sold their land to black Kenyans decades ago, a few hundred big land owners who remain continue to live in a bubble of wealth and privilege, even as the vast majority of Kenya's indigenous population is mired in poverty.

Parselelo Kantai captures this situation in his observation: 'The Delamere family owns 50,000 acres in the Rift Valley, in a country where people fight for a quarter of an acre. Their lives are a 1920s fantasy' (cited in Hammer 2006: 4).

In his incisive essay, 'In the Grip of the Vampire State: Maasai Land Struggles in Kenyan Politics' (2007), Parselelo Kantai offers an account of the loss of the Maasai tribal lands to the British colonial administration. The Maasai presented a challenge to British settlement, in part because their legendary reputation as ferocious and war-like had preceded them, raising anxieties about British settlement as they controlled massive stretches of land which lay adjacent to land earmarked for European settlement (Kantai 2007: 108). To solve 'the Maasai

---

[2] See Anderson (2005: 23–31) and Kantai (2007) for discussions of European land seizure in colonial Kenya.

problem', the British persuaded Maasai elders to thumb-print two Anglo-Maasai treaties. In the first treaty of 1904,

> the Maasai had, so the agreement states, willingly ceded their territory in the central Rift Valley to move to two reserves, one to the north of the newly-constructed Kenya–Uganda railway and the other to the south of it. The agreement, the Maasai were assured, would last 'as long as the Maasai existed as a race'. A second agreement made seven years later in 1911 reneged on the earlier assurance. The Maasai were forced to leave the Northern Reserve of Laikipia and settle in an expanded Southern Reserve [Kantai 2007: 107].

According to the Maasai, the second agreement ceded the Laikipia lands to the British for 99 years. The lease expired on 15 August 2005, and on this date, the Maasai community organized demonstrations in Nairobi, demanding their land back. However, the Kenyan government argued that the second agreement ceded the Laikipia lands for 999 years and not 99 years as the Maasai believed. Although the majority of the land in question is in white ownership, successive Kenyan elites have since laid claim to some of this land too.

In *Slow Violence and the Environmentalism of the Poor*, Rob Nixon describes what he terms the racialized ecologies of looking as an 'environmental dynamic between seeing and not seeing, between remembering and forgetting [that] is forcefully exemplified by the game reserve' (2011: 176). He describes the African adventure offered by wildlife tourism to an international, non-African clientele as shielding them from inconvenient interactions with Africans in ahistorical 'free-floating Edenic enclaves … [with the] blended aura of colonial time and prehuman natural time' (ibid.: 181).

In view of the outlined historical context, the Delamere killings were inevitably yoked to the Maasai land struggles in a discourse that questioned the validity of Cholmondeley's ownership of the Delamere Estates, which remain among the most visible chunks of the formerly Maasai-owned Laikipia lands. Three issues are of particular interest for us in this chapter: the tensions between hunting, farming and wildlife conservation in colonial Kenya, the alienation of Maasai land for wildlife conservation, and the postcolonial tourism and wildlife conservation industry. These three issues have their roots in arrangements put in place in colonial Kenya.

Colonial Kenya is often understood to have attracted a particular calibre of British settlers, different from those in other British African colonies such as Rhodesia. In a book titled *Black Poachers, White Hunters: A Social History of Hunting in Colonial Kenya*, Edward Steinhart describes them as wealthy, landed, often aristocratic gentlemen, a good number of whom were hunters who were drawn to Kenya's hunting opportunities, eventually making hunting and sportsmanship 'the chief feature of self-identification of the Kenya settler elite' (2006: 92). Elsewhere, David Anderson explains that while this demographic distinction between Kenya and Rhodesia – its sister British settler colony – is often understood to have been the result of deliberate government policy of excluding poor whites by demanding that new settlers prove economic stability, lest white poverty compromises 'white prestige' in the eyes of Africans, in reality this was partly a result of historical developments as indentured Indian labourers, initially brought in to build the Kenya–Uganda railway, not only outnumbered whites, but had taken up most available artisan positions leaving no room for the growth of a European artisan class as had been the case in Rhodesia (Anderson 2005).

Both Anderson and Steinhart outline the socio-economic texture of pioneer Kenyan settler society and the twin attractions of Kenya to the settler community: farming and hunting. The latter resulted in the popularization of Kenya as the hunter's paradise, which in turn laid the foundation for the subsequent branding of the country as the tourist's paradise – a brand that remains to date. An important figure in the Kenyan settler traditions was the white hunter. Largely affiliated with this settler aristocracy, the white hunter was part of a specific tradition in which hunting, according to the dictates of the English hunt exported to the colony, soon came to form a distinctive register of whiteness, further distinguishing itself from those who hunted for the meat, skin or trophy markets. For these white hunters, who saw themselves as embodying honesty, probity and courageous sportsmanship, '*whiteness would be worn as a badge of honour, distinguishing sporting gentlemen from the lesser breeds outside the law and custom of the hunt* (Steinhart 2006: 132, emphasis added).

Steinhart gives a fascinating exploration of this tension between hunting and farming leading up to the development of a wildlife conservation ethos in Kenya. For him though, one contradiction in this twin pursuit lay in the need to clear tracts of land for cultivation, the need to protect crops and livestock from destruction by marauding herds of wildlife, and the need for wildlife conservation. Tracing the history of hunting and conservation discourse in Kenya from colonial to postcolonial Kenya, and drawing on the auto/biographies of various pioneer settlers and hunters, Steinhart notes that settler destruction of wildlife habitat for purposes of farming, coupled with intense predation and trade in game products made white settlement the main driver of decline in game numbers in the early twentieth century (2006: 98). Yet poaching in Kenya has historically been framed as a black affair. Steinhart's thinking rhymes with Rob Nixon's observation that colonial conservationist mythology considers slaughter of wildlife by rural Africans to be the cause of decimation of game, yet historically the real factor was 'an imported European ethos of killing as an ennobling sport' using advanced weaponry that deflected hunting from the more-sustainable subsistence need for protein and hide clothing (Nixon 2011: 189–90).

When it eventually took root, the ethos of wildlife conservation largely excluded the local communities living near these conservation areas, especially the Maasai, the Waata and the Kamba. In many ways, this may have been a spin-off result of the privileging of sport hunting and the denigration of subsistence hunting in keeping with the dictates of the white hunter tradition. Predictably, Steinhart notes, African conservation approaches and methods were totally ignored in the emergent game conservation enterprise. In a bizarre twist, Africans soon found themselves being treated as the prime suspects in poaching, while wildlife conservation remains whitened, an ethos captured in the title of Steinhart's book, *Black Poachers, White Hunters*. This discourse laid the foundation for the appropriation of wildlife conservation as an important cultural practice of whiteness. This history outlines the construction of the hunting safari and later wildlife photography, wildlife safari and conservation as white cultural practices in Kenya.

These discursive practices were continued in postcolonial Kenya, further deepened by the profiling of Kenya as a prime wildlife tourist destination for international markets. The fascination with wildlife watching and wildlife tourism in Africa has historically been constructed as a white preoccupation. At the core of wildlife tourism, lies what Steinhart describes as 'the mystical oxymoron of safe-danger' (2006: 132).

The tourism industry in Kenya is officially touted as one of the key drivers of the country's economy. In popular imaginaries, however, the figure of the tourist is associated with whiteness, wealth and privilege. Indeed, in Kenya, as in many parts of Africa, wildlife tourism lay at the core of colonial leisure, and despite the gradual emergence of the black wildlife tourist, it remains embedded in a white cultural bedrock.[3] Will Jackson underlines the continuities and discontinuities in Kenyan tourism cultures, with the 1920s travel writers and white hunters' legacies remaining discernible in contemporary white writing and power relations remaining entrenched while the key players' biographies and worldviews change over time (Jackson 2011b: 346).

Despite the official promotion of the tourism industry in Kenya, there is bitter resentment towards tourists among the local populations living near key game reserves. This resentment is based on, among other things, perceptions of tourist arrogance and of preferential treatment of tourists, and feelings of exclusion from the economic gains of the tourism industry. John Akama for instance writes that the Maasai incur the social and environmental costs of tourism development and wildlife conservation in addition to ceding land they would otherwise use for agricultural production, but 'insignificant amounts of the country's tourism receipts trickle to the Maasai in areas adjacent to the

---

[3] See for instance Njabulo Ndebele's 'Game Lodges and Leisure Colonialists: Caught in the Process of Becoming' (1999) for a fascinating reflection on wildlife tourism and black tourists' encounters with it.

attractions' (1999b: 716). A Maasai elder Nkonina Songoi candidly captures this resentment of tourists and the tourism industry broadly:

> Tourists pass here constantly from one park to another. We have no relationship with them. They come and leave, knowing nothing of us. If someone is dying by the road, they don't stop. They knock down calves and goats and don't stop. These people must be human. It's our land they cross to get to the park. Surely they must stop and talk to us if they kill an animal. [In addition] wildlife coming off the parks – particularly Amboseli – are all over our land now. They don't ask permission. But if we cross into the park, with our cattle, the Rangers chase us out with Land Rovers and helicopters [Sayer 1998: 60].

To a large degree, the postcolonial tourism and wildlife conservation industry continues the exploitative relationship set in place in colonial Kenya, most visibly in the manner in which Maasai participation is confined to the very bottom of the food chain, as curio vendors, traditional dancers and photographic subjects.

In view of this history, the two Delamere killings – both of which evoked the question of poaching and game conservation – the concern with poaching in Kenya in the film *Ivory Hunters*, and the framing of the Julie Ward death along discourses of wildlife tourism and conservation speak to each other in ways that surface the mobilization of wildlife and conservation as an important vector in postcolonial whiteness. However, it is a vector which has been unable to, or disinterested in, shedding the cloak of contradictions and tensions embedded in the formation of settler Kenya as 'white man's country'. This is the background against which we read wildlife tourism and conservation as white cultural practices in the film, *Ivory Hunters*, the Cholmondeley killings and the Julie Ward case.

Poachers and Murderers: *Ivory Hunters* and the Cholmondeley Killings

An important clue to understanding whiteness as a constructed cultural hegemon lies in the fact that empire 'was an act, a theatrical performance staged before a captive audience of millions of colonized subjects' (Steinhart 2006: 209 citing Cannadine 2001) or, as Alfred López puts it, understanding 'the power of whiteness as contingent upon a performance of white power' (2005: 13). This observation' speaks to James Scott's idea of the importance of public transcripts in the maintenance of hegemonic power. As he reminds us, 'if subordination requires a credible performance of humility and deference, so domination seems to require a credible performance of haughtiness and mastery' (1990: 11).[4] One

---

[4] George Orwell's 'Shooting an Elephant' (1950) is an excellent illustration of this pressure of performing mastery that attached to colonial whiteness, in the context of colonial Burma.

medium that has repeatedly lent itself to the construction and performance of whiteness across the world is film. The film *Ivory Hunters*, released a year after Julie Ward's death in Kenya continued this tried and tested tradition in the construction of whiteness in Africa.

Alongside its reputation as a wildlife tourism paradise, Kenya also enjoys a reputation as a preferred destination for wildlife conservation. Over the years, Kenya has produced dozens of conservationists and attracted an array of wildlife conservation projects and ranch-owning game farmers. Among the better-known figures are Joy and George Adamson of the Born Free Foundation and Kuki Gallman of the Gallman Foundation. The three conservationists' work gained greater publicity through wildlife documentaries and feature films set in Kenya, one of the better-known ones being Adamson's *Born Free* (1966) that tells the story of Elsa an orphaned lioness cub that the Adamsons rescue from the wilds and nurse to adulthood. Kuki Gallman's feature film, *I Dreamed of Africa* (2000) is an autobiographical narrative about her life in Kenya and her involvement in wildlife conservation. *Ivory Hunters* is therefore a continuation of a distinct, well-developed film genre in Kenya, which tells the narrative of white involvement in wildlife conservation. Over time, the white wildlife conservationist has grown into a stock figure in Kenyan white society: the white hunter reincarnate. Dr Maria Edmonson, a zoologist based in a game reserve in Kenya in *Ivory Hunters*, is moulded around such a figure, a fictional version of Kuki Gallman or Joy Adamson.

Ivory Hunters' Maria Edmonson is passionate about wildlife conservation, and particularly, protecting the elephant from imminent extinction through poaching. Liz Page, an American research assistant to an American novelist Robert Carter, travels to Kenya, and goes to the game reserve to do research for Carter's next novel about the poaching industry. Liz goes on a game drive and in the process she accidentally stumbles upon elephant poachers in the act and takes their photographs. The poachers notice and capture her. Liz disappears for a few days, as her host, Maria, and the writer, Rob Carter, search all over for her. Days later, her mutilated body is recovered. This murder is followed by a long search for her killers, and their eventual arrest, with the assistance of the novelist – now turned conservationist – and Maria.

Liz Page's murder in the film echoes aspects of the Julie Ward case. Liz's trip to the game reserve and her murder as she photographs elephants echoes Julie Ward's trip to Maasai Mara and her interest in wildlife photography. Further, the narrative in *Ivory Hunters* strongly echoes speculation about the circumstances surrounding the Julie Ward death and the possibility that she may have stumbled across poachers in the vast Maasai Mara Game Reserve. These close parallels and allusions to the circumstances surrounding Julie Ward's death make the film an interesting text for our study. Despite the vast differences in narrative and the fiction-fact divide between the murders of Julie Ward and Liz

Page, it is an important text in making visible what Gillian Whitlock calls 'a paradigmatic circuitry' (2000: 116) that may shed light on our understandings of postcolonial whiteness.

In *Ivory Hunters*, after Liz's disappearance, subsequent murder and the finding of the photographs of her murderers, Maria and the novelist, Carter, join hands with the local police in their hunt for the poachers. The Kenyan police, having failed to catch the poachers, who are decimating elephants at an alarming rate, decide to use captured ivory as bait, through Carter, who pretends to have turned from writing to implementing the narrative of his upcoming novel, by actually doing what his protagonist in the novel does: stealing captured ivory from a warehouse in Mombasa. He therefore persuades the poachers to team up with him and steal this ivory. The poachers buy into this idea and are eventually caught and stand trial for murder and poaching.

Although the idea of baiting the poachers with captured ivory is initially conceived by the Kenyan Commissioner of Police, the ultimate victory belongs to Carter, to whom the film grants agency, as the Kenyan police are portrayed as having been hitherto incapable of meaningful interventions in breaking the poaching ring. The film evokes the Christian missionary interventions of earlier times. Underpinning this messianic intervention is a scripting of a proactive whiteness which stands in contrast with African helplessness. In the film, Liz Page literally lays down her life in an attempt to protect the elephants; later, Carter risks his life as he sets the trap to catch the poachers, since, if they catch on to his mission, they will kill him too.

The trope of messianic intervention in African crises in the film speaks to what López describes as 'the self-sacrificing, self-destructing white male rebel as a trope of the new postcolonial whiteness, a paradoxically self-serving figure who would allow whites to retain their central status as 'emancipators' and thus their power and privilege' (López 2005: 22). Citing Richard Dyer, López underscores the ways in which white subjects adopt a distancing mechanism that sustains a wilful blindness that sustains white cultural hegemony and the '"exquisite agony" of white liberal guilt [which] appeals to the other's capacity for orderly dissent while surrendering little of its own entrenched privilege' (ibid,: 22–23). López' and Dyer's ideas underscore the mobilization of the messianic figure of the white wo/man in the construction of postcolonial whiteness, and its continued maintenance of the privileges that accrue from whiteness, at a time when colonial myths of white supremacy and black subordination are no longer viable. This figure of the white messiah is an example of the new grammars of postcolonial whiteness, which re-invent the colonial missionary grammar, and to that end retains the notion of Africans' lack of initiative, and their need for redemption.

This messianic figure in *Ivory Hunters* stands in contrast with the two Cholmondeley killings, in which wildlife feature prominently. The paradox in the case over the protection of wildlife would seem to reduce it to a question of contested ownership of the wildlife in Soysambu Ranch. In the first incident, Cholmondeley shoots dead a KWS warden who was in the process of arresting his employees on charges of illegal trade in game meat, seemingly with Cholmondeley's full knowledge. In the second incident, he kills a man for poaching impala on his ranch.[5] At the core of this conflict seemed to be the old question of ownership of wildlife. This is an issue that has haunted wildlife conservation in Kenya since colonial times (Steinhart 2006: 212–14). For KWS spokesperson Connie Maina, 'all the wildlife in the country belongs to the government and KWS is the custodian. You have to go with what is the law, but Tom Cholmondeley made his own rules' (quoted in Hammer 2006: 6).

In both *Ivory Hunters* and the Cholmondeley killings, the master narrative of wildlife conservation represents an important platform for the performance of whiteness in postcolonial Kenya. Like the white hunter described by Steinhart above, in postcolonial Kenya the white conservationists too would seem to wear their whiteness as a badge of honour, now distinguishing animal conservationists from poachers. Thus, in *Ivory Hunters*, Maria with her doctoral degree and her sensitive passion for conservation, would seem to have inherited the mantle of whiteness from the white hunter, as she epitomizes animal conservation as an important marker of contemporary whiteness in which, as Whitlock writes in a different context, 'humane feelings towards animals [are] associated with an enlightened view and a revolution in perceptions of relations between human and animal worlds' (2000: 136). On the opposite extreme are the poachers, who, in both *Ivory Hunters* and the Cholmondeley killings, are associated with blackness – a reversal of roles when read against settler history in Kenya and the extermination of wildlife.

Ivory Hunters further speaks to the contradictions inherent in the modernity – savagery nexus that remains at the core of constructions of white subjectivities and their relationship with wildlife tourism in Africa. This is more so in view of Donna Harraway's reminder about 'nature's discursive construction as "Other" in histories of colonialism, racism, sexism and class domination' (1992: 296).

---

[5] Joshua Hammer's 'The Kenyan Cowboy' sheds some light on the conflict between Cholmondeley and the KWS:

In November 2003, the KWS banned the practice of animal culling on the country's private ranches, claiming that the existing programme – in which ranchers were permitted to shoot a small amount of their wildlife each year to prevent overgrazing and other environmental damage – was poorly controlled and that many ranchers were cheating. Connie Maina, the KWS spokesperson, told me, 'The system was being abused and ignored, and the numbers of zebra, gazelles, and buffalo were dropping fast'. Cholmondeley allegedly ignored the KWS prohibitions, claiming they were hurting the ranch's cattle … Cholmondeley had been appointed an honorary game warden by the KWS in the nineties, and he and fellow ranchers claimed that he had the right to shoot wild animals that he deemed a threat to his property, his cattle, or his staff (2006: 6).

She underlines the tensions that lay at the core of wildlife tourism's fascination with 'safe danger', which in many ways replicates colonialism's ambivalent construction of the Other as at once an object of desire and derision (Bhabha 1983: 19). The contradiction in Julie Ward's death, as in *Ivory Hunters*, lies in the intersection between fascination with the wild, and the simultaneous construction of Africans as both living outside modernity and defiled by an aborted modernity. This contradiction illustrates the tensions that beset constructions of postcolonial whiteness using discursive tools curved out of colonial whiteness. But how did Julie Ward's presence, death and the subsequent quest for her killers as narrated in the three books speak to these discourses?

Julie Ward and Postcolonial Whiteness in Kenya

Ivory Hunters' narrative reveals postcolonial whiteness to be preoccupied with the contradictions of modernity's claim to progress and civilization at the expense of the moral duty of protecting nature for posterity. To some degree, the film enacts a certain battle of conscience, a performed atonement for the destructive effects of modernity, which has created networks of markets for ivory. Yet while interrogating the destructive aspects of modernity, this performed battle of conscience simultaneously clings to the privileges afforded white characters by modernity. In the film then, we see the deployment of Africa as a discursive terrain for dramatizing postcolonial whiteness and its challenges. Whitlock notes this discursive capacity of Africa, in this case Kenya as a useable terrain for articulating these concerns: 'the natural environment [in Kenya] is particularly responsive to very different kinds of intellectual and physical uses of Africa for the West: on the one hand, the plains and the highlands, the vegetation and the variety of wild animals available for romantic visions of the loss or discovery of an essential life in nature (2000: 113–14).

In her analysis of settler fiction in Kenya, Elsie Cloete describes the pervasive representation of Kenya as an idyllic land, often captured in the 'sense of landscape, location and space untrammelled by Europe's urban congestion' (2002: 9). Simon Gikandi (1984), too, notes that settler fiction celebrated the land as a dual icon of a wilderness to be tamed and conquered through modern agricultural technology and an eroticized landscape that appears like a work of art and promises healing and rejuvenation.[6] These readings allowed African landscapes to be constructed as Edenic wildernesses endowed with a certain

---

[6] Anne McClintock makes a similar argument in her discussion of what she terms 'porno-tropics'. As she writes: 'renaissance travellers found an eager and lascivious audience for their spicy tales, so that, long before the era of high Victorian imperialism, Africa and the Americas had become what can be called a porno-tropics for the European imagination – a fantastic magic lantern of the mind onto which Europe projected its forbidden sexual desires and fears' (1995: 22).

savage innocence and beauty for which the fast-modernizing West yearned as a rejuvenating breath of primordial purity and tranquillity. Yet, as David Dunn cautions, this primordial object of desire was also a source of significant fear, in part rooted in the feminizing tropes through which the continent was understood: 'Africa, once feminized, becomes the object of the male gaze: she promises rewards to the hardy adventurer, yet she has a dark side that [is] lexically associated with primal ooze, fluids and menstruation' (Dunn 1988: 12).

A similar yearning persists in contemporary tourism in the case of Africa. Tom Selwyn points out that contemporary tourists often seek 'cognitively to create or recreate structures which modernity is felt to have demolished' (1996: 2). A similar logic emerges in the books describing Julie Ward's visit to Kenya. Contemplating the Maasai Mara landscape in *A Death in Kenya*, Michael Hiltzik laments the desecration of the once-authentic primordial jungle that was the Mara, by the trappings of modernity.

> For all its fame, Maasai Mara is not exactly the place to contemplate nature in an atmosphere of serenity. The songs of hundreds of species of birds are often drowned out by the engine drone of aircraft … It might even be true that some of the romance of seeing the wild animals in their natural habitat has been drained away by the Mara animals' easy familiarity with humans and their green tour vehicles [1991: 70].

These notions of purity, pure savagery and wilderness unpolluted by modernity which lie at the core of African tourism can be traced back to the colonial era, where figures such as the white hunter and safari were an important part of the colonial leisure repertoire. This repertoire mediated colonial knowledge of the people, wildlife and landscape of Kenya, which the tourists were seen to be best placed to negotiate, photograph and describe. Travel and settler fiction writers such as Karen Blixen, Robert Ruark and Elspeth Huxley played an important role in the construction of this archive and, with time, helped to define and construct Kenya as a tourist destination.[7]

While tropes of exoticism and the purity of nature owe their genesis to settler representations of Africa, they have continued to be produced in postcolonial Africa as part of the commodification of African countries as tourist destinations. Tourism, an industry which primarily thrives on the admiring foreign gaze, has been a core contributor to the economies of many African states for a long time. In Kenya, there has been sustained marketing of the country as a tourist destination, a process that has coded the beaches, wildlife, cultural artefacts and various ethnic groups into the recognizable brand of 'tourist Kenya'. Wildlife tourism represents another face of postcolonial whiteness in Kenya,

---

[7] See particularly Karen Blixen's *Out of Africa* (1937), Robert Ruark's *Uhuru* (1962) and Elspeth Huxley's *The Flame Trees of Thika: Memories of an African Childhood* (1959).

which rubs shoulders with wildlife conservation. Indeed, the two feed off each other and are largely mutually sustaining. The archive of tourist discourses about Kenya and Africa framed Julie Ward's presence in the Maasai Mara.

When she left Britain for Kenya on her first trip to Africa, Julie Ward told her parents she was going to Africa 'to photograph the Jumbos' (Ward 1991: 23). On her third and last trip to the continent, Julie Ward was part of an overland trip from England, across the Sahara desert, down through central Africa, into Kenya. As a tourist, she was positioned within this web of ideas about tourist Africa, a positioning that Jeremy Gavron (1991) and Michael Hiltzik (1991) reproduce in their reconstruction of her last trip to Africa. In the opening chapter of his book, Gavron describes Maasai Mara thus:

> The Maasai Mara National Reserve lies towards the south-west corner of Kenya, just one hundred and twenty miles, but a different world from the capital, Nairobi. Its high grass plains and shimmering hills, freckled with flat-topped acacia trees, have hardly changed, tourist lodges and prowling prides of Land Rovers and mini-buses apart, for a thousand years. During the day, a multitude of creatures – wildebeest, zebra, giraffe, elephant, lion, cheetah – swelter beneath the high, equatorial sun and a vast blue sky that seems to stretch up for ever. On moonless nights, the darkness is so absolute that whole galaxies invisible in the European sky wink and glitter like dust caught in a distant shaft of light [1991: 1].

In this opening paragraph of his novel, Gavron sets in place the lens of his Edenic Africa. This Africa retains a certain purity, undamaged by the modernity which seems to have clogged European skies.

A similar template is evident in Hiltzik's description of the Maasai Mara as 'this place of primordial natural savagery' (1991: 4), a description that draws on a distinct lexicon in the grammar of African tourism. Hiltzik goes on to describe the impact of Africa on Julie Ward upon return from her first two trips to the continent:

> [Julie] packed the camera gear … and went off to photograph animals in the best place on earth to see them: Kenya. When she came back to work a few weeks later, Rowland [Julie's boss] could not help noticing something different. There was a new glow in her eyes, as if she had discovered a new possibility in life. A year later, she took a second trip to Kenya, and this time she seemed entirely changed. 'By the time she came back from that trip' Rowland said later 'her heart was there. She had just fallen in love with it' [ibid.: 15].

From her experience, Kenya and Africa live up to the rejuvenating, healing power associated with it in colonial/settler literature and which remains an important attraction in postcolonial tourism. The landscape and wildlife seem to revitalize Julie Ward, putting a new glow in her eyes and opening up new horizons of possibilities in life. As her father observes, 'Muff returned with a million magic memories of wild, remote places where at night huge stars hang low and bright in an unpolluted sky. A few of those stars stayed in her eyes' (cited in Buckley 1998: n.p.).

Hiltzik describes Africa as having 'a way of beckoning, unseen but deep in the spirit, to those given to wanderlust' (1991: 16), thereby lending the continent a spiritual mysticism, to which, he suggests, many have yielded. He gives us a roll-call, starting from Mungo Park, David Livingstone and Henry Stanley and coming down to the owner of Hobo Trans-Africa Expeditions, who organized the overland trip on which Julie Ward came to Africa, Jo Jordan. Jordan 'heard the beckoning' after completing her solicitor's training. Mystical Africa lived up to her legendary reputation and rescued Jordan from a monotonous career that 'stretched towards infinity' (ibid.).

Imaginings of Africa as an exotic landscape with this revitalizing power sit side by side with another set of representations: Africa: the crisis-ridden continent. The two represent two sides of the same jungle: Africa the tourist's paradise, boasting a broad range of wildlife, spectacular landscapes and exotic cultural practices on the one hand, and Africa the crisis-ridden jungle teeming with disease, poverty, violence and corruption, epitomized by the failed postcolonial state on the other. The two imaginings of Africa are separated by a thin wall, which frames them as belonging to two different planes of experience: the Edenic paradise reserved for the pleasure of an elite, predominantly white tourist market, and the crisis-ridden jungle is the preserve of underprivileged locals.

In the light of this, Julie Ward's violent death in the Maasai Mara Game Reserve constituted a discursive rupture. Ward's death crumbled the discursive edifice which clearly distinguishes the tourist as the acting subject and sampler of exotic pleasures, a script which excludes the possibility of violent death in a game reserve. In the mysterious murder, coupled with the various state institutions' poorly concealed attempts to sabotage the search for the killers, the two jungles – normally separated by a fairly rigid wall – were crudely conflated. The Garden of Eden had been defiled.

The title of Jeremy Gavron's *Darkness in Eden* succinctly captures this defilement of the innocence and beauty of tourist Kenya, by the callous murder of an innocent woman. By covering this Eden with darkness, Gavron captures the sense of rupture that Julie Ward's death in this primordial site represented. In this fall from grace, Africa relapses into the white wo/man's grave trope, ironically not from tropical diseases and equatorial heat – which modernity has successfully conquered – but at the hands of callous locals[8] in a rogue postcolonial state.

---

[8] P.D. Curtin (1961) describes the 'the white man's grave' as including the '"primitive tribes", burning heat, fever-laden swamps, swarming insects and miles of trackless jungle' associated

Describing his stay at Keekorok Lodge in Maasai Mara on the night of the day his daughter's remains were found, Ward writes:

> I was in the farthest room from the lodge restaurant, across the large lawn. A native show was on that night and drums beat continually. Dancers with spears and painted faces stamped and pranced to the rhythm. Out beyond the lights, loud across the bush came the sound of animals as they snarled, roared and screamed through the darkness. To me, the sounds were like some primitive prehistoric hell on earth. How I loathed that place [Ward 1991: 85].

Ward's loathing for the wilderness that had hitherto been eroticized, and which had attracted his daughter to Kenya and the Maasai Mara in the first place, is striking. Similarly notable are the audible echoes of Joseph Conrad's *Heart of Darkness*. The continuities between 'prancing' and 'stamping' natives, with the snarling, roaring and screaming wildlife just 'beyond the lights' in the bush is suggestive. But most interestingly, albeit inadvertently, Ward here captures the defilement of this Edenic tourist paradise. Yet at the same time, at the core of his book – itself a monument to his daughter's memory – and all the other tributes to Julie Ward's memory, lay the idea of wildlife conservation and protection, coupled with the idea of the vulnerability of wildlife and white women to black male violence, as Whitlock (2000) notes.

In the discourse of wildlife conservation, twined with the vulnerability of the white woman, we begin to understand John Ward's framing of his text *The Animals are Innocent*, in ways that foreground Julie Ward's love for wild animals. This is captured in the iconic picture of the Julie Ward case, with Julie Ward hugging an orphaned baby chimpanzee at an animal orphanage in Zaire. By selecting this as the emblematic photo of Julie Ward after her death, Ward underscores a shared vulnerability to black violence,[9] which Gavron further underlines by juxtaposing 'the innocence of the animals and the white woman, over and against the preparedness of black men to slaughter both' (Whitlock 2000: 115) by drawing parallels between the 1988 burning of ivory that Gavron describes, with the burning of Julie Ward's remains in the wilderness. Whitlock writes: 'the burning of the tusks episode in *Darkness in Eden* further harkens back to Gavron's graphic reconstruction of the burning of Julie Ward's body in the Maasai Mara by her killers, and so develops a further association between

with West and Central Africa. In our case, Julie Ward's killers were not profiled in the trope of primitive tribes *per se*, but in terms of a modern variant of the primitive tribes' violence.

[9] This pairing of both the white woman and wild animals as victims of the black man's violence can be traced further back to the writing of Robert Ruark on colonial Kenya. In *Uhuru* for instance, Ruark juxtaposes what he sees as African violence against animals – captured in the Mau Mau's oathing ceremonies, in which domestic animals are brutally killed – with their violence against white women, as seen in the decapitation of Katie Crane, an American tourist.

the woman and the wildlife as victims' (2000: 115). Incidentally, the burning of the ivory scene also emerges in *Ivory Hunters*, with similar echoes, as it reminds us of the cold-blooded butchering of the elephants and the research assistant in a callous spray of bullets. Like Gavron, *Ivory Hunters* presents the white woman and wildlife as equally susceptible to the same kind of (black male) violence.

It is unsurprising that the memorials to Julie Ward's life all had the theme of wildlife conservation at their core. Among these was the coffee-table book of pictures of wildlife that she had taken on her last trip to Kenya and her letters to her family, as she travelled across the continent towards Kenya. The book, meaningfully titled *Julie Ward: Gentle Nature*, is published by the Born Free Foundation and proceeds of the book went towards the creation of a lion sanctuary in Uganda as a memorial to Julie Ward. Her jeep was 'converted into an open-top with her name on the side and donated to the Gallman Memorial Foundation ... which provides sanctuary for wildlife' (Buckley, n.p.). The book remains a powerful expression of the vacuating gaze discussed above, in a sense, a fitting sequel to John Ward's equally loaded *The Animals are Innocent*. The privileging of wildlife in all the monuments to Julie Ward's memory was consistent with the selective gaze that mediates the practices of African tourism, which deploys a vacuating gaze that only picks up wildlife, wilderness and 'noble savages'.

If the enlightenment project and broadly Western modernity implied containment, discipline and boundary erection, then this was fissured in Africa's wilderness by the supposedly aggressive masculinity of the black man. For Anne McClintock, British imperial conquest entailed 'the feminizing of terra incognita [which] was, from the outset, a strategy of violent containment' (1995: 24). As she writes 'land is named as female as a passive counterpart to the massive thrust of male technology (ibid.: 26). These dynamics of white male authority would appear to play themselves out in the Julie Ward case, *Ivory Hunters* and the Cholmondeley killings. Read alongside each other, this set of texts further seem to point towards contestations between white male authority and the black male criminal – whether in the shape of Cholmondeley's and Carter's poachers, Ward's murderers or the Kenyan state's corrupt politicians. Given the shared vulnerability of white women and wildlife to black male violence, one question that suggests itself is whether these texts point towards the inauguration of the black male criminal as the black rapist reincarnate, in much the same way as the white (woman) conservationist emerges as the white hunter reincarnate.

Rob Nixon observes that 'the cultural spectacle around African Edens has a strongly masculine tilt: the white game guides, the black trackers, the bush pilots all carry forward – adapted for the contemporary global marketplace – a neo-Victorian obsession with risk (or at least with saleable performance of risk's illusions)' 2011: 186). In similar vein, the figures of white male authority suggest the possibility of postcolonial whiteness in Kenya being preoccupied with the re-insertion of white male authority. It is notable that the three sets of narratives – books on Julie Ward's death, *Ivory Hunters* and the Cholmondeley killings – all seem to figure white men engaged in a struggle with black men over wildlife and white women. Apart from the fact that all the three books on the Julie Ward murder are written by white men, her father stood at the forefront of the quest for truth and justice, and found himself taking on a predominantly black male Kenyan state infrastructure. Similarly, in *Ivory Hunters*, Robert Carter is the one to take on the black male poachers, while the Cholmondeley killings would seem to have been as much about wildlife as about the contestation for authority between the white male Cholmondeley, the black Kenyan poachers, and KWS. But it is the later institution that draws interesting links across the three sets of narratives, primarily in the figure of another white male Kenyan, Richard Leakey.

In a curious, yet telling coincidence, both Gavron and Hiltzik close their books on the Julie Ward case by lingering on the appointment of Richard Leakey as the head of the KWS. The two reveal strong optimism in Leakey's capacity to bring back stability to the chaos and rupture of the tourism industry illustrated by the mutual vulnerability of white women and wildlife to black male violence. Less than a decade later, the Moi government appointed Richard Leakey the head of civil service. Commenting on this, Apollo Amoko (1999) notes the paternalist representation of Leakey as Kenya's messiah in British media.

On the whole, wildlife tourism and conservation emerges as an important platform for the performance of whiteness in postcolonial Kenya, yet this register has failed to break away from its colonial roots, which were mired in tensions and contradictions that were later to haunt the Julie Ward case. Further, as our discussion reveals, this postcolonial whiteness in Kenya remains a highly gendered one, at the heart of which lies a nostalgic struggle to affirm and restore a white male authority reminiscent of that of the settler colony.

The one dimension of the Julie Ward death and the subsequent quest for truth that has remained under-scrutinized by media reports and the three books on the matter is the official British involvement in her family's search for the truth and justice. The Kenyan police's attempts to frame the death as accidental overwhelmingly focused both media and public attention on the Kenyan state actors and their attempt to conceal the truth. By implication, Britain was, for years, assumed to naturally support the quest for the truth in the matter. Britain's quiet and non-sensational involvement in the case reinforced this assumption, enabling it to go unexamined. Yet, on hindsight, there were several instances when the conduct of the British High Commission in Nairobi and the Foreign and Commonwealth Office in London invited more questions than were asked at the time.

In this chapter, I invert this focus on the Kenyan state institutions, by examining the nature of official British involvement in the search for the truth behind Julie Ward's death. Through a reading of John Ward's *The Animals are Innocent*, John le Carré's *The Constant Gardener*, and news articles drawn from Kenyan and British print media, the chapter reflects on the configurations of the official British interventions in the case. In his investigations, as documented in *The Animals are Innocent*, John Ward perceived British institutions and officials as honest, professional and committed to justice, in sharp contrast with Kenyan officialdom's unprofessionalism and lack of integrity. In this chapter, I hope to illustrate that these assumptions, though founded on his experiences with Kenyan and British officialdom in the course of his investigations, blinded Ward to the subterranean fault lines of competing interests in the official British involvement in the quest for his daughter's killers. By reading Ward's account of the quest for his daughter's killers alongside a fictional account of a similar quest in le Carré's novel *The Constant Gardener*, and the subsequent revelation of British complicity in the cover-up of the truth behind Julie Ward's death, I hope to illustrate that, contrary to Ward's belief, and indeed, popular wisdom about British moral integrity and commitment to justice as opposed to the failings of the Kenyan officialdom, there were underlying fault lines that suggest continuities and complicities between Kenya and Britain in the cover-up. These fault lines unmasked the contradictions embedded in Ward's assumptions about Kenya and Britain. They also urge us to question the notion of the unity of the subject, in the unstated assumption that Britain was a monolithic entity bound by the same ethical codes, empathy, moralities and uncompromising desire for justice. The chapter hopes to show that these binary lenses – often articulated through notions of Europe's commitment to justice and human rights as contrasted with postcolonial African states' abuse of these – work to mask the intersections between the two, marked by complicities largely mediated by the interests of capital, which fracture the myth of Europe's moral authority sanctioned by a value-neutral progress through modernity.

Binary Lenses in John Ward's *The Animals are Innocent*

John Ward's personal account in *The Animals are Innocent: The Search for Julie's Killers* constructs a set of binary lenses that sharply polarize Kenyan and British state institutions. In constructing this polarity, Ward's account departs from certain assumptions which he propagates throughout the book.

In his preface to the book, John Ward says that many people have asked why he wrote it. In response, he explains that firstly, he 'wanted the true story of Julie and her terrible murder to be recorded', because in the aftermath, the truth 'has been enveloped in lies and corruption' (1991: xix). Ward's second reason for writing the book is the hope that it will be a warning.

> Kenya is a dangerous place. I am continually contacted by distraught and angry relatives of tourists who have been murdered, attacked, robbed or have completely disappeared ... 'Why didn't someone warn us it was dangerous? And why can't we get any information from the Kenyans about what happened?' ... If something goes wrong – you're on your own. *The Kenyans complain, 'why pick on us? Tourists sometimes get murdered in New York or London.' This is true but the difference is that in those cities, the authorities will not try to sweep the murder under the carpet* [1991: xix–xx, emphasis added].

Ward's resentment of Kenya is evident from his preface, which provides a fitting introductory frame to his polarization of the Kenyan cover-up against what he sees as British commitment to truth and justice. At the time of writing this, Ward was convinced that the attempt to 'sweep the murder under the carpet' was a Kenyan affair in its entirety. This polarity recurs throughout the book.

While the subject of the book – the grisly murder of the author's young daughter, and consistent attempts by Kenyans to undermine his search for answers – would provoke anger and resentment in anyone, Ward tells us that his dislike for Kenya develops on his very first visit to the country, immediately after his daughter goes missing, but before her fate is known. Ward describes his first encounter:

> Africa, Africa, Africa. I believe that if I were to be blindfolded and deposited anywhere on this earth, I'd know instantly if I were in Africa. *The sounds, smells, the*

'feel' of the continent that bombard the senses trigger in me a wary unease and, as always, I'd want to leave again as soon as possible. I don't like being in Africa. So much is
beyond my understanding. I'm sure this sensation of foreboding is not induced entirely
by my experiences [1991: 45, emphasis added].

On his first visit to Kenya, Ward collapses the entire continent under a homogeneous blanket of smells, sounds and opaqueness all of which make him
uneasy. As the book is written after the tragedy, it is possible to argue that this
memory of his first day in Kenya is inevitably tinted by rage and grief. But Ward
underlines that this 'sensation of foreboding' was not induced by his experiences. He seems to ascribe an inherently perilous status to the continent, which,
as a first-time visitor, he intuitively senses, and the subsequent discovery that
his daughter has been brutally murdered merely confirms his intuition. In this,
Ward draws on the semantics of preconceived ideas about the strangeness of
Africa and its opaqueness to the familiar, normative 'rational' tools of knowing/
understanding a place available to a non-African.

The subsequent tragedy of his daughter's death and the discovery of her
mutilated and burnt remains understandably spark a bitter hatred and anger
in John Ward, an anger that official attempts to pass off the death as suicide
or an attack by wild animals seals (1991: 88). In the ensuing drama of alterations on the autopsy report and the Police Commissioner's reluctance to open
a murder inquiry, Ward's mistrust for Kenyans and Kenyan state institutions
deepens further. It is no wonder that on subsequent visits to Kenya, he always
looks forward to his departure, and always 'feels a sense of total relief when the
[aircraft] door is closed and Kenya is shut outside' (1991: 93).

In his narrative, Ward constructs a binary lens, in which the British institutions are upright, professional and committed to truth, justice and integrity,
while the Kenyan state institutions display duplicity, inefficiency, corruption
and utter unprofessionalism. On his first visit to Kenya, when his daughter
is missing, Ward contrasts Kenyan police disinterest with the typical British
police's response.

I was only used to an English environment. If a young woman was missing in Hyde
Park, in the centre of London for just one night, two hundred policemen would be
out searching the park and every other copper in the land would be keeping his eyes
open. Yet here in Nairobi, I was being told that it was a real achievement to get any
police officer to even take the matter seriously [1991: 52].

Such comparisons recur throughout the book and, increasingly, Ward's distrust
for Kenyans grows.

In Kenya, John Ward interacted closely with the officials at the British High
Commission, among these Jenny Jenkins and John Ferguson. The two were
particularly helpful with logistics, contacts, processing paperwork and general

support at various stages of the investigations. Jenkins and Ferguson were also actively involved in John Ward's investigations and Ferguson often accompanied Ward to meetings with Kenyan state actors, including the Police Commissioner Philip Kilonzo and the government pathologists Dr Shaker and Dr Kaviti. In the process, Ward came to develop great trust and respect for the officials at the British High Commission in Nairobi, who provided an indispensable support base for him in Kenya, where he was a total stranger, grieving his daughter's brutal death and faced with official attempts to derail his search for answers. It is in gratitude for this support that Ward writes approvingly of the British High Commission in Nairobi:

> So many times I have read newspaper reports where Britons abroad have complained of the service, or lack of it, that they received from our Embassy or High Commission. But I could not have wished for better assistance than that which I have received from the consular staff in Nairobi. I have had nothing but good advice and solid support [1991: 102].

Ward has similar sentiments about the Foreign Office: 'In 1988 the Kenya desk in the Consular section at the Foreign Office was run by a young man named Nigel Wicks. He was very sincere and endlessly helpful and while he ran the Kenya desk, I was always kept fully briefed of any developments. Like Jenny Jenkins in Nairobi [British High Commission], [he] always offered help' (1991: 96).

Despite these glowing tributes to the two British institutions, there were slight hiccups in Ward's relationships with them. Two incidents stand out in this regard. For days after the finding of his daughter's remains, the Kenyan Commissioner of Police, Phillip Kilonzo refuses to acknowledge that they are looking at a case of murder. During this period, Kilonzo is often quoted in the media insinuating that Julie Ward's death is a case of misadventure, as opposed to murder. Suspicious of this misrepresentation of the case – coming soon after the altered autopsy report – Ward decides to hold a press conference in Nairobi, and set the record straight. Before the press conference, Ward writes:

> [Jenny Jenkins] informed us that while the British High Commission had considerable doubts [about the Kenyan police], the line they advocated for that morning was to support the Kenyan police ... At about 10.55 a.m. John [Ferguson] rushed in. 'I've just had a phone conversation with Kilonzo, who now says that the whole matter of the press conference is unfortunate. He insists that no mention be made of the possibility of murder, foul play or a murder inquiry. Also, he doesn't want any details of the post-mortem report released to the press ... I must ask you to abide by his request for this morning' [1991: 111].

It is puzzling that the High Commission asks John Ward to abide by the Kenyan police's instructions, with full knowledge that the Kenyan police were hardly taking the case seriously, and that they seemed bent on presenting Julie Ward's death as misadventure. Ward's close friend, Frank Ribeiro, who had accompanied him to Kenya, found this questionable. 'Personally', Frank stated, 'I'd be very cautious with the British High Commission too. They were very anxious you didn't say anything they didn't want you to this morning. Who are they supposed to be looking after anyway, you or Kilonzo?' (Ward 2012: 115). However, Ward explains this away by observing that 'whilst the Consular section were supportive, there were other sections more concerned with avoiding a diplomatic incident – people whose job it was to try to prevent anyone from "rocking the boat"' (1991: 111). Persuasive as this rationalization is, Ward's failing here was in not subjecting these anxieties about 'rocking the boat' to close scrutiny.

In the second instance, when the Kenyan police finally decide to set up an inquest into Julie Ward's death – a seemingly unnecessary step given the overwhelming evidence of murder – a Foreign Office representative, David Muat phones Ward and delivers this news, further indicating that the family has two options.

> The matter could be left to the Kenyan police to give evidence, entirely at their discretion. The other alternative was for my family to be legally represented, produce the evidence we had gathered and support that evidence with witnesses. The recommendation of the Foreign Office was that the former course be adopted and the submission of evidence should be left to the Kenyan police … I couldn't believe my ears! Knowing the record of the Kenya police over the last seven months, here was Muat telling me that the official Foreign Office recommendation was we should leave it all to the police [1991: 229].

As Ward rightly points out, this was a bizarre recommendation, in light of the Foreign Office's full knowledge of the Kenyan police's unbending investment in a verdict of misadventure and of the post-mortem report, which appeared to have been altered to validate this position. In this instance, Ward rejects the Foreign Office's recommendation and, to ensure that there is no confusion about his decision, he writes a letter to the Foreign Office and confirms that his family would be legally represented. As it turned out, this was hardly a straight-forward matter, notwithstanding a short-list of reputable local firms offered by an employee at the British High Commission. Most firms were hesitant to be involved, as the risks of contesting the official police and government view on the matter seemed too high, but he managed to secure the services of Byron Georgiadis of Kaplan and Stratton Law Firm (Ward 1991: 175). Despite this curious incident with Muat, Ward immediately goes to the Foreign Office's defence once again.

> All this must give the impression that my relations with the Foreign Office were at a low ebb. Generally this was not the case. While there was an attempt to influence events, to limit diplomatic damage, once such schemes were firmly rejected … the majority at the FO extended such solid unwavering support, which was gratefully

accepted. It would, indeed, have been a difficult battle in Nairobi, without the help of the British High Commission – and their instructions come from London [ibid.: 230].

For a long time, Ward remains convinced that his quest for his daughter's killers has the British High Commission and the Foreign Office's blessings. Whenever the two appear to err towards the Kenyan police's preferred approaches to the matter, Ward excuses it as typical but harmless diplomatic caution.

Although increasingly frustrated by the Kenyan police's seeming disinterest in the case, Ward nonetheless continues to hold the belief that the British High Commission was on his side on the matter. Thus convinced, he attempts to persuade the then British High Commissioner to Kenya, Sir John Johnson, to exert diplomatic pressure on whoever was behind the attempted cover-up, he advises that a private approach by Ward might be better as official contact 'might cause the Kenyans to "put up the shutters"' (1991: 202). Johnson advises Ward to approach President Moi personally, as Moi is also a father and would be empathetic. In this, Ward was convinced about British commitment to justice. Elsewhere, Ward demands that Britain withholds aid if Kenya refuses to hold a new investigation as 'only pressure from the highest office could lead Kenyans to reopening the case' (Campbell 1995: 5).

It from this line of thought that Ward feels Police Commissioner Kilonzo is embarrassed when confronted about the attempted cover-up in the presence of John Ferguson, a diplomat: 'Kilonzo was clearly furious at the cover-up being so obviously exposed. I knew though, that the main cause of his embarrassment was not Frank [Ribeiro, Ward's friend] or me, but John Ferguson. *Because, with John present, the British Government "knew"*' (1991: 206, emphasis added). Ward here presents Kilonzo like a child who had been 'caught out' as it were, by a representative of Her Majesty's government. For him, the cover-up is an entirely Kenyan affair and Britain is as scandalized as he was. This view was built on his conviction that the British diplomatic corps officially took strong exception to his daughter's murder and the attempted cover-up, and fully supported his quest for truth and justice. While indeed certain individuals – including Johnson, Wicks, Ferguson and Jenkins – may have shared his anger, and fully supported his quest for justice, Ward's assumption that this was the official line may have been too trusting. So too, it would appear, was his belief that the Kenyans were on their own in the cover-up and that they could be pressured into reconsidering this position by the British.

On the whole, Ward's narrative illustrates his construction of a binary lens through which he read Kenyan and British state institutions. Ward's resentment and distrust of Kenya and Kenyan official institutions is balanced against his faith in the British officials and institutions. Thus, for instance, he is dismissive of the investigating officer in charge of the case, Inspector Wanjau, while retaining great respect for the two Scotland Yard detectives sent to Kenya to investigate the murder – Supts Dave Shipperlee and Graham Searle.

In this polarized attitude, Ward once again illustrated his positioning in a broader architecture of ideas, which associates Europe with modernity, efficient state institutions and strong senses of integrity, ethics and justice. These ideas echo what Anne McClintock terms the 'metaphysical Manicheanism of the imperial enlightenment' (1995: 15). It is from this moral high ground for instance, that in a confrontation with Dr Kaviti for altering the post-mortem report, Ward angrily informs him: 'In England you would be struck off the medical register for doing what you have done. Don't you know it is a serious offence to falsify an official document?' (1991: 119). This outburst captures Ward's conviction about the ethical and moral integrity of British state institutions.

Behind the Scenes: The Foreign Office, the Secret Intelligence Service and the British High Commission in Kenya

Looking at the ever-helpful staff at the British High Commission in Nairobi, one would believe, as Ward was inclined to, that he had official British support in his search for answers in the mystery of his daughter's death. To a certain degree, Ward's trust grew into an unquestioning faith and even defence of the British High Commission's codes of diplomacy, in ways that may have obscured nuances of competing British interests in the matter. One particular incident which Ward narrates in his book stands out in this regard. Two weeks after the finding of his daughter's remains, Ward goes to the British High Commission in Nairobi, accompanied by his friend and business partner Frank Ribeiro.

> At one point, I was asked to go to another room, leaving Frank [Ribeiro] behind with Jenny. On the way, a request was made to which I agreed. I was to meet a man who had very good contacts at the highest level with the Kenyan police. I was to meet him on the understanding that his name was never disclosed for fear of jeopardizing his position ... He told us that the latest suggestion being put about by the Kenyan police was that Julie had been struck by lightning.
> 'They can't be serious. Surely they don't think I'm going to buy that, do they?'
> 'A lightning strike can cause an injury with the appearance of a cut,' he said.
> 'In my career, I've seen injuries like that and, of course, it would explain the burning.'
> His attempt to justify this ludicrous theory immediately rang warning bells with me. He affected to be there to help us but I formed the impression that his real assignment was to deliver a message. He seemed to be trying to sound me out, to see if I'd accept any different theory other than murder. I wondered who this man really worked for ... I satisfied myself that the Kenyans paid his salary. Whether anyone else did too, I never bothered to find out [Ward 1991: 133].

This curious incident should have merited closer scrutiny at the time. But Ward completely brushes it aside. The relevance of this incident dawns on him over a decade later.

After the Kenyan inquest confirmed that Ward had been murdered, there was a long silence on both the Kenyan and British sides, while the Ward family demanded an investigation into the murder. Finally, in November 1989 there was a meeting between President Moi and the then British Foreign Secretary Douglas Hurd, after which, Ward writes, the Foreign and Commonwealth Office (FCO) contacted Scotland Yard, which in turn appointed Supt Ken Thompson to travel to Kenya and investigate the merits of the case, and how Scotland Yard could assist, on Kenya's invitation (Ward 1991: 341). Thompson was fully briefed by the FCO on the case and read the file [in the FCO's possession], which featured 'the 10 reports showing murder, the post-mortem report by Dr Shaker and the altered post-mortem report by Kaviti [and] the complete transcript of the inquest [which] detailed how the state witnesses had admitted, under cross-examination, that their testimonies were false' (Ward 2012: 51). Ward was fully supportive of Thompson, and he shared the evidence and findings he had made so far, in his investigations. He also revealed the secret whereabouts of his daughter's jeep, which remained uncontaminated, and might have fingerprints and DNA clues. Upon his return from Kenya, Thompson recommended that Scotland Yard detectives be assigned to the case. Detectives Inspector Dave Shipperlee and Supt Graham Searle were soon off to Kenya to investigate the murder, with Ward's full co-operation.

Having shared his suspicions about Chief Game Warden Simon ole Makallah, with the Yard detectives, Ward was surprised that they recommended that two junior wardens, Jonah Magiroi and Peter Kipeen, be charged with the murder. He agreed with the acquittal of the two by Judge Fidahussein. At this stage, Ward is at pains to justify the Scotland Yard detectives' puzzling decisions as partly stemming from limited resources, a fact that came up, with initial confusion over whether Kenya and/or Britain would cover the detectives' expenses in Kenya. Media reports in 1998, when Makallah was charged with the murder, cited Ward as saying he never believed Magiroi and Kipeen were guilty, but he understood the constraints under which the Yard detectives were working. 'It's really not their fault; they're not bad detectives, it's a question of time. It was a cosmetic exercise really, with Foreign Office funding constraints. They only had two weeks in Kenya' (Sweeney 1998: 3). This 1998 statement, however, would seem to contradict a subsequent statement in 2012 by Ward, when he underlines his alarm at Graham Searle's inaccurate claims in court, during Kipeen and Magiroi's trial, particularly his claim that there was a track off the main road, which Julie Ward must have taken before getting stuck in the gully. On hindsight, writing in 2012, Ward accuses Searle of ignoring the established evidence, homing in on Makari Outpost and the two junior wardens, then 'inventing' a track to reinforce the claim that Julie Ward drove into the gully on her own accord. This view was consistent with the Kenyan police's view, regarding her getting stuck then walking in the park seeking help. The difference though, was that, since the inquest had proved the Kenyan police's version about an animal attack to be inaccurate, the Scotland Yard detectives' investigations implicated the two junior wardens who were at the time based at the nearby Makari Outpost, as the chief suspects. Searle's dishonesty about the non-existent track worried Ward and he reports that he alerted Kipeen and Magiroi's defence lawyer, James Orengo, to the fact that Searle's claim about a track was inaccurate. Unknown to Supt Searle, the prosecutor, Salim Dhanji, had visited the Mara just before the trial, to familiarize himself with the landscape and the scenes that would be up for discussion in the case. So, when Supt Searle insisted during interrogation, '[n]ot only does the road exist, it is particularly clear and well defined, and I drove along it with the prosecution party, three or four days before this trial commenced' (Ward 2012: 52), the case was effectively closed; Searle narrowly escaped arrest for deliberate and wilful perjury, reportedly thanks to Dhanji's intervention with the Judge. For Ward, while his family desperately wanted justice to see their daughter's murderer convicted, 'it did not satisfy [their] objective if the wrong person was convicted or someone was convicted on the basis of false evidence' (ibid.). By the time Makallah was charged and acquitted in 1998, Ward was suspicious enough of the various British units he had interacted with in the case.

In 2000, Ward lodged a formal complaint about Scotland Yard and the Foreign Office's involvement in the case with the Independent Police Complaints Authority (IPCC). An investigation was undertaken by the Lincolnshire Police, on behalf of Scotland Yard. Lincolnshire Police were instructed: 'To fully investigate allegations made by John Ward that there has been a conspiracy, implicit or explicit, between the following parties: That is, the Kenyan Government, the Foreign and Commonwealth Office and the Metropolitan Police, with the intention of preventing those person(s) responsible for the murder of Julie Ward being identified and brought to justice' (Ward 2012: 53). The investigation ran from 21 June 2001 to 16 September 2004 and their Report was presented to Scotland Yard, IPCC and the FCO (ibid.).

To Ward's surprise, once completed, the inquiry and its findings were classified: 'on 24 September 2004, at a meeting at the IPCC offices, instructions were given that the Lincs report, relating to allegations of a British and Kenyan Government conspiracy, was to be classified secret. Everyone present complied. I set about obtaining a copy of the report, using the UK Freedom of Information Act. It was a costly enterprise, involving lawyers etc. Eventually, after two years, a copy was obtained. It had been heavily censored and all names of FCO officials had been obliterated' (Ward 2012: 53). The investigation reportedly 'found clear evidence of "inconsistency and contradictions, falsehoods and downright lies" but no "firm evidence" of a criminal conspiracy' (*East Anglian Daily Times*, 2013). The report's summary further acknowledges that a Nairobi-based British Secret Intelligence Service Agent Mr A. and his contact person, David Rowe 'have been economical with the truth in relation to their knowledge of events surrounding Ward's murder' (ibid.).

By 2012, when Ward writes his second detailed report on his investigations and his conclusion that *Mr B.* was the man behind his daughter's murder, he could, with the benefit of hindsight, see that various British units were complicit in the cover-up from the point his daughter's remains were discovered. Thinking back to the course of British responses to his daughter's murder, Ward speculates that once Chief Pathologist Kaviti altered the post-mortem report, the British High Commission's political section was on high alert: 'From that moment, they knew Moi's government was intent on concealing the murder. Also, at that point, the BHC's political section assumed control of the matter. While the consular section was still portrayed as the public face of the BHC, it was the political section that issued instructions' (2012: 47). This line of thought might explain the initial, seemingly earnest support Ward receives from the consular officials; but might also suggest that these officials too, find themselves compelled to be part of sabotaging a grieving father's quest for justice, whatever their personal views on the tragedy. A year later, in 2013, a newspaper reported that Ward had lodged a new complaint against the Metropolitan Police, because they 'failed to properly investigate the murder and attempted to shut down an unfinished investigation'. Reportedly, 'a sample of excrement found at the crime scene and passed on to the Met for forensic testing was said to be soil, a "mistake" only corrected when Mr Ward revealed forensic testing he commissioned showed the sample was excrement' (*East Anglian Daily Times*, 2013).

Looking back, Ward revisits his encounter with the 'contact' who suggested that his daughter had been struck by lightning, a mere ten days after her remains were found. The role of this 'contact' in the case emerged during a second inquest into Julie Ward's death, held in Ipswich, Suffolk in 2004. The court had ordered both this lightning theory 'contact' and SIS agent code-named Mr A. to testify at the inquest. Mr A. testified via audio link from a secret room in the building, to protect his identity. At this inquest, it would become public news that not only was the lightning theory 'contact' a former assistant Commissioner of Police in the Kenyan police force, but that he was at the time a contact person to Nairobi-based British Intelligence agent code-named Mr A. At the inquest, Mr A. admits that he paid the then Commissioner of Police, Phillip Kilonzo, a 'courtesy call', soon after Julie Ward's death. Further, he admits that he was 'asked by the [British] High Commission to bring in Mr Rowe whom he knew well socially, and who was partly paid by the British government' (Barkham 2004b).

In his initial description of the meeting with Mr A. and the contact at the British High Commission, Nairobi, Ward indicates that he was asked to meet 'a man who had very good contacts at the highest level with the Kenyan police' (Ward 1991: 133). Ward writes that the meeting was 'on the understanding that his name was never disclosed, for fear of jeopardizing his position. And so it shall remain now' (ibid.). At the time of publishing his book in 1991, Ward's relationship to the High Commission was still good, hence he honoured the request to keep the contacts' identities secret. Decades later, in 2012, Ward retells this incident in his detailed feature article in the March 2012 issue of the *Nairobi Law Monthly*. In this version, Ward identifies the lightning man as David Rowe – the former Assistant Police Commissioner of Kenya, and his contact as SIS agent Clive Willy aka Mr A. Ward's 2012 retelling of the incident is worth citing for its insights into seeming British complicity in the cover-up and other concerns that were at play.

> On the 24th September, 1988, I was visiting the consular section at the BHC, clearing formalities to enable City Mortuary to release Julie's remains. I and a colleague were asked to go to another room. I was told not to mention the meeting to anyone, as it would compromise the men's position. One man, David Rowe, did the talking. The other man said virtually nothing. Rowe had a message to give to me. He said that he had many years' experience in the police, specialising in Scenes of Crime. He had seen the injuries to Julie's leg and had noticed the burning. Rowe said he knew I suspected murder, but in his opinion, that was completely wrong. Further, he said, the Masai Mara experienced very violent storms. In Rowe's opinion, Julie had not been murdered but struck by lightning! 'You are not looking at a murder Mr Ward,' he told me. 'This was an act of God.' I was informed the usual procedure was to have the remains cremated in Kenya then only take the ashes home ... Rowe is an endless talker – but a poor liar. Everyone at the meeting, including the consular official thought Rowe was lying. The question was, who had put Rowe up to it – and why? The answer lay with the other man, Clive Willy. Willy was one of the British Security Service officials, embedded in the political section of the BHC. David Rowe was one of his informers. David Rowe was an invaluable informer. For many years, he had been an Assistant Commissioner in Kenyan Police. Although now retired, he still undertook training for Kenya Police ... Rowe reported to Clive Willy, then reported to London. In this way, the Security Services in the UK became aware of most things that occurred at Kenya Police Headquarters in Nairobi. Years later, Rowe and Willy were confronted about their activities. Both immediately denied any wrongdoing and pretended that the meeting with me in the BHC had happened entirely by chance. In fact, subsequently, a very astute and thorough UK police officer found a contact note that Clive Willy had sent to SIS headquarters in London. It was dated several days before the BRC [*sic*] meeting with me. The note reported a meeting between Rowe and Willy, which had taken place at one of their homes, several days before the BRC [*sic*] meeting. The subject they had

discussed was the Julie Ward [*sic*]. An agreement had been reached as to what action was to be taken. That action was manifested in the meeting with me at the BRC [*sic*, Ward 2012: 48].

I have quoted Ward's retelling of the encounter with David Rowe and Clive Willy in detail, because it paints an engaging portrait of the ways in which Britain too, was invested in particular fictions on the case. These incidents represent what I term the 'invisible' face of the official British interventions in the case. These were the behind-the-scenes activities of officials affiliated with the High Commission.

A few issues stand out for us in this series of events. The meeting between the British intelligence agent, his contact and Ward, is facilitated by the British High Commission, takes place in the High Commission's offices, and comes just before a meeting with the ambassador John Johnson and immediately after a meeting with John Ferguson and Jenny Jenkins. Further, Clive Willy holds a meeting with the Kenyan Commissioner of Police, Phillip Kilonzo, a few days after Julie Ward's remains are found and, soon after, Clive Willy apparently tasks David Rowe with securing John Ward's buy-in to the theory of lightning, which closely approximates the Kenyan police's theories of accidental death. The note of the meeting between Clive Willy and David Rowe, and the agreed course of action, lodged in the SIS headquarters suggests that the two were acting with the blessings of the SIS and not in their personal capacities. In other words, it would suggest British Intelligence's official endorsement of attempts to sabotage a British citizen's quest for answers in his daughter's brutal murder. Meantime, Rowe's attempt to justify his lightning theory by claiming his extensive experience in police work, and 'insider's' knowledge of the Mara's violent storms is reminiscent of the logics of the rumour narratives described in the previous chapter; while his recommendation to Ward to cremate the remains, is equally noteworthy, as possibly intended to preclude a second, more reliable autopsy, given that this conversation happens just a few days after the controversial Kenyan autopsy. Remarkable too are the kinds of exchanges and deals between the two countries' secret services, at the marketplace of intelligence, where a retired Kenyan-British policeman, having served in post-independent Kenya's police force, becomes a useful middle-man informant to British Intelligence, thanks to his rich connections to the Kenyan police network, and his seeming investment in Britain, whether for material or patriotic reasons. The entangled transaction at play here – a former Kenyan-British policeman, paid by British Secret Service for Kenyan intelligence, supporting, at the request of British Intelligence, a Kenyan cover-up in a murder of a British citizen – is quite an eye opener. Rowe and Willy's position at this intersection between Kenyan and British state interests is an intriguing and powerful metonym for the complex layers of sometimes coinciding and complementing interests that are negotiated between Britain and her former colonies, and were at stake in the Ward case.

Aside from Clive Willy and David Michael Rowe, Ward further discovered that Scotland Yard's investigations were hardly above board, as he had imagined them to be. A look at Supt Thompson's report from his initial trip to Kenya revealed his theory to have been that

> Julie had left Sand River Camp Ground and driven to the place in the trackless wilderness, where her body was found. Once there, she had set up a camp, with the obvious intention of staying for a few days. She had then gone on a game drive to view and photograph the animals. During this drive, she had got her vehicle stuck in the gully. Not being able to extricate it, she had walked back to her camp, before perhaps being attacked by animals or even passing bandits … Thompson briefed senior officials at the BHC. Tom Bryant, the deputy High Commissioner, was present and David Alexander Warren, head of the Political Section … In fact, Supt. Ken Thompson provided his FCO masters with exactly what they had asked for. The FCO involvement in the cover-up was still on [Ward 2012: 51].

But the most damning development was that having trusted Thompson with the whereabouts of his daughter's jeep (which were unknown to Kenyan police) because he at the time he felt he could entrust information to a British police officer, 'Thompson guided the Kenya police to the location of Julie's vehicle. Two weeks after he had returned to the UK, the vehicle vanished. Months later, it was discovered, miles away in a breaker's yard. It had been completely dismantled and forensic opportunities were lost forever' (Ward 2012: 51). The vehicle, which had still not been 'swept' for DNA evidence, was an important source of information as, for Ward, available evidence pointed to someone else driving the vehicle and getting it stuck in the gully, after his daughter's murder, so as to make it seem like she had got stuck in the gully then walked around the park in search for help, before being attacked by the animals. In revealing the vehicle's whereabouts to the Kenyan police, Thompson deeply compromised the chances of resolving the case.

By 2012, John Ward, who had initially believed in the fundamental differences in integrity between the Kenyan and British authorities, had changed his mind: 'In reality, there is no difference between the Government of Kenya and the British Government' (Ward 2012: 53). At the time of writing this, in 2012, over two decades after his daughter's death, Ward had a better grasp of the political landscape in which his daughter's murder had happened, and had come to realize what many Kenyans had taken for granted from the beginning: it was not a case of Kenyan police incompetency, as Ward was inclined to assume, but a question of power and the kind of impunity that power afforded the people behind the murder. It is this power that also afforded them the silence of all the key people complicit or in the know of, the circumstances surrounding Julie

Ward's murder and disposal of her body. As Ward eventually acknowledges, 'when confronted with the truth and asked why they had forged or lied or falsely reported, their responses were always the same. A plaintive, 'I had to', 'I was told to', 'I was threatened', 'I have a family'. The rewards for compliance were good and they knew they would be protected from any consequences of their wrongdoing. *They also knew that non-compliance attracted ruthless penalties*' (Ward 2012: 53, emphasis added). The ruthless penalties Ward mentions in passing here, appear to have been seen in the earlier-discussed case of the hasty execution of Nahashon Njenga, the gunman who killed Tom Mboya.

From the above incidents, contrary to Ward's belief that the cover-up was an exclusively Kenyan affair, the British Secret Intelligence Service would seem to have been complicit in the Kenyan police's preferred 'truths' on the case as suggested by Mr A's involvement in the matter. The possible involvement of influential people in Kenyan politics in Julie Ward's death was later to figure as a reason behind the British High Commission's reluctance to be outspoken about the case. At the second inquest into Julie Ward's death held in Suffolk, Jenny Jenkins of the British High Commission in Nairobi, acknowledged that rumours regarding the possible involvement of a prominent political figure in the matter meant that the High Commission in Nairobi had to handle the matter carefully, in the interests of the diplomatic relations between Kenya and Britain. Years later, John Ward was to speculate that perhaps Britain chose not to pressure the Kenyan Government out of fear of the 'volatile' President Moi: "'President Moi was a volatile man who could kick the British out of Kenya just by flicking his fingers and the boys who look at the big board have to take that into consideration" he said. They probably thought "We cannot bring Julie back, so there is nothing to be gained by being kicked out of Kenya"' (McVeigh 2004).

Beyond interrogating Ward's polarization between Kenya and Britain's involvement in the quest for justice in his daughter's death, another issue of interest in this chapter is the masking of these shared interests. What discursive masks are produced to mask the contradictions that fracture hegemonic discourses?

The British involvement in the cover-up remained under wraps and unexplored in the media, the popular imaginary and the books on the case. In its place, the British narratives – both the media and the books on the case – produced the idea that Kenyan officials' cover-up of the truth behind the Julie Ward case was an attempt to protect the tourism industry. Commenting on this, Michael Hiltzik observes:

> This time however the context was not Kenya's valiant fight against wildlife poachers, but the country's inability to keep its famed tourist venues safe and secure. Legions of reporters came into the country to document the hazards of game safaris. (KILLERS PROWL PARADISE was one British headline) … Adding to the dis-

comfiture of a tourism industry trying to mollify hundreds of thousands of skittish tourists, the inquest into Julie Ward's death in Kenya's most renowned game reserve was about to reconvene [1991: 238].

While the tourism industry is indeed a key contributor to the country's economy, this argument was not wholly persuasive. In fact, the attempted cover-up drew greater negative publicity to both the industry and the country. Second, the interests in the Kenyan tourism industry are largely multinational, with investors from across the world, including Britain who would be as likely to be concerned about negative publicity around the industry as the Kenyan Government, if not more. In Kenya, as in many African countries, there is a large body of multinational economic interests in the tourism industry, in the shape of travel agents, tour, hotel and transport investments. As John Akama notes, 'the establishment and development of tourism in most Third World countries is usually externally oriented and controlled, and mainly responds to external market domains. In consequence … the management and long-term sustenance of the tourism establishment depends on external control and support (1999a: 7–8). In this respect, the economic interests of protecting the tourism industry would conceivably be shared by other countries whose interests at the time lay in the Kenyan tourism industry, in which they controlled the bulk of the industry's luxury resorts, lodges and tour companies. In the Maasai Mara Game Reserve, for instance, the majority of the accommodation facilities were at the time owned by multinational companies. These multinational investments in the tourism industry fracture the accepted wisdom that the Kenyan Government attempted to cover up the case in a bid to protect its tourism industry. What further stands out is the silence on these international economic interests in the tourism industry – a significant chunk of which are British. To date, neither the books on the case nor the British media have acknowledged Britain's economic interests in the Kenyan tourism industry and how these may have contributed to the official silence on the matter by Britain.

But the emphasis on the Kenyan tourism industry further serves as a mask that deflects attention from Britain's other strategic interests in Kenya, primarily in the shape of military arrangements between the two countries.[1] In a different context, commenting on British strategic interests in Kenya at independence, Daniel Branch notes Britain's keenness to protect its political and economic interests, most notably access to the Mombasa port facilities, infantry training

---

[1] Godwin Murunga underscores Kenya's status as the bastion of capitalism in the region, which made it 'a useful bulwark against communism in the region' for the US with the added bonus of the 'entrenchment of foreign capital', which soon controlled 'key sectors of the economy including the main productive arteries in agriculture, manufacturing and the service sectors' (Murunga 2007: 266–7).

in the Mount Kenya area, overfly rights and being Kenya's primary vendor for its defence needs (2012: 39). Later, Ward would acknowledge that, faced with the prospect of supporting a British citizen's pursuit of justice or preserving its relationship to Kenya for strategic, commercial, military and political interests, Britain opted for the latter:

> the British had all manner of commercial interests in Kenya to protect. The British Army had a training base near Mt. Kenya. The crack British SAS troops underwent jungle training in Kenya, sometimes in the Masai Mara. In 1988, the Cold War was still lurking on the international scene. There was tacit agreement between the West and Moi that the Port of Mombasa could be used as a NATO naval base if need be. The political section of the British High Commission was there to ensure all these interests were protected and preserved. The Julie Ward death and Moi's clear statement that he did not want the matter to be a murder caused concern [Ward 2012: 43].

Ward ends his article noting that the conspiracy continues, now in attempts to protect officials who were part of the conspiracy, from prosecution: 'the longer they can conceal, the more likely the affair will simply be lost in time' (ibid.: 53).

A range of issues emerge from a reading of these dynamics 'behind the scenes'. We realize that Kenya had no monopoly over corruption and the derailment of the course of justice in the Ward case. While it may be the case that British institutions and professionals had access to better facilities, which Ward opted to mobilize in his quest for the truth, this was no insurance against manipulation of truth. In this regard, Ward's claim that while tourists get attacked, robbed or murdered in Europe too, *'the difference is that in those cities, the authorities will not try to sweep the murder under the carpet* (1991: xix) disintegrates in light of alleged official British complicity in the cover-up. These incidents underscore certain continuities across the British–Kenyan divide, in terms of their political strategies, and their pursuit of their own interests at whatever costs.

Read against the earlier mentioned implicit polarization of Kenya and Britain, these contradictions alert us to the fault lines that often lie beneath the surface of accepted Manichean tenets of received wisdom. In this sense, the concept of fault lines, drawn from geology, provides a useful metaphor for conceptualizing the contradictions and competing interests that lay beneath the visible face of British support for Ward's quest for justice. Faulting is a particularly apt metaphor for understanding the textured nature of hegemonic enterprises by penetrating the outer crust of a unified position, to catch glimpses of the cracks that lie beneath the seemingly solid surface. In geology, fault formation is the result of fracturing of solid rocks due to pressure and the movement of rock planes in different directions. Although the earth's surface often appears to be continuous, the earth's crust beneath is made up of layers of different rock compositions, which are constantly under pressure. These rock plates often push and pull sometimes towards each other or in different directions, resulting in cracks or faults. For the most part though, these faults do not rupture the earth surface. However, under extreme pressure, or significant movement of the rocks within the earth's crust, there may be substantial movement of the rocks, which results in visible shifts on the earth's surface leading to sinking or protrusion of sections of the earth surface. These geological ideas on faulting processes offer a useful metaphoric handle on ways of understanding internal contradictions inherent in structures and discourses because these geological processes in many ways mirror the tensions and contradictions that underpin seemingly homogeneous discourses. In the Julie Ward case, discourses such as the Kenya–Britain moral polarity, British commitment to justice and human rights, British diplomatic caution in dealing with the 'volatile' President Moi, and Kenyans' cover-up to protect the tourism industry all worked to mask the underlying fault lines of British involvement in frustrating the Ward family's quest for truth and justice. By extension, this unmasks the popular discourse of Western/centre domination of the periphery.

These fault lines, if surfaced, would crumble Britain's discursive veil and, in this case, unmask the fact that its commitment to human rights and justice is contingent on its other interests in a given context. Despite the self-evident injustice and brutality of Julie Ward's death and the implicit admission of a high-level cover-up by the state, Britain appeared to prioritize its other interests in Kenya. Put differently, in this instance, unstated interests seemingly made it inconvenient for Britain to 'walk the talk' of human rights and justice.

The apparent British complicity in the cover-up further raises interesting thoughts about the notion of complicity, especially in contexts of sharp, hierarchical polarizations such as the Kenya–Britain relationship. Here, one is interested in the shapes of relationships that unfold in what Mary Louise Pratt has termed contact zones. Although she uses the phrase specifically in reference to those zones of interaction between black and white people in colonial setups, where 'black and white interests collided in a thousand different ways' (1992: 7), I see the term as equally useful in describing those sites of convergence between overlapping spheres of control – similar to the layers of rocks, described above – in contexts marked by multiple epicentres of power, that defy linear hierarchies, especially when they operate in concurrent orbits. The under-explored issue here becomes the shapes of relationships that ensue in contact zones where overlapping spheres of influence dispense with simple hierarchies.

Feminists often emphasize the 'simultaneity of oppression' of black and African women, where they are confronted with race, class and gender subordination at the same time.[2] Implicit in this is what I term the simultaneity of domination, which can be seen to unfold at the juncture of these sets of identities

---

[2] See for instance Nnaemeka (1997; 1998); Ogundipe-Leslie (1994).

or discursive structures, where, to use the case of African women, they find themselves confronted by three concurrent sets of dominant discourses articulated through race, gender and class. The idea of simultaneity of domination was at play in Julie Ward's death in Kenya, which presented a complex contact zone between Britain and Kenya, with multiple overlapping spheres of control or epicentres of power that created significant configurations of power relations.

Geographically, Julie Ward died in the Maasai Mara Game Reserve, itself a space marked by several power centres, including the Narok County Council, the surrounding Maasai community, local and international investors in the tourism industry and, nationally, the Kenyan state institutions, including the police and the judiciary. At the same time, as a British citizen, Julie Ward's death further drew the interest of the British High Commission and by extension, Britain, both of which found themselves in a complex position, caught between the Ward family's desperate demand for justice, the Kenyan state actors' keenness to pass off the death as a natural accident and the pursuit of Britain's multiple interests in Kenya and the East African region which included diplomatic, military, economic and socio-political interests. In essence, Julie Ward's murder was situated in this complex cartography of interlinked nodes of power centres, with multiple and conflicting interests. These layers of interests in the case alert us to the concentric nature of power, and the co-existence of sometimes coinciding circles of influence, which re-configure hierarchical patterns of power relations between the dominant group and the subordinate group. These concentric circles of control and interests gesture towards the highly nuanced textures of complicity that often lie beneath superficial constructions of polar binaries such as the centre–periphery moral scheme that Ward constructs in his book.

Fictive Imaginings of British Interests in *The Constant Gardener*

John le Carré's novel *The Constant Gardener*, published a decade after John Ward's book, offers interesting parallels with the Julie Ward case. When read side by side with Ward's *The Animals are Innocent* (1991), le Carré's novel invites us to reconsider three important issues in Ward's narrative: the essentialized polarity between Kenya and Britain, British diplomatic concerns about the case as purely routine, innocent caution and, broadly, the myth of British moral authority.

Le Carré's *The Constant Gardener* is a fictional narrative set in the 1990s during the Moi regime. Although this is a fictional narrative, within its fictional truths are a range of important insights which, when read beside the Julie Ward narrative, shed important light on the perception of the British official institutions' support for the Ward family's quest for the truth outlined above. In the novel, Tessa Quayle, wife of diplomat Justin Quayle prepares a detailed report in which she outlines details of human rights abuses, corruption and the use of violent repression by the Moi government, and submits this to Sandy Woodrow,

Head of Chancery at the British High Commission in Nairobi. When she asks why the High Commission does nothing about the report, Woodrow retorts:

> Because we are diplomats and not policemen, Tessa. The Moi government is termi-
> nally corrupt, you tell me. I never doubted it ... Ministers are diverting lorry-loads
> of food aid and medical supplies earmarked for starving refugees. Of course they
> are ... The police routinely mishandle anybody unwise enough to bring these mat-
> ters to public attention. Also true. You have studied their methods. They use water
> torture, you say. They soak people, then beat them, which reduces visible marks.
> You are right. They do ... *The High Commission shares your disgust, but we still do
> not protest. Why not? Because we are here, mercifully, to represent our country, not
> theirs.* We have thirty-five thousand indigenous Britons in Kenya whose precarious
> livelihood depends on President Moi's whim [le Carré 2001: 52, emphasis added].

Woodrow's response here provides an important qualifier to both the notion of British power over Kenya and the myth of its commitment to human rights protection. For Woodrow, Britain's position in Kenya is a delicate one, in which they have to be careful not to upset the president, as this would be to put the welfare of the British expatriate community at risk.

This fictional portrait of Britain's compromising position on Kenya would seem to mirror Britain's actual choices in its relationship with post-independent Kenya, perhaps most notably in the 1980s and 1990s, at the height of struggles for democracy. In an essay on the role of foreign donors in Kenya's democratic transition, Stephen Brown observes that despite the perception that donors were instrumental in facilitating the country's transition to democracy by encourag-ing opposition parties and enforcing donor conditionality, they played a 'second, less publicized role' (2001: 725).[3] After opposition parties were legalized, donors consistently discouraged the quest for deeper democratization by 'knowingly endorsing unfair elections (including suppressing evidence of their illegitimacy) and subverting domestic efforts to secure far-reaching reforms' by prioritizing political and economic order at the expense of legitimizing authoritarian rule (ibid.: 726).[4]

---

[3] This idea, though true, often overshadows the contribution of local actors in Kenya's democratic transition by over-emphasizing donor-pressure, which in any case, as our discussion
here reveals, was both interested and qualified.

[4] Brown further discusses a more specific case of the donor representatives' caginess in the face
of gross human rights abuses in his essay 'Quiet Diplomacy and Recurring "Ethnic clashes"
in Kenya', where the international community was content to support the UNDP's intervention in the 1992 'ethnic clashes' in Kenya, thus avoiding direct involvement, while simultaneously turning a blind eye to overwhelming evidence that the clashes were instigated by high
ranking officials in the Moi government, with apparent state support, as suggested by the
state security officers' refusal to intervene, and even cases of state security officers disarming
victims who attempted to defend themselves (Brown 2003: 78–79). For Brown, this reticence
was a strategic decision, since donors and diplomatic missions in Kenya were reluctant to

Brown considers Kenya's strategic and economic importance to Western countries as the key reason behind their reluctance to compromise their relationship with the Moi government: the United Kingdom 'values close ties with Kenya rooted in colonial history and strong financial and commercial relations' (Brown 2003: 82). Further, 'donors use their generally friendly relationship with Kenya to further other foreign policy goals in the region' (ibid.: 83). In similar vein, Godwin Murunga notes that donors' preference for negotiating reforms with a small handful of technocrats to the exclusion of the wider public played into the hands of the state in depoliticizing and delaying the reform process and, ironically, reinforcing an undemocratic process which precluded public opinion on policy (Murunga 2007: 275). Le Carré's fictional character Sandy Woodrow sums up this position, in his response to Tessa's questioning of the British High Commission's unconcern about the Kenyan Government's corruption and human rights abuses: 'we are here, mercifully, to represent *our* country, not *theirs*' (le Carré 2001: 53, original emphasis). Woodrow's response to a certain degree echoes Ward's justifications about the delicate position that the British diplomats in Kenya found themselves in: 'I am aware of an element in the Foreign Office, whose only function is to ensure the status quo is maintained between the UK and other countries, including Kenya. Probably there are very sound political or commercial reasons for their activities' (1991: 211–12).

While both Woodrow and Ward's arguments here would justify a restrained attitude towards local politics in the spirit of non-interference, they do not explain active involvement in such activities. In reality, the notion of quiet diplomacy would seem to be a useful discursive mask, behind which Britain hides its interests, the contradictions underpinning the macro-discourses it progresses in the Third World (chiefly democracy, good governance, and human rights), and the reality of its compromising economic, military and political pursuits in these countries.

In *The Constant Gardener*, Tessa is murdered to end her interference with the activities of a huge multinational company, House of ThreeBees, owned by a Nairobi-based British businessman, Sir Kenny Curtiss. ThreeBees, Tessa finds, is '[q]uite an amazing outfit. Finger in everyAfrican pie but British to the core. Hotels, travel agencies, newspapers, security companies, banks, extractors of gold, coal and copper, importers of cars, boats. Plus a fine range of drugs … And they're hugger-mugger with Moi's Boys too' (le Carré 2001: 114). ThreeBees not only serves the interests of the British Government, but these investments are also sustained by a mutually beneficial patronage relationship with the Kenyan Government, which compromises Britain's ability to question the Kenyan Government's misdeeds. Further, for Britain, ThreeBees' new merger with a large

antagonize the government because this might have jeopardized their programmes as their activities predominantly required them to work with the government (ibid.).

Swedish pharmaceutical company Karel-Vita-Hudson (KVH), not only means bigger profits for ThreeBees, but KVH has also offered to build a pharmaceutical factory in an economically depressed region in the United Kingdom.

The novel's portrayal of an intermeshed relationship between commercial interests, British Foreign Service and the British Secret Intelligence Service provides a fascinating multi-dimensional view that, though fictional, is nonetheless enlightening regarding some of the dynamics that played out in the Julie Ward case. From the novel, we learn about a symbiotic relationship between the intelligence unit and business, in this case through Kenny Curtiss and the Nairobi arm of the British Secret Service, housed in the British High Commission. This relationship is highly complicit, as the Secret Service not only uses Curtiss – a private businessman – to help do their dirty work, including supplying arms to war-torn Sierra Leone in exchange for political protection (le Carré 2001: 414), which in turn assures his business' success, and feeds British economic growth, but he also gives cash hand-outs to British political parties and classified intelligence to the Secret Service. As he reminds Tim Donohue of the Secret Service's Nairobi office: 'I'm *Sir* fucking *Kenneth* Curtiss! I have subscribed – last year alone – half a fucking *million* quid to party funds. I have provided *you* – British fucking Intelligence – with nuggets of pure gold. I have performed *voluntarily*, certain services for you of a very, very tricky sort' (ibid.: 409, original emphasis).

Although *The Constant Gardener* insists on its fictiveness, the narrative is nonetheless enlightening about the symbiotic relationships between British politics, commercial interests and its foreign missions. What is important here is not so much whether this reflects the reality or not, but the possibility – even in fictional imaginaries – of the fault lines that fissure Britain's mythical mantle of virtue and uncompromising moral integrity. The novel becomes an interesting reference point when read from the perspective of the conventions of documentary realism. Lars Ole Sauerberg defines documentary realism as 'a narrative mode which, while adhering in principle to the time-honoured narrative conventions of realistic narrative, draws on verifiable reality to various extents, but invariably in such a way as to call attention explicitly or implicitly to the difference between the fictional and the factual' (Sauerberg 1991: 6). According to him, documentary realism includes isolated reference to a factual phenomenon, which works through the double-reference technique. This double reference typically manifests itself 'either as integration of more or less obviously factual material in the form of quotations or references into the narrative's otherwise quite fictitious universe, or as the adaptation of a wholly factual series of events to a traditionally fictional narrative pattern, and sometimes as a combination of both' (Sauerberg 1991: 7). Arguably, *The Constant Gardener* deploys the double-reference technique, not only in its allusion to real places, institutions and individuals in Kenya, but also in the ways in which the narrative is grafted onto a familiar Kenyan topography with such identifiable features as police brutality, corruption in the Moi regime and, broadly, a recognizable geo-political topography. Indeed the apparent complicity of the British Secret Intelligence Service in the Julie Ward cover-up, the SIS agent Mr A.'s secret rendezvous with the Commissioner of Police Phillip Kilonzo, and the attempts to persuade John Ward that his daughter was struck by lightning would seem to be a real-life precursor to the fictional narrative of Tessa Quayle's murder and the British High Commission in le Carré's novel. In the novel too, the High Commission attempts to persuade Justin Quayle that his wife was having an affair with Dr Arnold Bluhm and that he went berserk and killed her. This lingering focus on Tessa Quayle's sexuality is in some ways reminiscent of similar speculations on Julie Ward's alleged sexual interactions in the Mara.

These fictional portraits offer important overlaps with the Ward quest for truth and the British officialdom's involvement in the process. An interesting concurrence is the novel's use of the notion of ensuring that nobody 'rocks the boat', which Ward uses in his book. Ward's comment about 'people whose job it was to try to prevent anyone from "rocking the boat"' (1991: 111), gains suggestive meanings when read beside similar sentiments expressed in le Carré's novel by two Scotland Yard detectives – Rob and Lesley – who are sent out to Kenya to help investigate Tessa Quayle's murder. As they tell Justin Quayle, in confidence, soon after being pulled off the case for getting too close to the truth,

> The glorious House of ThreeBees is never to be mentioned again and that's an order. Not their products, their operations or their staff. Nothing's allowed to rock the boat. Lots of boats … Curtiss is untouchable. He's halfway to brokering a bumper British arms deal with the Somalis. The embargo's a nuisance but he's found ways of getting around it. He's a front-runner in the race to provide a state-of-the-art East African telecom system using British high-tech [le Carré 2001: 217].

Although Ward seems to take the notion of not 'rocking the boat' to be an innocent preservation of diplomatic relations between the two countries, le Carré's novel, though fictional, nudges us to consider that the concerns may have been less innocent than Ward initially took them to be.

The novel presents the Foreign Office, the British High Commission and Scotland Yard as all caught up in these complicities and power games, even though a few individual members remain upright, and act with integrity. A case in point here is the fictional British High Commissioner Sir Porter Coleridge who, like the actual British High Commissioner in Nairobi in the late 1980s, Sir John Johnson, finds himself in the middle of a high-profile murder, while having to maintain diplomatic stability and abide by the Foreign Office's dicta. In the novel, soon after Tessa Quayle's death, the High Commissioner receives instructions from the Foreign Office in London to cover up her death.

'The shit [Foreign Office Director of Affairs for Africa] Pellegrin says, shove the whole thing under the carpet' Porter Coleridge announced, slamming down the telephone. 'Shove it far and fast. Biggest bloody carpet we can find ... Off the record and only if asked, we respected her crusades but considered them under-informed and screwball'. A pause while he wrestled with his self-disgust. 'And we are to put it out that she was crazy ... The [Foreign] Office wants long-suffering. She was our cross but we bore her bravely. Can you do long-suffering? It makes me absolutely fucking *sick*' [le Carré 2001: 70–71, original emphasis].

The Foreign Office orders the British High Commissioner to completely cover up Tessa Quayle's murder along with the reasons behind it (the investigations into the activities of the British multinational, ThreeBees). Coleridge's failure to toe the official line is punished by a sudden removal from his post in Nairobi, when he is considered a threat to the web of political lies intended to discredit both Tessa and her cutting report on British complicity in corruption and fatal drug trials on Kenyans by ThreeBees. The official story put out to the staff at the High Commission is that, on the spur of the moment, the High Commissioner has decided to take some home leave and find his brain-damaged daughter Rosie a special school in Britain (le Carré 2001: 301).

Similarly, soon after Tessa's death, the fictional Scotland Yard sends two young detectives, Rob and Lesley to Kenya to investigate. The two piece together evidence of British involvement in Tessa's death and submit a detailed report to Scotland Yard, with recommendations about the involvement of key British figures and institutions. In response, their Scotland Yard boss rejects their report, pulls them off the case and appoints two new detectives, under strict instructions on the bounds of their investigations. They inform Tessa's husband, Justin:

> '[We] are off the case. Gridley has sent two new officers to Nairobi to help and advise the local police in the search for [Tessa's close friend Arnold] Bluhm. No looking under stones, no deviations. Period ... And our replacements aren't allowed to talk to us in case they catch our disease' [le Carré 2001: 216].

Rob and Lesley are angered by the realization that there is a high-level cover-up in the case, and that the very institutions they have worked for with loyalty and a strong sense of integrity, are morally bankrupt, driven by an intense greed that is endorsed by state institutions, including the High Commission, the Foreign Office, the Secret Intelligence Service, the national political parties and Scotland Yard, all of which present a front of commitment to justice and integrity. Rob and Lesley find themselves unmasking the depths of lies and complicities, which Tessa had earlier unmasked, when she observed that the 'mother of democracies is once more revealed as a lying hypocrite, preaching liberty and human rights for all, except where she hopes to make a quick buck' (le Carré 2001: 53).

Tessa's observation here – and indeed the entire novel's portrayal of the multiple interests that underpin the Kenya–Britain relationship – offer important points of reflection for Ward case. Though fictional, the novel dismantles assumptions about an inherent British commitment to justice, truth and moral integrity as contrasted with Kenya's lack of these values. Although the novel's narrative mirrors Ward's experiences in so far as the existence of some upright wo/men of integrity like Nigel Wicks, John Ferguson and Jenny Jenkins are concerned, such people's commitment to justice, the novel suggests, remains constrained by the broader institutional structures under which they work, and which dictate the limits of their interventions, as illustrated by the fictional Justin Quayle, Rob, Lesley and Porter Coleridge in the novel, all of whose efforts to counter the system are clipped.

Le Carré's novel eloquently articulates the power of capital and its interests. In the novel, it is capital that mediates the fault lines in the Kenya–Britain relationship. Le Carré suggests that faced with the interests of capital, the moral integrity and commitment to justice that Ward initially associates with British institutions melts down, and the artificial moral distinction between the ex-colonies and the mother country fizzles out, as the two work in partnership towards capital accumulation, and the mother country finds itself deploying the very strategies it publicly condemns in the postcolonial African state, through its discursive mask of the promotion of justice and democracy.

In sum then, there are indications that contrary to popular assumptions about Britain's support for the quest for Julie Ward's killers, the British Secret Intelligence Service, working with the High Commission in Nairobi, may have been complicit in the Kenyan attempts to cover up the truth behind Julie Ward's death. At a certain level, Kenyan interest in hiding the truth behind Julie Ward's death appears to have resonated with certain British interests. The relationship between Kenya and Britain over the Julie Ward case is revealing about the inner workings of hegemonic structures and discourses. Our discussion indicates that beneath hegemonic structures and forces, which often present an image of coherence, often lurk fault lines which contradict accepted wisdom. The British–Kenyan interactions in the Julie Ward matter highlight two key concerns. First, that hegemonic groups' pursuit of the discourses they endorse is often in flux, and contingent on a range of other interests that determine the earnestness with which such discourses will be pursued. To a large degree, this approximates James Scott's (1990) idea of public transcripts of the dominant group, which co-exist with hidden transcripts that are at times in direct opposition to the public transcripts they perform and through which they earn legitimacy. The patterns of interactions between Kenya and Britain in the Julie Ward matter though, stretch Scott's work further by revealing that, sometimes, the dominant group and the subordinate group's hidden transcripts overlap when their shared interests resonate, as was the case with the shared interest between Kenya and Britain in the Julie Ward matter.

Our discussion further suggests that apart from Ward's cultural illiteracy which prevented him from accessing local textualities, as discussed in the previous chapter, Ward's quest for his daughter's killers was further impeded by his assumptions about Kenya and Britain, in which he constructed a binary lens that placed the two countries at opposite ends of the moral spectrum. Ward's polarity placed British official institutions on an irreproachable pedestal of moral authority, integrity and commitment to justice. Yet unknown to Ward, these notions of moral authority and indeed, even the very polarization between Kenya and Britain was merely a discursive mask that, alongside the idea of diplomatic caution, worked to mask Britain's seeming complicity in the cover-up of the truth behind his daughter's murder.

From another perspective, Ward and le Carré's narratives are instructive on the workings of narrative in relation to dominant discourses, and the ways in which the narrative space allows for the possibility of either the reproduction of dominant discourses, as in the case of Ward's unquestioning replication of the polarized lenses, or the destabilization of such ideas, as suggested by le Carré's fictional narrative. Yet this is never a clear-cut process as, often, narratives challenge certain hegemonic discourses while simultaneously constructing others.

Despite our focus on the social truths that were inscribed in the Ward case, and the ways in which Julie Ward's death in Kenya and the subsequent quest for her killers convened a set of contact zones, providing important forums where various concerns were debated in the course of the interactions between the different constituencies, it is hard to overstate the horrible human tragedy at the centre of this book: a young woman was brutally murdered and her body was disposed of in a most inhumane way. For more than 25 years, a family has been subjected to layer upon layer of deceit, sabotage and contempt in its search for truth and justice.

The search for the murderer(s) is still on, and new reports and allegations continue to emerge. On 11 October 2009, reports of a new collaborative investigation between the Scotland Yard and Kenyan police emerged; their hopes lay in human DNA collected from the scene of the remains and preserved since then. In November 2011, BBC News reported that a team of six Scotland Yard investigators had flown to Kenya to launch new investigations into the murder.

This book has offered a reflection on the conceptual and empirical reach of binary categories of understanding the relationship between the colonizer and the colonized and, by extension, Africa and Europe. Where much of the existing literature dismisses such binaries as a thing of the past, and celebrates their demise with such 'inclusive' discourses as multiculturalism, hybridity and globalization, our reflection on the developments and narratives regarding the Ward murder points to different conclusions. First, far from being extinct, these binaries continue to be mobilized in understanding contemporary Africa and Africans, perhaps not with the same crudeness, but certainly from the same impulse. Second, far from fixing them immutably under an oppressive gaze, within the deployment of these binaries are interesting sites for subversion, resistance and critique. In this respect, our exploration of the contact zones that were convened by the Julie Ward case revises our understandings of modernity, especially in relation to its pillars of rationalism/reason, unity of the subject and their assumptions about Africa. The book revealed that Julie Ward's death in Kenya took place in a complex discursive terrain marked by layer upon layer of interests, values and anxieties. These discursive terrains inevitably tinted interpretations of the Julie Ward case, and to a large degree, framed the concerns that were later to be inscribed on the death. Thus, while the Ward family and the authors of the three books approached the case from their vantage point within British colonial archives about Africa and Africans, Kenyan publics positioned themselves at the fourth corner of the quadrilateral comprised of themselves, the Ward family, British state institutions and the Kenyan state. It is from this position that they speculated on the circumstances surrounding Julie Ward's death, arriving at conclusions that differed from those offered by both the courtroom processes and the three authors of the books on the case – John Ward, Jeremy Gavron and Michael Hiltzik.

In the contestations over the portrait of Julie Ward in Kenyan and British imaginaries, there seemed to be a consistent focus on her sexual relations. Both sides appeared to celebrate a virginal, victimized Julie Ward, whose virtue was a hotly contested issue in their narratives, whether in the British fixation on the 'black peril' rape model or in the Kenyan lingering on a criminal political elite's deployment of sexual violence, and the attendant figure of the sexually adventurous tourist. This was a remarkable discursive continuity across the British–Kenyan divide, in which we see the interpenetration of the two social imaginaries' concern with policing female sexual and racial purity. Notably, in the British case, this policing of female sexuality goes beyond bland patriarchy, to gesture at a preoccupation with the re-insertion of white male authority in Africa, indeed, a nostalgic struggle to affirm and restore a white male authority reminiscent of that in the settler colony.

If as Mary Douglas notes, 'margins are dangerous [and s]ocieties are most vulnerable at their edges, along the tattered fringes of the known world' (1966: 63), then we can see why, in negotiating the contact zone between Kenya and Britain, Ward, Hiltzik and Gavron grasped at colonial memory, and drew on this archive in making sense of the Julie Ward death in Kenya. These archives in a way provided a familiar cartography for navigating both this moment of rupture and the unfamiliar postcolonial Kenyan terrain. In many ways, the resurgence of ideas drawn from an outdated colonial archive suggests their continued availability and easy re-activation in reading contemporary realities. Indeed, our discussion suggests that fragments of myths and prejudices about Africa and Africans remain embedded in European society's cultural psyche. It is this cultural psyche that helps us to understand the persistent enactment of a certain 'return of the repressed' in British imaginaries, in the form of tropes such as the 'noble savage' that were deployed in understanding the contact zones between Britain and Kenya. These tropes, it would seem, having been successfully internalized, return in moments of crisis, such as the Ward murder, as part of an ancient yet familiar grammar of making sense of Otherness, when more contemporary and 'rational' logics fail. Here, one is reminded of Rita Felski's notion of the 'transtemporal movement and affective resonance of particular texts' and the possibilities of 'tracing cross-temporal networks' (2011: 574, 577), or what Angela Davis (2013) would term the reproduction, retooling, recasting and adaptation of ideas drawn from the colonial library and remobilized in making sense of contemporary experiences.

The retrieval of these discursive tropes in British imaginaries echoes an older binary opposition between what Gikandi, in a different context, describes as 'European modernity, epitomized by the rule of reason, and African primitivism embodied in non-rational systems of cognition' (2002: 140). Our discussion revealed the unproblematic transition from a discourse of pre-modern primitivism and savagery, to another variant of savagery, in the political jungle of the postcolonial African state. We see the transition from a subhuman, uncorrupted 'noble savage' status, still closely aligned to nature and to an amoral, monstrous variant of savagery, embodied by the morally bankrupt Kenyan state institutions and its officials. Implicit here is the notion that Europe's purportedly inherent morality can survive the corrupting potential of modernity – in part because it is also a successfully conceived modernity, rooted in science and the law. African moral faculty however, fails to survive beyond the child-like 'noble savage' stage, as, with the aborted project of modernity, the sense of integrity expected to be achieved concurrently with progress, through rationality, science and law, is also stillborn. Put differently, African morality can only be safeguarded by 'irrational' forms such as metaphysics and religion – an element that variously figured in the elements of African ethnoculture in the murder.

While this recourse to available social imaginaries and discursive tools largely drawn from colonial archives is arguably understandable as a 'summoning of the familiar', these epistemological templates were nonetheless ill-suited to the layered realities of the Julie Ward death in Kenya, which remained illegible to the logics of modernity privileged by John Ward and the Scotland Yard investigators. In part due to this reliance on inappropriate templates drawn from British social imaginaries, Julie Ward's presence in Kenya, her death and the subsequent quest for her killers was consistently haunted by neat dichotomies, derived from the various master narratives that the murder of the young British woman seemed to evoke. One important concern for this book has been the empirical reach of these dichotomies. The study found that these binaries were both disrupted and disruptive. First, the realities of the Ward case – both Kenyan and British – subverted the logics of the received knowledge about Africa and Africans that underpin these dichotomies. Second, these master narratives created blind spots which impeded the visibility of the underlying fault lines of deceit and complicity across the British–Kenyan divide. In fact, these polarities were revealed to work as discursive masks which conceal subterranean fault lines, complicities and shared interests. As seen from our discussions, John Ward's binary lenses of the Kenya–Britain dichotomy unfortunately created a naïve faith in the mirage of an uncompromising British sense of justice and moral integrity, blinding him to possible British complicity in the cover-up and, paradoxically, made him too trusting and open to manipulation by the British.

If we consider what Jorge Larrain calls the 'civilising mission of capitalist expansion and colonialism throughout the world' (1994: 21) as one of the products of European enlightenment, then the Ward case offers important commentary on the workings of capital, in the contradictions of British complicity in covering up the truth behind Julie Ward's death. This complicit relationship between Kenya and Britain over the Julie Ward case offers further insights into the inner workings of hegemonic structures. Our discussion suggests that beneath hegemonic structures and forces that present an image of coherence often lurk fault lines contradicting the public transcripts they perform, and suggesting that hegemonic groups' pursuit of the discourses they endorse is often in flux, and contingent on a multiplicity of sometimes conflicting interests which shatter the myth of the unity of the subject.

Our discussion on the rumours and allegations regarding the Julie Ward case is particularly insightful in this regard. Perhaps what stands out here is the way in which an oft-neglected and largely discredited medium was able to offer a powerful critique of modern institutions in the postcolonial state, and colonial modernity's legacy. As responses to formalized truths, the rumours and allegations surrounding Julie Ward's death represented an important process of reconfiguring the conventional regimes of truth and evidence privileged by modern state institutions' drawing on the dictates of science and law to formulate their truths, while simultaneously rejecting those two disciplines' hegemonic status in the Julie Ward case. To this end, the rumours critique the notion that 'it is precisely in the breakdown of the process of rationalization that life in the postcolony becomes intelligible', which Gikandi (2002: 144) situates in Achille Mbembe's work on the postcolony. In fact, the rumours worked within their own system of logics and rationalities, which were founded on a critical engagement with local realities, even though they rejected hegemonic notions of truth as based on legally admissible evidence. In the process, these rumours challenge what Gikandi describes as the re-inscription of the postcolony as a system of signs that differentiates between mind and sense, in an economy of discourse which 'posit[s] a split between an autonomous, rational subject and its field of experiences' (ibid.), by illustrating the co-valence of both the rational subject and its experiences.

In an essay titled 'The Triple Helix: Nation, Class and Ethnicity in the African State', Michael Schatzberg proposes a useful metaphor for understanding the shifting and often concentric identities to which people lay claim in the postcolonial African state. Using the metaphor of a triple-stranded helix of state, class and ethnicity, Schatzberg argues that the three components interact with each other, each strand variously occupying a dominant position depending on the context and the strategic benefits to be reaped from such foregrounding of a given identity. While Schatzberg uses this metaphor to understand the nature of the state in Africa and its accompanying social dynamics, his ideas are instructive in making sense of the unstable nature of popular sentiment on the Julie Ward death among Kenyan publics. In our case, popular publics laid the blame for Julie Ward's death at the doorstep of a violent state, a state with dark secrets to hide, a state controlled by a powerful elite. Thus, at this level, Julie Ward's death became symptomatic of a predatory state. Yet at the same time, this incrimination of the state did not necessarily translate to sympathy with John Ward's investigations into the circumstances surrounding his daughter's death. Thus, local publics saw no contradictions between the incrimination of the political elite and revelling in a sensational portrait of Julie Ward as a woman of loose sexual mores.

This was an important differentiator between the local imaginaries on the case and the British imaginaries, as articulated in the three books on Julie Ward's death. While the British appeared to cling to their neat dichotomies, local imaginaries were more versatile and nursed a healthy suspicion of absolute truths produced through the modern state institutions. In a different context, Ikem, a character in Chinua Achebe's *Anthills of the Savannah*, observes:

> In the vocabulary of certain radical theorists, contradictions are given the status of some deadly disease to which their opponents alone succumb. But contradictions are the very stuff of life. If there had been a little dash of contradiction among the Gadarene swine some of them might have been saved from drowning [1987: 100].

Ikem's observation here could easily be applied to investigations into the Ward murder. John Ward resolutely clung to received wisdom about Africa and Africans and failed to nurse the cautionary scepticism needed in dealing with both the Kenyan and British individuals and institutions. Yet, one must hasten to add, although local imaginaries were resilient, and despite their strong critique of the state, this dash of contradiction was far from healthy in our case, further serving to underscore the often limited reach of popular discourses' oppositional impulses.

In the end, there were two important impediments in the Ward case. First was the failure to imagine new grammars of whiteness, independent of the grammars of colonial whiteness. This went beyond the Wards particularly, and related more broadly to the hegemonic regimes of whiteness in Africa, of which Julie Ward, John Ward and the Scotland Yard detectives merely partook. This failure to cut loose from the logics of colonial whiteness and its aesthetics is seen in the continued deployment of the missionary impulse with regards to modernity in Africa. Thus, acceding to a popularized discourse of the failure of modernity – and by extension the civilizing mission – in Africa, whiteness in postcolonial Africa continues to be produced through a messianic trope, largely re-directed to the humanitarian and wildlife conservation industries in the continent. In both cases – well-meaning as they may be – there is an implicit indictment of the failures of the postcolonial African state and its violence, coupled with a white male benevolence, still scripted in grammars reminiscent of colonial messianism. The difference here, though, is a new dialectic of cynicism towards the project of modernity in Africa, coupled with disengagement, best articulated through the resort to wildlife conservation, combined with forays to select pockets of the human world to distribute relief to victims of African violence and state inefficiency. The vulnerability of such victims has earned them a place beside the wildlife as worthy of protection and rescue. In many ways, this is a shade of the same vacuating gaze that underpins wildlife tourism in Africa, and goes back to colonial annexation of land that was presumed 'vacant'. As David Dunn argues in his reading of one of the classics of colonial romance, Rider Haggard's *King Solomon's Mines*, 'the foreign landscape appears as an uncharted "virgin" zone that waits to be inscribed by masculine colonizing zeal' (Dunn 1988: 12). What stands out here is the total refusal, failure or inability to engage with Africans outside the logic of white messianism or paternalism.

A second impediment lay in the unquestioning faith in modern legal apparatuses whose definitions of credible truths and admissible evidence were too narrow and stifling, and which were, furthermore, stained by the imprint of colonial modernity's selective distribution of its privileges, a convention the postcolonial African state was sure to inherit, perfect and even re-invest in its incestuous relationships with capital and the mother country. Perceived to be – for whatever reasons – potentially disruptive to this tripartite marriage, the Ward case was unlikely to be resolved in either the Kenyan or British legal institutions. Given the knack of the other tripartite marriage between capital, state power and modernity (and their institutions) for re-inventing itself, while keeping the mask of modernity-as-progress in place, it is important to heed Gikandi's (2002) call to interrogate the privileged tenets of Western modernity, particularly rationality and the attendant logocentric impulse as they manifest themselves in Africa. The insights developed in this book are a contribution towards that project.

Afterword

Julie Ward was among the group of tourists I travelled with in 1988 on the Hobo Trans-Africa truck. We set off from Dover in the freezing February weather and arrived in Nairobi five months later. All the way from Europe to East Africa we slept in small but sturdy tents that we pitched by the side of the road, and we cooked meals over an open fire in canteen saucepans.

We all liked Julie. She was gentle without being a pushover, quiet without being introverted. While the raging tinnitus in her ears prevented her from easily participating in conversations when our noise was in full flow, she made several close friends and talked with excitement about her plans to set up a new life in Kenya.

When our truck got stuck in the mud trying to cross the River Niger in Mali, Julie and a few others set up a makeshift clinic for the mothers who brought infants with conjunctivitis, or needed antiseptic wipes and painkillers. We did not carry anything stronger than aspirin, TCP and plasters on the truck.

Julie's gentle manner and quiet way of engaging with people made the news of her violent death all the more difficult for us to comprehend. I heard it on a Radio Four newscast while sitting in a traffic jam in London. Was this the same Julie Ward, I wondered? I could not imagine what had caused this to happen. I read all the newspapers. Again and again, there was the photograph of Julie holding the orphaned chimpanzee. All over the media in Europe and East Africa, a multiplicity of stories was mapped onto this unassuming woman.

Julie crossed continents in search of a new beginning. That life did not have the chance to begin. Grace A. Musila has captured the complicated layers of speculation that accompanied Julie's death and shows how Julie was reconstructed again and again by different commentators, each one striving to understand what really happened in the Maasai Mara. But this book does not attempt to offer a definitive truth or to solve the mystery of Julie's murder. It is a tribute to the author that, in amongst all the criss-crossing and contradictory stories, Julie's personality shines through the pages of this book.

Stephanie Newell
Series Co-Editor, African Articulations

Bibliography

Achebe, Chinua (1974). *Arrow of God.* London: Heinemann.

—— (1987). *Anthills of the Savannah.* London: Heinemann Educational.

Adar, Korwa G. and Munyae, Isaac M. (2001). 'Human Rights Abuse in Kenya under Daniel arap Moi, 1978–2001'. *African Studies Quarterly* 5 (1): 1–17.

Africa Centre for Open Governance (AfriCOG) (2007). 'A Study of Commissions of Inquiry in Kenya'.

Africa Confidential (2015). 'ICC Murder Mystery'. *Africa Confidential* 56 (3). Available at www.africa-confidential.com/article-preview/id/5962/ICC_murder_mystery. Accessed 27 February 2015. Aganyanya, Judge Daniel K.S. (1999) Judgement, Case no 55 of 1988 *Republic of Kenya vs. Simon Basha ole Makalla*, delivered on 17 September 1999.

Aganyanya, Daniel (2014). *The Judicial Purge 2003 – That Never Was.* Nairobi: Amicable Printers.

Akama, John (1999a). 'The Evolution of Tourism in Kenya'. *Journal of Sustainable Tourism* 7 (1): 6–25.

—— (1999b). 'Marginalization of the Maasai in Kenya'. *Annals of Tourism Research* 26 (3): 716–18.

Amoko, Apollo O. (1999). 'The Missionary Gene in the Kenyan Polity: Representations of Contemporary Kenya in the British Media'. *Callaloo* 22 (1): 223–39.

Anderson, David (2002). 'Vigilantes, Violence and the Politics of Public Order in Kenya'. *African Affairs* 101: 531–55.

—— (2005). *Histories of the Hanged: Britain's Dirty War in Kenya and the end of Empire.* London: Weidenfeld and Nicolson.

—— (2010). 'Sexual Threat and Settler Society: "Black Perils" in Kenya, c. 1907–30. *Journal of Imperial and Commonwealth History* 38 (1): 47–74.

Appadurai, Arjun (1996). *Modernity at Large: Cultural Dimensions of Globaliization.* Minneapolis: University of Minnesota Press.

Ashcroft, Bill, Griffiths, Gareth and Tiffin, Helen (1998). *Key Concepts in Post-Colonial Studies.* London and New York: Routledge.

Attwell, David (2005). *Rewriting Modernity: Studies in Black South African Literary History.* Scottsville: University of KwaZulu-Natal Press.

Baderoon, Gabeba (2014). *Regarding Muslims: From Slavery to Post-Apartheid.* Johannesburg: Wits University Press.

Bakhtin, Mikhail; trans. Michael Holquist (1981). *The Dialogic Imagination: Four Essays.* Austin TX and London: University of Texas Press.

—— (1984); trans. Helene Iswolsky. *Rabelais and his World.* Bloomington: Indiana University Press.

Barber, Karin (ed.) (2006). *Africa's Hidden Histories: Everyday Literacy and Making the Self.* Bloomington: Indiana University Press.

—— (2007) *The Anthropology of Texts, Persons and Publics: Oral and Written Culture in Africa and Beyond.* Cambridge: Cambridge University Press.

Barkham, Patrick (2004a). 'Father Vindicated as Kenya Admits Obstructing Julie Ward Inquiry'. *The Guardian* 29 April. Available at www.theguardian.com/uk/2004/apr/29/kenya.world. Accessed 2 July 2015.

—— (2004b). 'MI6 Agent Hid Role in Julie Ward Murder Case'. *The Guardian* 30 April. Available at www.guardian.co.uk/kenya/story/0,,1206768,00.html. Accessed 20 March 2007.

—— (2004c). 'My Daughter was Killed and Thrown to Lions. Did You Expect Me to Walk Away? Coroner's Verdict Adds to Optimism that Julie Case will be Solved'. *The Guardian* 5 May. Available at www.theguardian.com/uk/2004/may/05/kenya.world. Accessed 2 July 2015.

Barritt, David (1988). 'Lion Girl's Last Sex-Crazed Night'. *Sunday Mirror* 7 November.

Bayart, Jean-François (1993). *The State in Africa: The Politics of the Belly.* London and New York: Longman.

—— (2000) 'Africa in the World: A History of Extraversion'. *African Affairs* 99 (395): 217–67.

BBC News (2011). 'Detectives Fly to Kenya in Julie Ward Murder Probe'. Available at www.bbc.co.uk/news/uk-england-15598775. Accessed 2 July 2015.

Bennett, Tony (1983). 'Texts, Readers, Reading Formations'. *The Bulletin of the Midwest Modern Language Association* 16 (1): 3–17.

—— (1990) *Outside Literature.* London: Routledge.

Bhabha, Homi (1983). 'The Other Question: The Stereotype and Colonial Discourse'. *Screen* 24 (6): 18–36.

Bland, Lucy (1995). *Banishing the Beast: English Feminism and Sexual Morality 1885–1914.* London: Penguin.

Blixen, Karen (1937). *Out of Africa*, London: Putnam.

Branch, Daniel (2012). *Kenya: Between Hope and Despair, 1963–2012.* New Haven: Yale University Press.

Brown, Barbara (1987). 'Facing the "Black Peril": The Politics of Population Control in South Africa'. *Journal of Southern African Studies* 13 (2): 256–73.

Brown, Stephen (2001). 'Authoritarian Leaders and Multiparty Elections in Africa: How Foreign Donors Help to Keep Kenya's Daniel arap Moi in Power'. *Third World Quarterly* 22 (5): 725–39.

—— (2003). 'Quiet Diplomacy and Recurring "Ethnic Clashes" in Kenya'. In Chandra L. Sriram and Karin Wermester (eds). *From Promise to Practice: Strengthening UN Capacities for the Prevention of Violent Conflict.* Boulder CO: Lynne Rienner: 69–100.

Buckley, Nick (ed.) (1998). *Julie Ward: Gentle Nature.* Horsham: The Born Free Foundation.

Campbell, Duncan (1995). 'Father wants Kenya Aid Blocked over Killing'. *The Guardian* 25 September: 5.

Cannadine, David (2001). *Ornamentalism: How the British Saw their Empire.* Oxford: Oxford University Press.

Carter, Helen (1998). 'I Will Feel a Certain Contentment if I get a Murder Verdict' *The Guardian* 22 July: 12.

Chakrabarty, Dipesh (2010). 'Provincializing Europe: Postcoloniality and the Critique of History'. In Stephen Howe (ed.). *The New Imperial Histories Reader*. London and New York: Routledge: 55–71.

Chege, Michael (1998). 'Africans of European Descent'. *Transition* 73 (7): 74–86.

Citizens for Justice (2003). *We Lived to Tell: The Nyayo House Story*. Nairobi: Friedrich Ebert Stiftung.

Clark, Heather A. (2012). *Chai Tea Sunday*. Toronto: ECW Press.

Cloete, Elsie (2002). 'Re-Telling Kenya: Wambui Waiyaki Otieno and Mau Mau's Daughter'. Unpublished PhD. Thesis, University of the Witwatersrand.

Coetzee, Carli (2013). *Accented Futures: Language Activism and the Ending of Apartheid*. Johannesburg: Wits University Press.

Coetzee, J.M. (1988). *White Writing: On the Culture of Letters in South Africa*. New Haven CT: Yale University Press.

Cohen, David and Odhiambo, Atieno (1992). *Burying SM: The Politics of Knowledge and the Sociology of Power in Africa*. London: James Currey.

—— (2004). *The Risks of Knowledge: Investigations into the Death of the Hon. Minister John Robert Ouko in Kenya, 1990*. Athens: Ohio University Press.

Comaroff, Jean and Comaroff, John (eds) (1993). *Modernity and its Malcontents: Ritual and Power in Postcolonial Africa*. Chicago: Chicago University Press.

Cooper, Frederick (2002). *Africa since 1940: The Past of the Present*. Cambridge: Cambridge University Press.

—— (2005). *Colonialism in Question: Theory, Knowledge, History*. Berkeley and Los Angeles: University of California Press.

Cornwell, Gareth (1996). 'George Webb Hardy's *The Black Peril* and the Social Meaning of "Black Peril" in Early Twentieth Century South Africa'. *Journal of Southern African Studies* 22 (3): 441–53.

Cruise O'Brien, Donal (1972). 'Modernization, Order, and the Erosion of a Democratic Ideal: American political science 1960–70'. *Journal of Development Studies* 8 (4): 351–78.

Curtin, P.T. (1961). '"The White Man's Grave": Image and Reality, 1780–1850'. *Journal of British Studies* 1 (1): 94–110.

Davis, Angela (1982). *Women, Race & Class*. New York: Women's Press.

—— (1999 [1998]). *Blues Legacies and Black Feminism: Gertrude 'Ma' Rainey, Bessie Smith, and Billie Holiday*. New York: Vintage Books.

Devereux, Cecily (1999). 'New Woman, New World: Maternal Feminism and the New Imperialism in the White Settler Colonies'. *Women Studies International Forum* 22 (2): 175–84.

Diamond, Larry (1987). 'Class Formation in the Swollen African State'. *Journal of Modern African Studies* 25 (4): 567–96.

Deutsch, Jan-Georg Probst, Peter and Schmidt, Heike (eds) (2002). *African Modernities: Entangled Meanings in Current Debate*. Portsmouth NH and Oxford: Heinemann and James Currey.

DiFonzo, Nicholas and Bordia, Prashant (2007). 'Rumor, Gossip and Urban Legends'. *Diogenes* 54 (1): 19–35.

Dlamini, Jacob (2014). *Askari: A Story of Collaboration and Betrayal in the Anti-Apartheid Struggle*. Johannesburg: Jacana Media.

Douglas, Mary (1966). *Purity and Danger*. London: Routledge and Kegan Paul.

Duder, C.J.D. (1991). 'Love and the Lions: The Image of White Settlement in Kenya in Popular Fiction, 1919–1939'. *African Affairs* 90 (360): 427–38.

Dunn, David (1988). 'Embodying Africa: Woman and Romance in Colonial Fiction'. *English in Africa* 15 (1): 1–28.

Dyer, Richard (1997). *White*. London: Routledge.

East Africa Protectorate Economic Commission (1919). 'Final Report I & II' Nairobi: Government Printers.

East African Centre for Law and Justice 'Understanding the Law in the Nancy Baraza Case' 17 January 2012, http://eaclj.org/constitution/20-constitution-feature-articles/113-understanding-the-law-in-the-nancy-baraza-case.html Accessed 18 February 2015.

East Anglian Daily Times (2013). 'Twenty-Five years on from Murder of Julie Ward'. 31 August. Available at www.eadt.co.uk/news/twenty_five_years_on_from_murder_of_julie_ward_in_kenya_grieving_dad_asks_i_know_who_killed_her_so_why_won_t_they_convict_my_daughter_s_murderer_1_2361130. Accessed 27 February 2015.

Ekeh, Peter (1975). 'Colonialism and the Two Publics in Africa: A Theoretical Statement'. *Comparative Studies in Society and History* 17 (1): 91–112.

Elkins, Caroline (2005). *Imperial Reckoning: The Untold Story of Britain's Gulag in Kenya*. New York: Henry Holt.

Ellis, Stephen (1989). 'Tuning in to Pavement Radio'. *African Affairs* 88 (352): 321–30.

Ellis, Stephen and ter Haar, Gerrie (2004). *Worlds of Power: Religious Thought and Political Practice in Africa*. Johannesburg: Wits University Press.

Epstein, Arnold (1958). *Politics in an Urban African Community*. Manchester: Manchester University Press.

Fanon, Frantz (1967). *The Wretched of the Earth*. London: Penguin.

Felski, Rita (2011). 'Context Stinks!' *New Literary History*. 42 (4): 573–91.

Fidahussein (1992), Abdallah. Judgement: Republic of Kenya vs. Jonah Tejui Magiroi and Peter Kipeen Magiroi, Nairobi.

Fontanella-Khan, Amana (2014). 'India's Feudal Rapists' *New York Times* 4 June. www.nytimes.com/2014/06/05/opinion/indias-feudal-rapists.html. Accessed 6 July 2014.

Frankenberg, Ruth (1993). *White Women, Race Matters: The Social Construction of Whiteness*. London: Routledge.

Foucault, Michel (2002 [1969]). *The Archeology of Knowledge*. London and New York: Routledge.

—— (1979 [1976]) *The History of Sexuality Vol 1: An Introduction*. London: Allan Lane.

Fox, James (1983). *White Mischief: The Murder of Lord Erroll*. New York: Random House.

Gates, Henry Louis, Jr (1997). *Thirteen Ways of Looking at a Black Man*. New York: Vintage Books,

Gavron, Jeremy (1991). *Darkness in Eden: The Murder of Julie Ward*. London, Harper-Collins.

Gikandi, Simon (1984). 'The Growth of the East African Novel'. In G.D. Killam (ed.). *The Writing of East and Central Africa*, London: Heinemann.

—— (2000a). 'Africa and the Idea of the Aesthetic: From Eurocentricism to Pan-Africanism.' *English Studies in Africa* 43 (2): 19–46.

—— (2000b) 'Reading the Referent: Postcolonialism and the Writing of Modernity'. In Susheila Nasta (ed.). *Reading the 'New' Literatures in a Postcolonial Era*. Cambridge: D.S. Brewer.

—— (2001). 'Globalization and the Claims of Postcoloniality'. *The South Atlantic Quarterly* 100 (3): 627–58.

—— (2002). 'Reason, Modernity and the African Crisis'. In Jan-Georg Deutsch, Peter Probst and Heike Schmidt (eds). *African Modernities: Entangled Meanings in Current Debate*. Portsmouth NH and Oxford: Heinemann and James Currey: 135–57.

—— (2007). 'The Ghost of Mathew Arnold: Englishness and the Politics of Culture'. *Nineteenth Century Contexts* 29 (2–3): 187–99.

—— (2012). 'African Literature and the Colonial Factor'. In Abiola Irele and Simon Gikandi (eds). *The Cambridge History of African and Caribbean Literature* Vol. 1. Cambridge University Press: 379 –97.

Gqola, Pumla Dineo (2015). *Rape: A South African Nightmare*. MFB: Johannesburg.

Graff, Gerald (1989). 'Narrative and the Unofficial Interpretive Culture.' In James Phelan. *Reading Narrative: Form, Ethics, Ideology*. Columbus: Ohio State University Press.

Graham, Lucy (2006). '"Bathing Area – For Whites Only": Reading Prohibitive Signs and "Black Peril" in Lewis Nkosi's *Mating Birds*'. In Lindy Stiebel and Liz Gunner (eds). *Still Beating the Drum: Critical Perspectives on Lewis Nkosi*. Johannesburg: Wits University Press; Amsterdam: Rodopi: 147–66.

Gregory, Derek (2000). 'Edward Said's Imaginative Geographies'. In M. Crang and N. Thrift (eds) *Thinking Space*. London: Routledge: 302–48.

Grove, Richard H. (2010). 'The Colonial State and the Origins of Western Environmentalism'. In Stephen Howe (ed.) *The New Imperial Histories Reader*. London and New York: Routledge: 209–18.

Gunn, Robin Jones (2012). *Finally & Forever*. Grand Rapids MI: Zondervan.

Gqola, Pumla (2006). 'After Zuma: Gender Violence and our Constitution'. Ruth First Lecture, 15 November, Constitution Hill, Johannesburg.

Habermas, J. (1981). 'Die Moderne – Ein Unvollendetes Projekt'. In J. Habermas. *Kleine Politische Schriften*, Vols I–IV. Frankfurt am Main: Suhrkamp: 444–64.

Hacking, Ian (1986). 'The Archaeology of Foucault'. In Michel Foucault and David Couzens Hoy (ed.). *Foucault: A Critical Reader*. Oxford: Blackwell: 27–40.

Hall, Stuart (2002). 'The Television Discourse: Encoding and Decoding'. In Dennis McQuail (ed.). *McQuail's Reader in Mass Communication Theory*. London: Sage.

Hammer, Joshua (2006). 'The Kenyan Cowboy'. *Outside Magazine*, December. Available at www.outsideonline.com/1825141/kenyan-cowboy. Accessed 8 June 2015.

Harraway, Donna (1992). 'The Promises of Monsters: A Regenerative Politics for Inappropriate/d Others'. In Lawrence Grossberg, Cary Nelson and Paula A. Treichler (eds). *Cultural Studies*. New York: Routledge.

Haugerud, Angelique (1995). *The Culture of Politics in Modern Kenya*. Cambridge University Press.

Hiltzik, Michael (1991). *A Death in Kenya: The Murder of Julie Ward*. New York, Delacorte Press.

Hoch, Paul. *White Hero, Black Beast: Racism, Sexism, and the Mask of Masculinity*. London: Pluto, 1979.

Hodgson, Dorothy (1999). '"Once Intrepid Warriors": Modernity and the Production of Maasai Masculinities'. *Ethnology* 38 (2): 121–50.

Hornsby, Charles (2012). *Kenya: A History Since Independence*. London: I.B. Tauris.

Horton, Susan R. (1995). *Difficult Women, Artful Lives: Olive Schreiner and Isak Dinesen, In and Out of Africa*. Baltimore MD: Johns Hopkins University Press.

hooks, bell (1994). *Outlaw Culture: Resisting Representations*. New York: Routledge.

—— (1995). *Killing Rage: Ending Racism*. Henry Holt, New York.

Huxley, Elspeth (1980 [1935]). *White Man's Country: Lord Delamere and the making of Kenya*. London: Chatto and Windus.

—— (1983 [1959]). *The Flame Trees of Thika: Memories of an African Childhood*, Leicester: Ulverscroft.

Indian Ocean Newsletter (1995). 'Memoirs of a Secret Agent'. *Indian Ocean Newsletter*, 8 July.

Jackson Robert H. and Rosberg, Carl G. (2003). 'Personal Rule'. In Tom Young (ed.) *Readings in African Politics*. Oxford and Bloomington: James Currey and Indiana University Press: 28–33.

Jackson, Will (2011a). 'Bad Blood: Poverty, Psychopathy and the Politics of Transgression in Kenya Colony, 1939–59'. *The Journal of Imperial and Commonwealth History* 39 (1): 73–94.

—— (2011b). 'White Man's Country: Kenya Colony and the Making of a Myth.' *Journal of Eastern African Studies* 5 (2): 344–68.

Jameson, Elizabeth (1984). 'Women as Workers, Women as Civilizers: True Womanhood in the American West'. *Frontiers: A Journal of Women's Studies* 7 (3): 1–8.

JanMohamed, Abdul Razak (1983). *Manichean Aesthetics: The Politics of Literature in Colonial Africa*. Amherst: University of Massachusetts Press.

Jones, Branwen Gruffydd (2013). '"Good Governance" and "State Failure": Genealogies of Imperial Discourse'. *Cambridge Review of International Affairs* 26 (1): 49–70.

Kaiser, John Anthony (2003). *If I Die*. Nairobi: Cana Publishing.

Kagwanja, Peter M. (2003). 'Facing Mount Kenya or Facing Mecca? The *Mungiki*, Ethnic Violence and the Politics of the Moi Succession in Kenya, 1987–2002'. *African Affairs* 102: 25–49.

Kantai, Parselelo (2007). 'In the Grip of the Vampire State: Maasai Land Struggles in Kenyan Politics'. *Journal of Eastern African Studies* 1 (1): 107–22.

Karimi, Joseph and Ochieng, Philip (1980). *The Kenyatta Succession*. Nairobi: Transafrica Press.

Kariuki, James (1996). '"Paramoia": Anatomy of a Dictatorship in Kenya'. *Journal of Contemporary African Studies* 14 (1): 69–86.

Kariuki-Machua, Rosemary (2008). *I am my Father's Daughter*. Nairobi: Flamekeepers.

Kaviti, Jason (n.d.). 'Statutory Declaration'. CD 42(iii): 3.

Kennedy, Dane Keith (1987). *Islands of White: Settler Society and Culture in Kenya and Southern Rhodesia, 1890–1939*. Durham NC: Duke University Press.

KHRC. 'Lest we Forget: The Faces of Impunity in Kenya'. Nairobi: Kenya Human Rights Commission, 2011.

Kibicho, Wanjohi (2003). 'Tourism and the Sex Trade: Role Male Sex Workers Play in Malindi, Kenya'. *Tourism Review International* 7 (3–4): 129–41.

Kimondo, James (1978). 'Judy: Blood Clues Found'. *Daily Nation* 10 June: 1, 4.

Koross, Kibiwott (2012). 'Mr B. Denies Killing Julie Ward'. *The Star* 7 March.

Lacey, Marc (2006). 'Keystone Kops? No, Kenyans, but Often Similarly Inept'. *New York Times* 18 April. Available at www.nytimes.com/2006/04/18/world/africa/18kenya. html. Accessed 27 February 2015.

Larrain, Jorge (1994). *Ideology and Cultural Identity: Modernity and the Third World Presence*. Cambridge MA: Polity Press.

Law Society of Kenya (2007). 'Countering the Culture of Short Memory in Combating Human Rights Violation in Kenya', Law Society of Kenya Human Rights Report 2005/2006'.

Lazarus, Neil (2005). 'Representation and Terror in V.Y. Mudimbe'. *Journal of African Cultural Studies* 17 (1): 81–101.

—— (1993). 'Disavowing Decolonization: Fanon, Nationalism and the Problematic of Representation in Current Theories of Colonial Discourse'. *Research in African Literature* 24 (4): 69–98.

le Carré, John (2001). *The Constant Gardener*. London: Hodder & Stoughton.

Lewis, Simon (2003). *White Women Writers and their African Invention*. Gainesville: State University Press of Florida.

Lipsitz, George (2006). *The Possessive Investment in Whiteness: How White People Profit from Identity Politics*. Philadelphia PA: Temple University Press.

López, Alfred (ed.) (2005). *Postcolonial Whiteness: A Critical Reader on Race and Empire*. Albany: State University of New York Press.

Loughran, Gerald (2010). *Birth of a Nation: The Story of a Newspaper in Kenya*. London: I.B. Tauris.

Lovelace, Earl (1998 [1979]). *The Dragon Can't Dance*. London: Faber & Faber.

Macamo, Elísio Salvado (2005). 'Negotiating Modernity: From Colonialism to Globalization'. In Elísio Salvado Macamo (ed.). *Negotiating Modernity: Africa's Ambivalent Experience*. Dakar: CODESRIA: 1–18.

—— (2005). 'Denying Modernity: The Regulation of Native Labour in Colonial Mozambique and its Postcolonial Aftermath'. In Elísio Salvado Macamo (ed.). *Negotiating Modernity: Africa's Ambivalent Experience*. Dakar: CODESRIA: 67–97.

Macharia, Keguro (2013). 'Blogging Queer Kenya'. *Journal of Commonwealth and Postcolonial Studies* 1 (1): 103–21.

Mail & Guardian (2005). 'Kenya Prosecutor Sacked in Murder Row'. 26 May. Available at http://mg.co.za/article/2005-05-26-kenyan-prosecutor-sacked-in-murder-row. Accessed 27 February 2015.

Makali, David (1996). 'So Near Yet So Far: The Story of Julie Revisited'. *Nairobi Law Monthly* March: 25.

Mamdani, Mahmood (1996). *Citizen and Subject: Contemporary Africa and the Legacy of Late Colonialism.* Kampala: Fountain Publishers.

Margolick, David (2001 [2000]). *Strange Fruit: Billie Holiday, Café Society and an Early Cry for Civil Rights.* Edinburgh: Canongate.

Maughan-Brown, David (1985). *Land, Freedom and Fiction: History and Ideology in Kenya.* London: Zed Books.

Mayaka-Gekara, Emeka and Sigei, Julius (2013). 'Philip Murgor: How cocaine choked me out of Kibaki State job'. *Daily Nation* 10 August. www.nation.co.ke/ Features/weekend/Philip-Murgor-How-cocaine-choked-me-out-of-Kibaki-State-job--/-/1220/1942634/-/item/2/-/n5eibxz/-/index.html. Accessed 27 February 2015.

Mbembe, Achille (1992). 'Provisional Notes on the Postcolony'. *Africa* 62 (1): 1–33.

—— (2001). *On the Postcolony.* Berkeley: University of California Press.

Mbogo, Fredrick (2012). 'The "Comical" in the Serious and the "Serious" in the Comical: A Reading of *Vioja Mahakamani*'. PhD. Dissertation, Moi University, Eldoret.

McArthur, Benjamin (1995). '"They're out to get us": Another Look at our Paranoid Tradition'. *The History Teacher* 29 (1): 37–50.

McClintock, Anne (1991). 'The Scandal of Whorearchy: Prostitution in Colonial Nairobi'. *Transition* 52: 92–99.

—— (1995) *Imperial Leather: Race Gender and Sexuality in the Colonial Contest.* New York: Routledge,.

McVeigh, Karen (2004). 'Hunt for Julie's Killers to Resume'. *The Scotsman,* Online Edition, 5 May. Available at http://thescotsman.scotsman.com/index.cfm?id=510352004. Accessed 20 March 2007.

Moeller, Susan (1999). *Compassion Fatigue: How the Media Sell Disease, Famine, War and Death.* New York: Routledge.

Moore, Jack (1984). 'Africa Under Western Eyes: Updike's *The Coup* and Other Fantasies'. *African Literature Today* 14: 65–78.

Morrison, Toni & Lacour, Claudia Brodsky (eds) (1997). *Birth of Nation'hood: Gaze, Script, and Spectacle in the O.J. Simpson Case.* London: Vintage,.

Muchangi, John and Mwangi, Kelvin (2012). 'Bishop Muge Murdered, Says Ex-Spy'. *The Star* 6 March. Available at http://allafrica.com/stories/201203061097.html. Accessed 1 July 2015.

Mudimbe, V.Y. (1985). 'African Gnosis Philosophy and the Order of Knowledge: An Introduction'. *African Studies Review* 28 (2–3): 149–233.

Murunga, Godwin (2007). 'Governance and the Politics of Structural Adjustment in Kenya'. In Godwin R Murunga and Shadrack W Nasong'o (eds). *Kenya: The Struggle for Democracy,* Dakar and New York: CODESRIA and Zed Books: 263 –301.

Musila, Grace Ahingula (2008). 'Kenyan and British Social Imaginaries on Julie Ward's Death in Kenya'. PhD. dissertation, University of the Witwatersrand, Johannesburg.

—— (2009). 'Phallocracies and Gynocratic Transgressions: Gender, State Power and Kenyan Public Life'. *Africa Insight* 39 (1): 39–57.

Mutahi, Wahome (1981). *Three Days on the Cross.* Nairobi: Heinemann.

Mutonya, Maina (2004). 'Writing Human Rights in Kenya: Mwakenya Prison Literature of Wahome Mutahi'. *L'Afrique Orientale*: 181–99.

Mutonya, Njuguna (2010). *Crackdown! A Journalist's Personal Story of Moi Era Purges 1986–1989*. Nairobi: JC Press.

Mwangi, Paul (2001). *The Black Bar: Corruption and Political Intrigue within Kenya's Legal Fraternity*. Nairobi: Oakland.

Nairobi Law Monthly (1996a). 'Julie Ward Murder: Starting All Over Again. Will Probe Name these Killers?' *Nairobi Law Monthly* 62: 21–26.

Nairobi Law Monthly (1996b). 'Two of a Kind: Striking Similarities between Julie and Ouko Murders'. *Nairobi Law Monthly* 62: 27.

Nation Reporter (1980). 'US Sailor Goes Free'. *Daily Nation* 1 October: 1–2.

Nation Reporter (2004). 'Julie Ward's Father has got "Fresh Clues"'. *Daily Nation* 9 September: 3.

Nation Team (2007). 'Cover-up Alleged at Julie Ward Inquest'. *Daily Nation*, 27 April: 3.

National Assembly of Kenya (1975). Report of the Parliamentary Select Committee on the Disappearance and Murder of the Late Member for Nyandarua North, The Hon. J.M. Kariuki, M.P. Nairobi: National Assembly.

Ndebele, Njabulo (2007). 'Game Lodges and Leisure Colonialists'. In his *Fine Lines from the Box: Further Thoughts about our Country*. Capetown: Umuzi.

Nead, Lynda (1988). *Myths of Sexuality: Representations of Women in Victorian Britain*. Oxford: Basil Blackwell.

Ngotho, Kamau (2004a) 'Murder Mystery that Shook Kenya'. *Daily Nation: Outlook Supplement* 22 March: 2–3.

——(2004b) 'Julie Ward Inquest Could Unearth New Evidence'. *East African Standard* 19 April: 4.

Nixon, Rob (2011). *Slow Violence and the Environmentalism of the Poor*. Cambridge MA: Harvard University Press.

Nkosi, Lewis (1987 [1983]). *Mating Birds*. Johannesburg: Ravan Press.

Nnaemeka, Obioma (1997). *Politics of (M)othering: Womanhood, Identity and Resistance in African Literature*. London: Routledge.

——(ed.) (1998). *Sisterhood, Feminism and Power: From Africa to the Diaspora*. Trenton NJ: Africa World Press.

Nuttall, Sarah (2001). 'Subjectivities of Whiteness'. *African Studies Review* 44 (2): 115–40.

Nyairo, Joyce (2007). '"Modify": Jua Kali as a Metaphor for Africa's Urban Ethnicities and Cultures'. In James Ogude and Joyce Nyairo (eds). *Urban legends, Colonial Myths: Popular Culture and Literature in East Africa*. Trenton NJ: Africa World Press: 125–54.

Nyamnjoh, Francis (2001). 'Expectations of Modernity in Africa or a Future in the Rear-view Mirror?' *Journal of Southern African Studies* 27 (2): 363–9.

——(2005). *Africa's Media: Democracy and the Politics of Belonging*. London: Zed.

Nyamweru, Celia (2001). 'Letting the Side Down: Personal Reflections on Colonial and Independent Kenya'. In Grant H. Cornwell and Eve W. Stoddard (eds). *Global Multiculturalism: Comparative Perspectives on Ethnicity, Race, and Nation*. Oxford: Rowman & Littlefield: 69–192.

Ochola, Aloo (1992). 'Ethnic Clashes: Civil War Looms in Kenya'. *Nairobi Law Monthly* 43: 24–27.

Odhiambo, Atieno (1987). 'Democracy and the Ideology of Order in Kenya'. In Michael Schatzberg (ed.). *The Political Economy of Kenya*. New York: Praeger: 177–201.

—— (2002) 'Hegemonic Enterprises and Instrumentalities of Survival: Ethnicity and Democracy in Kenya'. *African Studies* 61 (2): 223–49.

Odinga, Oginga (1976 [1967]). *Not Yet Uhuru: An Autobiography*. Nairobi: East African Educational Publishers.

Ogola, George (2006). "Stirring Whispers: Fictionalising the "Popular" in the Kenyan Newspaper'. PhD. Dissertation, Johannesburg: University of the Witwatersrand.

Ogude, James (2007). "'The Cat that Ended up Eating the Homestead Chicken": Murder, Memory and Fabulization in D.O. Misiani's Dissident Music'. In James Ogude and Joyce Nyairo (eds). *Urban legends, Colonial Myths: Popular Culture and Literature in East Africa*. Trenton NJ: Africa World Press: 173–202.

Ogundipe-Leslie, Molara (1994). *Re-Creating Ourselves: African Women and Critical Transformations*. Trenton NJ: Africa World Press.

O'Kane, Maggie (1992). 'No Matter What, These People are Not Going to Get Away With It'. *The Guardian* 30 June: 2.

Okello, Sam (2005). *The Night Bob Died*. West Conshohocken: Infinity Press.

Omamo, Steven 2004). *The Men do not Eat Wings*. Kampala: Richardson-Omamo Books.

Omondi, Rose (2003). 'Gender and the Political Economy of Sex Tourism in Kenya's Coastal Resorts'. Paper presented at the International Symposium on Feminist Perspectives on Global Economic and Political Systems, Tromso, Norway, September 24–26.

Orwell, George (1950 [1938]). *Shooting an Elephant and Other Essays*. New York: Harcourt, Brace & World.

Outhwaite, William (1996). *The Habermas Reader*. Cambridge: Polity.

Owuor, Yvonne Adhiambo (2013). *Dust*. Nairobi: Kwani.

Oyono, Ferdinand 1966 [1960]). *Houseboy*. London: Heinemann Educational.

Pape, John (1990). 'Black and White: The "Perils of Sex" in Colonial Zimbabwe'. *Journal of Southern African Studies* 16 (4): 699–720.

Pflanz, Mike (2005). 'Prosecution Chief in Happy Valley Murder Case Fired'. *The Telegraph*, 27 May. Available at www.telegraph.co.uk/news/worldnews/africaandindianocean/kenya/1490882/Prosecution-chief-in-Happy-Valley-murder-case-fired.html. Accessed 27 Feb 2015.

Pratt, Mary Louise. *Imperial Eyes: Travel Writing and Transculturation*. London: Routledge, 1992.

Print Craft (1966). *Pio Gama Pinto: Independent Kenya's First Martyr*. Nairobi : Print Craft. Available at www.goacom.com/biographies-of-goans-in-africa/829-pio-gama-pinto. Accessed 16 April 2015.

Priyadharshini, Esther (1999). 'The Rhetoric of Otherness in the Discourse of Economics'. Paper presented at the Critical Management Studies Conference 14–16 July. Sourced from www.mngt.waikato.ac.nz/ejrot/cmsconference/documents/PostColonialism/ECOREH3.pdf. Accessed 24 June 2006.

Randall, Vicky (1993). 'The Media and Democratisation in the Third World'. *Third World Quarterly* 14 (3): 625–46.

Richards, Terri (2012). *Mission of Desire*. New York: Bold Strokes Books.

Roberts, Diane (2005). 'The Body of the Princess'. In Alfred López (ed.). *Postcolonial Whiteness: A Critical Reader on Race and Empire*. Albany NY: SUNY Press: 31–52.

Robinson, Jennifer (2006). *Ordinary Cities: Between Modernity and Development*. London and New York: Routledge.

Roediger, David R. (2000 [1991]). *The Wages of Whiteness: Race and the Making of the American Working Class*, revised edition. London: Verso.

Ruark, Robert (1962). *Uhuru*. London: Hamish Hamilton.

Samuelson, Meg (2007). *Remembering the Nation, Dismembering Women? Stories of the South African Transition*. Scottsville: University of Kwazulu-Natal Press.

Sartre, Jean-Paul. trans. MacCombie, J. (2001 [1948]). 'Black Orpheus'. In R. Bernasconi (ed.) [1952] *Race*. Malden MA: Blackwell: 115–42.

Sauerberg, Lars Ole (1991). *Fact into Fiction: Documentary Realism in the Contemporary Novel*. Basingstoke: Macmillan.

Saute, Alda Romao (2005). 'Mozambican Convert Miners: Missionaries or a Herd without a Shepherd? The Anglican Mission of Santo Agostinho – Maciene, 1885–1905'. In Elísio Salvado Macamo (ed.). *Negotiating Modernity: Africa's Ambivalent Experience*. Dakar: CODESRIA: 98–134.

Sayer, Geoff (1998). *Kenya: The Promised Land*? Oxford: Oxfam.

Schatzberg, Michael (1988). 'The Triple Helix: Nation, Class and Ethnicity in the African State'. In his *The Dialectics of Oppression in Zaire*. Bloomington: Indiana University Press.

Scott, James (1985). *Weapons of the Weak: Everyday Forms of Peasant Resistance*. New Haven CT: Yale University Press.

——(1990). *Domination and the Arts of Resistance: Hidden Transcripts*. New Haven CT: Yale University Press.

Selwyn, Tom (ed.) (1996). *The Tourist Image: Myths and Myth Making in Tourism*, New York: John Wiley.

Shaw, Carolyn Martin (1995). *Colonial Inscriptions: Race, Sex, and Class in Kenya*. Minneapolis: University of Minnesota Press.

Sheffield, Carole J. (1992). 'Sexual Terrorism'. In Patricia A. Samuel (ed.). *Reading Women's Lives: An Introduction to Women's Studies*. Needham Heights MA: Simon & Schuster: 271–6.

Sörlin, S. and Vessuri, H. (eds) (2007). *Knowledge Society vs. Knowledge Economy: Knowledge, Power, and Politics*. New York: Palgrave Macmillan.

Steinhart, Edward (2006). *Black Poachers, White Hunters: A Social History of Hunting in Colonial Kenya*. Oxford: James Currey; Nairobi: EAEP, Athens: Ohio University Press.

Stern, Chester (1996). 'Is this the Truth at Last of Julie's Death?' *Nairobi Law Monthly* 62: 23–24.

Steyn, Melissa (2001). *Whiteness Just Isn't What It Used To Be: White Identity in a Changing South Africa*. Albany: State University of New York Press.

Stoler, Ann L. (1989). 'Making Empire Respectable: The Politics of Race and Sexual Morality in 20th-Century Colonial Cultures'. *American Ethnologist* 16 (4): 634–60.

——(2010). 'Carnal Knowledge and Imperial Power: Race and the Intimate in Colonial Rule'. In Stephen Howe (ed.) *The New Imperial Histories Reader*. London and New York: Routledge: 177–94.

Strinati, Dominic (1995). *An Introduction to Theories of Popular Culture.* New York and London: Routledge.

Sturma, James (2002). 'Aliens and Indians: A Comparison of Abduction and Captivity Narratives'. *Journal of Popular Culture* 36 (2): 318–34.

Sweeney, John (1998). 'Father Scents Justice at Last as his Prime Suspect is Held'. *The Observer* 19 July: 3.

Tebbutt, Judith, and Kelly, Richard T. (2013). *A Long Walk Home: One Woman's Story of Kidnap, Hostage, Loss – and Survival.* London: Faber & Faber.

TJRC (2013). *Report of the Truth, Justice and Reconciliation Commission* Vol. IV. Nairobi: TJRC.

The Guardian (1992). 'One Man and his Daughter'. 30 June: 22.

The Kenya Gazette (1983). Notice No. 4648 of 16th December.

The People (1996). 'If only Julie Ward were a Kenyan...' *The People* 12 to 21 March: 4.

Turner, Patricia (1993). *I Heard it through the Grapevine: Rumor in African-American Culture.* Berkeley: University of California Press.

Turner, Simon (2004). 'Under the Gaze of the "Big Nations": Refugees, Rumours and the International Community in Tanzania'. *African Affairs* 103 (411): 227–47.

Vessuri, Hebe (2007). 'The Hybridization of Knowledge: Science and Local Knowledge in Support of Sustainable Development'. In S. Sörlin and H. Vessuri (eds). *Knowledge Society vs Knowledge Economy: Knowledge, Power, and Politics.* New York: Palgrave Macmillan: 157–74.

Wainaina, Binyavanga and Macharia, Keguro (2011). 'The Pursuit of Ordinariness in Kenyan Writing'. *McSweeney's* 37: 151–4.

wa Mungai, Mbugua (2007). '"*Kaa Masaa*, Grapple with Spiders": The Myriad Threads of Nairobi Matatu Discourse'. In James Ogude and Joyce Nyairo (eds). *Urban legends, Colonial Myths: Popular Culture and Literature in East Africa.* Trenton NJ: Africa World Press: 25–58.

wa Ngugi, Mukoma (2013). *Killing Sahara.* Kwela Books: Cape Town.

wa Njenga, Gitau (2004a). 'My Encounter with Sleuth – Turned Villain'. *East African Standard* 29 May: 1–2.

—— (2004b). 'I Saw Julie Raped and Killed'. *East African Standard* 29 May: 1.

Ward, Jan (1998). Preface. In Nick Buckley (ed.). *Julie Ward: Gentle Nature.* Horsham: The Born Free Foundation.

Ward, John 1991). *The Animals are Innocent: The Search for Julie's Killers.* London: Headline.

—— (2012). 'Mr B. Raped and Killed Julie Ward'. *Nairobi Law Monthly* 5 March.

Ware, Vron (1992). 'Moments of Danger: Race, Gender and Memories of Empire'. *History and Theory* 31 (4): 116–37.

Warner, Michael (2002). *Publics and Counterpublics.* New York: Zone Books.

Waters, Anita (1997). 'Conspiracy Theories as Ethnosociologies: Explanation and Intention in African American Political Culture'. *Journal of Black Studies* 28 (1): 112–25.

wa Thiong'o, Ngugi (1965). *The River Between.* London: Heinemann.

—— (1967). *A Grain of Wheat.* London: Heinemann.

—— (1982). *Devil on the Cross.* London: Heinemann.

—— (1993). 'Her Cook, Her Dog: Karen Blixen's Africa'. In his *Moving the Centre: The Struggle for Cultural Freedoms*. Portsmouth NH: Heinemann: 132–5.

White, Bob (2004). 'The Elusive *Lupemba*: Rumours about Fame and (Mis)fortune in Kinshasa'. In Theodore Trefon (ed.). *Reinventing Order in the Congo: How People Respond to State Failure in Kinshasa*. Kampala and London: Fountain and Zed Books: 174–91.

White, Hayden (1978). *Tropics of Discourse: Essays in Cultural Criticism*. Baltimore MD: Johns Hopkins University Press.

—— (1987). *The Content of the Form: Narrative Discourse and Historical Representation*. Baltimore MD: Johns Hopkins University Press.

White, Luise (1995). 'Tsetse Visions: Narratives of Blood and Bugs in Colonial Northern Rhodesia, 1931–9'. *Journal of African History* 36 (2): 219–45.

—— (2000). *Speaking With Vampires: Rumor and History in Colonial Africa*. Berkeley and Los Angeles: University of California Press.

—— (2003). *The Assassination of Herbert Chitepo: Texts and Politics in Zimbabwe*. Bloomington: Indiana University Press; Cape Town: Double Storey Books.

Whitlock, Gillian (2000). *The Intimate Empire: Reading Women's Autobiography*. New York and London: Cassell.

Williams, Raymond (1977). *Marxism and Literature*. Oxford: Oxford University Press.

Young, Crawford (1982). 'Patterns of Social Conflict: State, Class and Ethnicity'. *Daedalus* 111 (2): 71–98.

Zack-Williams, Alfred (2004). 'Africa and the Project of Modernity: Some Reflections'. In Ola Uduku and Alfred Zack-Williams (eds). *Africa Beyond the Post-Colonial: Political and Socio-Cultural Identities*. Farnham: Ashgate Publishing: 20–38.

Index